African American Single Mothers

SAGE SERIES ON
RACE AND ETHNIC RELATIONS

Series Editor:
JOHN H. STANFIELD II
College of William and Mary

This series is designed for scholars working in creative theoretical areas related to race and ethnic relations. The series will publish books and collections of original articles that critically assess and expand upon race and ethnic relations issues from American and comparative points of view.

Volumes in this series include

1. Roger Waldinger, Howard Aldrich, Robin Ward, and Associates, ETHNIC ENTREPRENEURS: Immigrant Business in Industrial Societies
2. Philomena Essed, UNDERSTANDING EVERYDAY RACISM: An Interdisciplinary Theory
3. Samuel V. Duh, BLACKS AND AIDS: Causes and Origins
4. Steven J. Gold, REFUGEE COMMUNITIES: A Comparative Field Study
5. Mary E. Andereck, ETHNIC AWARENESS AND THE SCHOOL: An Ethnographic Study
6. Teun A. van Dijk, ELITE DISCOURSE AND RACISM
7. Rebecca Morales and Frank Bonilla, LATINOS IN A CHANGING U.S. ECONOMY: Comparative Perspectives on Growing Inequality
8. Gerhard Schutte, WHAT RACISTS BELIEVE: Race Relations in South Africa and the United States
9. Stephen Burman, THE BLACK PROGRESS QUESTION: Explaining the African American Predicament
10. Bette J. Dickerson, AFRICAN AMERICAN SINGLE MOTHERS: Understanding Their Lives and Families
11. Davia Stasiulis and Nira Yuval-Davis, UNSETTLING SETTLER SOCIETIES: Articulations of Gender, Race, Ethnicity and Class
12. Robyn M. Holmes, HOW YOUNG CHILDREN PERCEIVE RACE

African American Single Mothers

Understanding Their Lives and Families

Bette J. Dickerson

**Sage Series on Race
and Ethnic Relations**

v o l u m e   10

SAGE Publications
International Educational and Professional Publisher
Thousand Oaks   London   New Delhi

For information address:

SAGE Publications, Inc.
2455 Teller Road
Thousand Oaks, California 91320

SAGE Publications Ltd.
6 Bonhill Street
London EC2A 4PU
United Kingdom

SAGE Publications India Pvt. Ltd.
M-32 Market
Greater Kailash I
New Delhi 110048 India

Printed in the United States of America

Library of Congress Cataloging-in-Publication Data

Main entry under title:

African American single mothers: understanding their lives and
   families / edited by Bette J. Dickerson.
      p. cm.—(Sage series on race and ethnic relations: v. 10)
   Includes bibliographical references and index.
   ISBN 0-8039-4911-1 (cl). —ISBN 0-8039-4912-x (pb).
   1. Afro-American single mothers. 2. Afro-American families.
   3. Women head of households—United States. I. Dickerson, Bette.
   1951-   . II. Series.
   HQ759.45A38 1995
   306.85'6'08996073—dc20   94-40084

95 96 97 98 99 10 9 8 7 6 5 4 3 2 1

Sage Production Editor: Diana E. Axelsen

Contents

Series Editor's Introduction

During the past 20 years, literary scholars have led the way in offering critiques of conventional male-centric and Eurocentric social scientific interpretations of women of African descent in the United States and their family traditions and structures. This volume is the first of its kind. It offers a culturally indigenous interpretation of what it means to be an African American single mother and parent. The Africentric perspectives that these women present are efforts to develop and present sophisticated analyses of the roles of African and African American histories and cultures in the formation of African American single mothering and parenting norms, traditions, and social organizations. The phrase "sophisticated analyses" is a critical one because the authors attempt to go beyond the romanticization of African-descent experiences that tend to hinder Africentric perspectives through reifying culture from historical, political, economic, and social processes and structures.

It is a great pleasure to publish this volume because it represents a needed new chapter in the ways in which scholars come to interpret the experiences of women of African descent in the United States as mothers and parents and in other family roles. It is hoped that the contents will encourage much debate not only over the empirical realities of African American women in mothering and parenting roles but, more important, over how we should conceptualize such complex and paradoxical experiences. Such discussion is needed because the culture of poverty paradigm, pathological or otherwise, that has guided most popular and social scientific thinking about so-called female-headed African American families has discouraged the kind of creative reconsiderations the authors in this volume offer. Thus, although the readers may hope to gain great insights into the empirical realities of African American mothers and parents, it is even more important that they be provoked to think more creatively and constructively about a most misunderstood and misconstrued topic in American social sciences and in the larger, dominant North American nation-state.

Another reason why this volume is a welcomed addition to the literature is that it is being published during a time of reassessment of studies of single European American woman parenting. It has been interesting to watch scholars grapple for normative explanations about why an increasing number of European American women, including those in the middle class, are raising their children alone out of choice or necessity. There is a need for child and family studies scholars as a whole to begin to study parenting by single women as simply an alternative way in which kinship institutions are organized, transformed, and function. Perhaps we even need to compare and contrast the experiences of such women across racialized ethnic categories. It is hoped this volume will provoke such thinking.

John H. Stanfield II
Series Editor

Introduction

Bette J. Dickerson

Misconceptions about African American single mothers and their families are insidious and deeply entrenched. They are stereotyped as inferior, nonproductive, and dysfunctional for themselves and society. Typically, research about them has been pursued through conventional paradigms based on models and concepts of the dominant culture that have created many myths and distorted portrayals. These conventional paradigms served as the core foundations for the study of "the Black family" when I was in college. Having been reared myself in a grandmother-headed extended family, I found little in the textbooks and journal articles that described my healthy, happy, wholesome experiences. During class lectures, I experienced a range of disturbing emotions from frustration to anger over the limited and biased information. But I knew that I was not "seasoned" enough yet for the tasks involved in refuting the information. When I finished my doctoral degree I began a self-directed process of re-education in works that I had not been exposed to during my formal education phases. I "was on a mission" and this anthology is one of the results.

AUTHOR'S NOTE: The quotation from "Mother's Day," by Marian Wright Edelman, is reprinted by permission of Parade Publications, copyright © 1994, and the Children's Defense Fund, copyright © 1994.

In this era of multiculturalism, America's diverse family forms are openly acknowledged, but the tendency still exists to revert to the "ideal" conjugal, nuclear unit as the universal model of comparison in determining the extent of familial stability and productivity. As a result, only part of the story of American families is legitimated, the part that supports the notion that they *all* emulate the ideal. Certainly, there are many nuclear families with kinship based primarily on spousal relationships, but a single definition of "family" is erroneous and insensitive to the realities of scores of single mothers and their families.

This book grew out of a long-standing concern with the persistent image of the "normal" American family and the recurring tendency to portray African American single mothers and their families as abnormal deviations. Historically, the "myth of the monolithic family form" has consisted of three elements: "(1) the family is a nuclear unit; (2) it consists of mother, father, and their children; and (3) it exhibits a sexual division of labor" (Zinn & Eitzen, 1990, p. 14). This mythical monolithic model is maintained and promoted in American society as the normative standard for the formation and composition of all families. Based on the ideals of the dominant culture, the criteria underlying this ideal image of the family are conjugality, or marriage; nuclearity, or two-generational domiciles, consisting of mother, father, and their children; and a division of labor based on the sexes (Zinn & Eitzen, 1990). In actuality, the conjugal, nuclear family is not, nor has it ever been, the only form of American family organization. There is no one form of the American family but, rather, a range of structures that meet people's needs at various points in their lives or that may be forced on them by circumstances. The monolithic ideal is in stark contrast to the considerable pluralism surrounding American family life, including the increasing numbers of households headed by single mothers; extended families consisting of kin, both blood and fictive, that extend beyond the nuclear family and are often multigenerational; egalitarian roles; and households whose productive functions often extend beyond immediate physical boundaries into interhousehold exchange networks.

According to Skolnick and Skolnick (1989), "The idea of the universal nuclear family is based on biology. A woman and a man must unite sexually to produce a child" (p.7). But no rigid or uniform kinship patterns or family forms are necessarily required by this natural biological order. The family appears to be natural and unchanging because many of the functions of family life are organized around several basic events—birth, death, sexuality, eating, and sleeping. These fundamental functions of the family are not just natural and biological occurrences; rather, they take place in and are affected by environmental contexts with varied cultural and economic resources.

When resources are limited, diverse family forms may be used as mechanisms for fashioning solutions to the problems of everyday life. Although the basic functions may remain the same, distinct cultural values and traditions may also cause the basic family functions to be creatively carried out. To illustrate, a poor, single, African American mother struggling to make ends meet has fewer legitimate opportunities and more imposed constraints that can influence her family form. Institutionalized economic inequality can have profound effects on the shape of her family and its quality of life, yet the basic functions remain the same. What, where, and how her family members engage in providing for their physical and emotional needs, including the reproduction and rearing of children, will depend on the resources available to them. To adapt to the world around it and to fashion solutions to the problems of daily living, her family's coping strategies may include diverse kinship and living arrangements and distinctive forms of interpersonal relationships. She may exhibit resilience and endurance in the face of economic uncertainty by participating in a *system of reciprocity* in which such families provide mutual aid for one another (Stack, 1974). It is based on trust within an extended family that consists of a network of blood kin and fictive kin—those friends who are included in the exchange network just like, and sometimes even more than, blood relatives. The mothers depend on these kinship ties and shared resources for the very survival of their households. This system of reciprocity in African American extended families and households is both a reflection of a distinct cultural characteristic and a response to structural conditions.

THE CONVENTIONAL PARADIGMS

The myth of the monolithic family form is rooted in a patriarchal norm that depicts the male/husband as the major breadwinner and power wielder. The use of this myth to gauge the extent of a very real legacy of resilience and endurance raises some pertinent questions. Why is the patriarchy model of the family, based on male dominance, used to assess the normalcy of African American single mothers and their families? Must examinations of African American single mothers always serve to reinforce the stereotypical views of the Black matriarchy? What must be done conceptually and methodologically to construct a new image? Why is a matriarchy model, based on female dominance, presented as the other option? It is important to deconstruct these stereotypes and to take issue with the whole idea of the patriarchy and matriarchy models.

The matriarchy view is best personified by Moynihan's (1971) infamous report that labeled African American single mothers and their families as dysfunctional, as major glitches in the otherwise smoothly running American familial system. Moynihan's report was developed through the *culture of poverty* perspective that maintains that the poor share a distinct set of values, which includes resignation to the conditions of poverty (Lewis, 1946). The culture of poverty thesis is based on the bias that considers two-parent families to be superior to single-mother-headed families (Brewer, 1988) and considers single female-headed families as the central mechanism through which poverty is transmitted to subsequent generations (Moynihan, 1965).

Academic and social policy explorations generally use the culture of poverty thesis to justify the treatment of female-headed families as units separate from the broader social milieu. The effects of the intersection of race, class, and gender within the broader U.S. social structure and its ingrained stratification system are downplayed or overlooked entirely. In addition, the interplay of interpersonal and cultural considerations with the larger society is not fully taken into account. The results are assessments, theories, practices, policies, and behaviors that perpetuate the myths and stereotypes about African American single mothers. The consequences deprive the mothers, their children and the entire family, the community, and society of the varied contributions they can make toward supporting themselves and their families and contributing to their communities and society. Such support and contributions exceed mere monetary resources and include an array of mutual benefits for the mothers, families, communities, and society.

Another consequence of the culture of poverty thesis is the unfair characterization of poor African American female-headed families as social problems and as evidence of the disintegration of *all* African American families. The concept *social problem,* as in people or groups that are labeled deviants and thus "problems," is central to the dominant Eurocentric perspective (Asante, 1990). Its use is particularly endemic to the study of African American single mothers and their families, as in "the problem of Black female-headed families." What happens when this group is no longer considered a "problem"? How can it be studied? What new insights and information can be gained?

We do not take the more typical social problem approach in this volume but, rather, explore the enduring legacy of resiliency and strength of African American single mothers and their families because "this other side—enduring, positive, and powerful—is more important because it is more generative" (Billingsley, 1992, p. 17). The intent of the illumination of "this other side" is to foster real empowerment and social transformation for African American single mothers and their families because they "have arrived at a point of maximum danger, which is also a point of maximum opportunity" (Billingsley, 1992, p. 18). African American single mothers and their families must continue to turn to these strengths to navigate and survive what may be the most difficult passage since the Middle Passage.

Only by taking on the task of examining African American single mothers' lives and families from this more generative position can they be fully empowered on their own terms to capitalize on opportunities. In this context, empowerment refers to the *power to,* in contrast to the *power over,* and is reflected in the knowledge, resources, and abilities to make, pursue, and achieve informed life choices.

This book attempts to address these limitations and to reconceptualize the issues for more effective social action. It responds to the continual use by social scientists, policy makers, and the media of the stereotypical distortions that emerge from the deviant approach to analyses of the African American single mother family. By debunking the myths and stereotypes and by illustrating the more generative legacy of resiliency, strength, and survival of the African American single mother family, this work is a tool for those committed to the ultimate goals of empowerment and social justice.

Our critiques of scholarly hegemony encompass a demand that other forms of discourse be included in the "Master Discourse" and that serious attention be given to the productive nature of empowerment. They are reflective of our consensus that not all knowledge is Western based or male centered and that any perspective or approach that aims to eliminate the processes that foster inclusive knowledge and that gives no credence to the worldviews of others holds the threat not of assimilation but of annihilation (Collins, 1990).

SINGLE MOTHERHOOD

"Motherhood without marriage" is becoming almost commonplace in the United States. One third of all female-headed families are headed by women who have never married, and almost 1 million babies are born out of wedlock each year, representing one in every four births. Single motherhood is usually attributed to births out of wedlock, but there are a number of other causes that are often overlooked, including marital separation, divorce, widowhood, and formal and informal adoptions. Births out of wedlock are typically thought to be the reason for the overall increases in single mothers, but divorce is actually the leading factor (U.S. Bureau of the Census, 1989a, 1989c).

Contrary to public opinion, African Americans and teenagers do not account for the majority of out-of-wedlock births. European American women actually have the majority of such births and are the fastest growing category of unwed mothers. Although teenagers have a substantial number of out-of-wedlock births, half of both European and African American mothers who give birth out of wedlock are age 23 or older (National Center for Health Statistics, 1989). African American women may not create the majority of out-of-wedlock births in the nation overall, but they make up a significant portion of the African American population and the number is growing at a staggering rate. In 1960, only 22% of African American families with minor children present were headed by women, compared to 32% in 1970 and 46% in 1980. By 1990, more than half (55%) of all African American families with children under 18 years of age were single-parent situations. The vast majority of these (94%) were maintained by single mothers (U.S. Bureau of the Census, 1991).

The inculcation of false information and the perpetuation of negative images are partially attributed to the continuing use of inadequate or inappropriate definitions. Standardized concepts and standardized categories can be misleading if they do not encompass variations that exist. The language used to describe and categorize groups of people is socially and politically constructed. Establishing normative standards entails making value judgments and leads to the question, by whose standards? Revising thinking to be more inclusive requires an accompanying revision of language, as illustrated by the following examples.

Family composition is being confused with *household* composition when the definition of family form is based on the criterion of place of residence, as in "The family to be a family, must live together" (Schneider, cited in Skolnick & Skolnick, 1989, p. 15). A household consists of all the individuals sharing a common dwelling, whereas a family might include kin living outside the household. Certainly, there are African American families that do fit the narrow definition of the family, but it is erroneous and insensitive to the realities of many single mothers' lives. Such a limited conceptualization literally ignores the extended network of kin relations that stretches beyond the household and within which household-related activities occur. The *extended family* is also blatantly disregarded when teenaged single mothers and their children are codified as "single mother families." This is extremely misleading if they, as they often do, reside in extended or multigenerational families where the parents or grandparents are the actual heads of the families.

Female-headed families are often portrayed as matriarchies when they might actually be matrifocal. *Matriarchy* refers to mother/woman dominance over males, whereas *matrifocality* refers to mother/woman centeredness. In a matriachal family system, the mother/woman is the dominant member holding the unit together, even if the father/man is present. In contrast, dominance is not a precondition for a matrifocal family system. Rather, it is a unit held together by the extended line of female kin: mother, daughters, and their children pooling resources and often sharing a household.

Despite the frequent use of the term "matriarchy" when referring to female-headed households there is relatively little empirical support for the view of female dominance over males. Sadly, the African American family has "been characterized as a matriarchy so often that the assertion is widely accepted as a truth rather than a proposition still in need of empirical evidence and critical analysis" (Hyman & Reed, 1971, p. 186). It is not uncommon to find that matriarchy is used interchangeably with matrifocality (Hyman & Reed, 1971). Because for decades the existence of African American matriarchal families has been viewed as a given, far fewer empirical studies have been undertaken to determine the viability of matrifocal families but what data are available do support its viability (Green, 1993; Wei, 1982). *Father-absent* single mother families are erroneously assumed to be *male-absent*, meaning that there are no supportive males present. Although demographic data may report the number of father/husband-absent households, seldom is there the accompanying information on whether or not other males serve father/husband roles in the family (Hyman & Reed, 1971).

THE RACIALIZATION AND
FEMINIZATION OF POVERTY

Even if it is a result of personal choices or circumstances, single mothering takes place within a larger sociocultural context that must also be understood because of what it contributes to the outcomes for all involved parties. One of the most critical problems from that larger context is that of inadequate economic resources. One third of the African American population lives in poverty and female-headed families represent more than 73% of these poor African American families (U.S. Bureau of the Census, 1989a, 1989b, 1989c, 1989d, 1990). The causes of poverty are often confused with effects of poverty. Wilson (1980, 1987) points out that female-headed households and unwed motherhood are symptoms, not causes, of poverty. They are not due to inherent weaknesses but to societal forces beyond their control. The most common example of an influencing outside force is that of a social welfare system that shortchanges African American families through governmental policies and programs that "force" fathers out of families by requiring that they be absent in order for the family to qualify for public assistance (i.e., if the father is present, or if he is absent but contributing financially, it may compromise the welfare classification of the family and void its qualification for Aid to Families with Dependent Children or public housing).

The combination of out-of-wedlock births and poverty conditions has fostered widespread interest in causal factors and fuels national debate over the racialization and feminization of poverty. Many societal problems that disproportionately impact African Americans are exacerbating the situation. Those that endanger African American men are particularly disconcerting and include the rising rates of underemployment and chronic unemployment, incarceration, homicide, drug abuse and distribution, and the HIV/AIDS epidemic that worsens their already precarious health status (Johnson, 1988). In addition, a frightening "pattern of intracommunity violence is sapping the very heart of the Black community and its future viability. It exacerbates the decline in married-couple families" (Billingsley, 1992, p. 163).

Some societal problems may be experienced episodically, but underemployment and unemployment have had the greatest long-term impact on the ability of African American men to marry and/or support families. Despite arguments to the contrary, marriage does not automatically ensure women of changes in their economic status. Marital stability and the patterns of one- and two-parent families are directly related to the economic status of males (Billingsley, 1990; Edelman, 1987; Johnson, 1988; McGhee, 1984, 1985; Wilson, 1987). The large proportion of out-of-wedlock births among African American females is reflective of the precarious economic status of the males. Many African American female-headed families are adaptations to the "double yoke" of underemployment-chronic unemployment that guarantees low socioeconomic status for most African American males. Wilson (1980, 1987) found a direct link between the high rates of joblessness among inner-city males and the high rates of out-of-wedlock births in these areas. Male joblessness is also a determining factor in many poor unwed mothers' personal choices because even if they marry the unemployed fathers of their children they will still be poor (Brewer, 1988).

Economic and employment considerations also appear to be affecting the attitudes of young African American males toward the institution of marriage. Anderson (1989) found that young African American women still want to marry and young African American men still promise love and commitment. However, if a young woman becomes pregnant, the young man responsible may experience a sense of inadequacy and anxiety over how he will support her and the baby. He may reach the conclusion that he should not marry. Financial considerations are primary influences in the young mother's out-of-wedlock birth once again (Johnson, 1988; McGhee, 1984, 1985).

THE AFROCENTRIC PARADIGM

One way to assure a better understanding of the subject matter is to center studies of the experiences and perspectives of a particular group in the group's own reality. An aim of this anthology is to present various centered studies that move beyond the traditional focus on "comparison to dominant group." Centrism in general, and Afrocentrism in particular, was felt to be the best approach for our examinations of the lives and families of African American single mothers. Using the Afrocentric approach, single mothers and their families become *subjects* rather than *objects* of the analyses. As a result, the information does not suffer from disconnectedness or marginalization by overobjectivity and detachment, as happens so often in scholarly works. The reader can sense the "feeling tone" (for more on the feeling tone, see "Carol Freeman" in Terkel, 1992).

We are providing culturally relevant "lenses" through which to examine, interpret, and understand the enduring resiliency of such women and their families. By using the Afrocentric paradigm as our guiding force and applying it to our individual examinations of the experiences of African American single mothers, we have been provided with invaluable information not ordinarily revealed by the application of other paradigms. Most analyses concerning the family-related roles of African American women begin with the slave era, confuse matriarchy and matrifocality, and contribute to the matriarchy stereotype. All of these errors are captured in the following statements by Moynihan (1971):

> Slavery vitiated family life. . . . Since many slave owners neither fostered Christian marriage among their slave couples nor hesitated to separate them on the auction block, the slave household often developed a fatherless (matrifocal, mother-centered) pattern. (p. 131)

> E. Franklin Frazier makes clear that at the time of emancipation Negro women were already "accustomed to playing the dominant role in family and marriage relations" and that this role persisted in the decades of rural life that followed. (p. 132)

Other analyses of the family-related roles of African American women are ahistoric. They do not even attempt to place the subject matter within the context of its African cultural background. It is virtually impossible to have an adequate understanding of what African American single mothers are today without having some understanding of what their African forebears' experiences were, especially those related to the roles, functions, and responsibilities traditionally held within the family unit and their relationship to the broader social contexts.

Afrocentrism is an ideology reappropriated by African descended peoples themselves in an effort to restore their own cultural heritage to its rightful place as the center of their experiences and to valuate attributes previously undervalued by others. It is a perspective vital to the reconceptualizations necessary for the study of African American single mothers and their families because it explores the way they view the world and documents their experiences. According to Asante (1990), Afrocentrism "is sustained by a commitment to centering the study of African phenomena and events in the particular cultural voice of the composite African people" (p. 12).

Afrocentrism is based on an assumption that the culture, history, and current experiences of African Americans are unique because the descendants of African people have retained elements of African culture (Kershaw,

1992) and melded them with American culture. It is based on the belief that there is an "African way of knowing," that there are a "number of family values, generated in Africa, which survived slavery and the exodus and which have relevance to African American family life today" (Billingsley, 1992, p. 135). Indeed, this assumption is the cornerstone of this book. In other words, not only do we argue that we cannot understand African American families without being grounded in the larger cultural and historical forces of such families, we further argue that, despite the impact of the larger social structure, African American families have been able to retain important positive values that have been passed down through generations by the descendants of Africans. It is these values, including respect for the wisdom and "motherwit" gained from experience, the high esteem for elders, the importance of the communality provided by extended family and fictive kinship ties, pragmatic spiritual ethics, and a collective survival ethos that help African American single mothers "to keep keeping on" for themselves and their families.

A SYNTHESIS OF AFROCENTRISM AND FEMINISM

There are some who may feel that the heading of this section is inappropriate or even improbable, but it best reflects our own efforts to use the Afrocentric framework to reconceptualize and redefine the issues related to African American women who are single mothers. The rationale for this synthesis is best captured by a statement made by Anna Julia Cooper in 1882 that still holds true. Cooper noted that an African American woman faces a twin dilemma because "she is confronted by a woman question and a race problem, and is yet an unknown or unacknowledged factor in both" (cited in Brewer, 1993, p. 14). More than 100 years later, African American women face the same dilemma and continue to combine "the fight against sexism with the fight against racism by continuously calling the public's attention to these issues" (Brewer, 1993, p. 14).

Within the context of this double bind, we attempt to advance understanding of African American single mothers by not only expanding the application of Afrocentricity but also providing insights into the theory's intersection with feminism in general. There is also the shared recognition that the interlocking systems of race/ethnicity and gender intersect with class oppression to simultaneously shape the experiences of all Black women. Therefore, our contributions extend beyond the additive "double bind" of race/ethnic and gender oppression to analyses of the multiplicative "triple jeopardy" of racism, sexism, and class oppression (King, 1986).

Afrocentrism and feminism present challenges to the basic tenets of positivist science, particularly the notions of *one truth* and *expert knowledge,* by rejecting social distancing, or the separation of investigator/subject relationship. The rejection of subjectivity, taken to its logical conclusion, is akin to the assumption of the "generic human" that underlies dominant thought, whether intentionally or unintentionally (King & Mitchell, 1990). This has severe implications for Afrocentric and feminist thought and practice: How can racism or sexism be fought or economic discrimination claimed to be harmful to the interests of African American single mothers if categorical truth claims are invalidated? How can specific battles be legitimately fought without invoking the categories *African American* and *woman*? In our efforts to move African American single mothers' experiences from "margin to center," we cannot afford not to make authoritative statements or rely on Afrocentric feminist truths.

Both modes of inquiry share a commitment to praxis and empowerment (Collins, 1990). People of African descent and women of European descent are oppressed groups under the same patriarchal system of the dominant society and share some of the same limitations imposed by their inferior status. But there is a significant difference for women of African descent. Sexism oppresses their "woman-ness," whereas racism enslaves their "woman-ness," their men, and their descendants. Mainstream feminist scholarship is committed to privileging women's experiences as they define them and legitimating the reality of conditions shaping women's lives to empower *women* (Spalter-Roth, 1986). But a fundamental aspect of Afrocentric scholarship is the examination of "the roles women have played in liberating Africans and others from oppression, resisting the imposition of sexist repression and subjugation, and exercising economic and political authority" for the empowerment of *all African peoples* (Asante, 1990, p. 10).

The inability, so far, of mainstream feminism to adequately integrate the concerns of women of African descent necessitated the engendering of our Afrocentric approach by what Steady (1981) calls "*intraethnic feminism*—that is, within the Black groups' experience" (p. 3)—or what is more commonly referred to as *Black feminism.* The dual allegiance to women's and to the Black community's empowerment are fused together, producing the knowledge base essential to any centered examination of the standpoint of African American women. Black feminism includes a respect for those nonsexist features of traditional African cultures; female autonomy and cooperation; the centrality of children; and multiple mothering and kinship (Steady, 1981). It consists of African women telling their own story and recognizes the common struggle with African men for the eradication of racist domination and exploitation. It is not antagonistic to African men but, rather, challenges them to acknowledge the unique aspects of women's subordination (Davies & Graves, 1986). As Ladner (1972) states, "Black women do not perceive their enemy to be Black men, but rather the enemy is considered to be oppressive forces in the larger society which subjugate Black men, women and children" (pp. 277-278). The synthesis of Afrocentric and intraethnic feminist insights is essential for challenging the oppressive race/ethnic-gender-class-based systems of domination that limit the advancements that African American women could make for themselves, their families, and the larger community.

OVERVIEW OF THE BOOK

The study of African American single mothers and their families does not fit neatly into any one scholarly discipline and requires information from more than one field of study to reach more holistic understandings. The diverse insights gained from a multidisciplinary approach that combines diverse research methodologies and resultant findings can lead to more accurate and holistic interpretations. But it is hard enough keeping abreast of the new developments in one's own field, let alone the other disciplines. So this anthology project consists of a collection of original works by women scholars from various disciplines whose previous works embodied efforts to break through intellectual balkanization. Each was also knowledgeable about the historical and cultural dynamics of the group under examination.

Conversely, interdisciplinary works can be problematic. Each discipline has its own paradigms—characteristic ways of viewing the world—and assumptions that may not be directly transferable to other disciplines. There can be difficulties in reconciling heretofore distinct disciplinary methodologies and models. In this instance, however, our confusion was lessened through forging the bonds of our commonalities. Each of us has had extensive, varied personal involvements with African American single mothers and their families. Despite immersion in different academic disciplines and specializations and disparate personal backgounds, we are shaped by shared historical and cultural experiences. As *African Americans,* we acknowledge our common racial group fate identification, making a cognitive decision to identify with the group with which we share a common history, kinship, and destiny (Jackson, 1991). As *women,* we offer distinct gendered insights to our effort to dispel false notions and to reconceptualize the subject matter. As *scholars,* we have honed our abilities to extensively engage in data collection, analyses, conclusions, and recommendations related to the subject matter. As *activists,* we bring our experiential knowledge to bear in a concerted attempt to maintain unity of theme as well as to preserve the diversity of voices, perspectives, and experiences. Taken together, these factors intensively affected the development of our respective essays and constitute the collective strength and legitimacy of this anthology.

Taken together, the topics selected for discussion provide a composite picture of issues affecting the lives of African American single mothers and their families. The objectives of this volume include specifying, analyzing, and reconceptualizing (a) applicable definitions, theories, and methods; (b) internal adaptations, survival strategies, and support systems to alleviate structural disadvantages; (c) intersections in and variations of race, gender, class, and cultural patterns; and (d) implications, recommendations, and strategies for social policy, action, and change.

The chapter by Bette J. Dickerson examines the three predominant analytical approaches taken by scholars when they study African American families: the *cultural deviant, cultural equivalent,* and *cultural variant* approaches. The cultural deviant and cultural equivalent approaches have been used more often in studies and have produced much of the misinformation available on single mothers and their families. Dickerson then establishes the parameters of a cultural variant approach, the Afrocentric paradigm, that is used by the other contributors in their respective chapters. A form of *centrism,* the Afrocentric paradigm encompasses the view that groups must be understood, or centered, in terms of their own cultural meanings, attitudes, and values. Centered methodologies gather data from the perspective, or *standpoint,* of the group being studied. The *freedom* that comes from the ability to conceptualize the world in terms of one's own culture and history heightens *literacy* or the capacity to apply historical and cultural knowledge as the confluence between personality and situation dictates. African originating and the intervening American historical and cultural influences are central to any examinations of the standpoints of people of African descent in general and, in this particular instance, of African American women who are single mothers and their families. Afrocentrism is not just a way of thinking. It is also a way of acting, in partnership with research subjects, because it requires knowledge be relevant to practice and social transformation.

Indeed, historical events do influence the development of multiple family forms as complementary alternatives to the conjugal nuclear family, as Norma J. Burgess asserts in her chapter. She uses a sociohistoric perspective to assess the effects of retained elements of the African heritage and of events during the slave era in the United States on the construction of female-headed households in African American families. Her analysis includes attention to two subjects that have been understudied: the often overlooked "free Blacks" and the composition of early female-headed households. She reviews findings regarding socioeconomic and demographic causes for the early formation of female-headed households. The stereotypes that characterize female heads of households stem from the lack of attention given to accurate descriptive and empirical historical data. This lack of adequate information has allowed the stereotypes to flourish, ignoring the many dimensions of this segment of the population.

One of the institutions that best overtly evidences the retention of Africanisms is that of religion and the varied belief and value systems. Annie Ruth Leslie offers a challenge to the social construction of the moral view of unwed motherhood as sinful on the part of Western Christianity. Some scholars have found that many poor African American women view motherhood as wrongdoing but not as sinful. They are indifferent to the idea of "original sin," in which unwed motherhood is equated with absolute corruption of the human essence. This view has also been found in many African Bantu, Egyptian, and Yoruba peoples and in certain African American working-class Southern Baptist groups. Yet although an indifference to sin is consistently observed in many distinct traditional African and African American belief systems, other scholars debate whether a unified Black cultural ethos actually exists. Leslie links together these observations about sin, suggesting that a distinctive Afrocentric female moral system does exist in the United States that is different from the Western Christian system in which absolute corruption is associated with human sexuality and social behavior.

The construction of meanings is also one of the central themes in the chapter by Sharon Elise. Based on findings from her own cross-cultural study of teenaged mothers, she analyzes the social construction of teenaged motherhood and the social reproduction of race/ethnicity, class, and gender in the lives of teenaged mothers through their own voices. Concepts like *family, sexuality, motherhood,* and *teenaged mother* are socially, culturally, and politically constructed and have diverse meanings. The multitude of meanings become even more problematic when they are racialized. Elise discusses various concepts and perspectives that affect African American teenaged single mothers and proposes an alternative framework that takes into account their "sense of self." She looks at the differing cultural proscriptions related to sexuality and motherhood that result in different levels of acceptance of teenaged motherhood. While race/ethnicity continues to play a key role in limiting the opportunities for social mobility, restrictive gender relations based on varying forms of male dominance also pervade all racial groups, leaving motherhood as one of the most viable options. Elise also found that African Americans have an alternative social construction of motherhood that does not require marriage and, despite the most conservative views on sexuality, that maintains the greatest family support for teenaged mothers.

The interface between the dominant popular culture and the general knowledge gained through the mass media affects the development of the social construction of meanings, personal prejudices, and aspirations. There is burgeoning interest by the mass media in subject areas which focus on African American single mothers and their families. This heightened attention can be partially attributed to the national debates over "family values," but to the extent to which the mass media have begun to pay attention to family planning, child care, and child support issues for single mothers it has been largely in response to the changing marital status characteristics of European American middle-class women while similar changes of women of African descent continue to be glossed over as being racialized social problems. Depictions of African American single mothers are still based largely on the same old stereotypes and misconceptions, whereas European American single mothers are affirmatively portrayed. Marian Wright Edelman argues that "Today, two out of every three Black babies, and one out of every five White babies are born to unmarried mothers. And if it's wrong for 13-year-old, inner-city girls to have babies without benefit of marriage, it's wrong for rich celebrities too" (Edelman, 1994, p. 4).

Dhyana Ziegler's essay leads to the question "Why is it that while the growing number of European American middle- and upper-class women who are choosing to be single parents are viewed as having 'alternative lifestyles' (e.g., "Murphy Brown"), the mass media portrays the lifestyle of African American female single parents as seemingly classless and deviant?" Ziegler argues for the importance of more accurate and diverse portrayals in mass media. Having been appalled by Bill Moyers's television documentary "The Vanishing Family: Crisis in Black America," Ziegler produced the documentary "Single Parenting: A Woman's Perspective," in which middle-class, professional African American single mothers discuss the problems, joys, and frustrations of parenthood. She purposely selected this sample because they are all too often overlooked when considering single motherhood in the African American community. Her analysis of the resultant themes emerging from the mothers' own voices refutes the misperceptions rampant in the mass media, a social institution, that, therefore, can be transformed through institutional change.

Willa Mae Hemmons's exploration of the legal system and the law takes up the call for institutional change. Hemmons examines how the legal responses to problems facing African American women are anchored in the interests of European American males—"the innocent." African American women in general, and single mothers in particular, are often treated as the causes rather than the victims of societal problems. This influences the formulation of laws that often result in the design of controversial public policies and the delivery of inappropriate program interventions. There are gender-based antagonisms inherent in many laws. As African American women benefit, European American men must relinquish some share of a fixed resource pool and lose. This approach becomes even more threatening (and thus politically and socially unacceptable) when its effects are targeted at all levels of society. Finally, laws rely on decisions that dictate rather than reflect widespread social norms and patterns. They usually flow from a centralized source down to recipients rather than flowing from the bottom up. As a consequence, although many far-reaching reforms have been mandated concerning women's status and privilege, de facto equality remains elusive. Along with her legal analysis of specific court decisions, Hemmons's socioeconomic analysis reveals the cumulative demographic effects of specific legal rulings.

According to Hemmons (Chapter 6, this volume), "As long as the African American woman does not have equal access and opportunity for getting hired and protection from being arbitrarily fired because of her race and gender, being alone with children will mean, for her, an impaired economic and political status" (p. 113). But what are the effects for the children? Research has shown that such children are at great risk for detrimental outcomes. Children from one-parent families have been found to be more likely to have emotional and mental illnesses and to engage in substance abusive and delinquent behaviors. Most commonly, it has been found they do not do well in school. Being raised in families headed by single parents, however, is not always a negative experience. Many female-headed families do provide a positive climate for the effective rearing of children. In cases where family income sources and the social supports—relatives, friends, day care facilities—are stable and adequate, children from African American single-parent families do quite well.

Suzanne M. Randolph discusses the problems and strengths surrounding children in single mother families. She specifies a range of household and family types among single mother families that results in an intriguing cultural matrix that supports and facilitates children's development. Randolph attempts to untangle this cultural matrix that shields these children from poor developmental outcomes. Adaptive strengths that have sustained African American families and communities are discussed as strategies for ensuring the optimal development of all children in single mother families.

Many of the supportive strengths come from the role of grandmothers and the network of extended kin relations, both unique cultural phenomena. Many single mothers depend on a network of kinship ties and shared resources for fulfilling child-care functions. This network of mutual support is both a reflection of cultural specificity and a survival response to structural conditions. Susan M. George and Bette J. Dickerson examine and clarify the intergenerational relationships exemplified by the supporting role of grandmothers in extended families and households. Attention is given to the relatively new phenomenon of "young grandmothers" and the possible breakdown of intergenerational support. By presenting the strengths and weaknesses of a model of familial adaptation to parental caregiving by grandmothers, George and Dickerson intend to inspire a critical evaluation of this and other models and, in this way, contribute to the construction and use of those more culturally relevant.

Unfortunately, the support provided by adaptive familial systems may not fully respond to the very real needs of the female-led families among poor African Americans. Three fourths of all never-married mothers receive some form of welfare assistance following childbirth. Many single mothers encounter less likelihood of child support and are more likely to be less educated, reducing their earning potential. In the past, public assistance programs have helped provide female-headed families at least a minimum level of support. However, such governmental programs were reduced significantly during the 1980s, adding significantly to the numbers living in poverty and reducing the standard of living even further. The irony is that while there is nationwide concern with the plight of the family, limited or nonexistent political support is given for those public programs designed to ensure sufficient economic resources, health care, housing, and education. African American women who head households have the same encounters with this patriarchal distribution of power and economic resources as do European American women but with the added burden of institutional racism.

Rose M. Brewer cuts through the distorted information regarding the "pathology" of poor African American families led by women and places this family formation in a theoretical context that entails an explication of the complex interplay of gender, race/ethnicity, poverty, culture, state, and economy. Brewer develops the following propositions:

1. Female-led families among poor African Americans are the product of the interplay of these social realities occurring at the micro and macro level.
2. The examination of issues of agency and social structure in the context of gender, culture, race, and class is essential to understanding this family form.
3. Social policy and change must be rethought in the context of the complex interplay among race/ethnicity, gender, class, culture, state, and economy so as to develop appropriate support strategies for families.

Policy makers and service providers have not become fully aware of or adequately responded to the needs of African American single mothers and their families. Programs are frequently implemented based on invalid assumptions.

A basic tenet of Afrocentricity is that practice must follow all research endeavors in order to directly benefit the studied groups. Meaningful efforts can be derived only from a centered understanding of both the micro- and macrolevel aspects of policy-related issues. In the preceding chapters, the authors reconceptualized old insights and developed new ones into the standpoints of African American single mothers. Having linked their scholarship to "ordinary knowledge," they then suggest implications for actions that can benefit African American single mothers and their families.

This information provides the basis for an examination by Bette J. Dickerson, Philipia L. Hillman, and Joanna E. Foster of strategies for affecting related policy changes. They identify and explore those conditions that can lead to new, productive action that links "ordinary" knowledge, scholarship, and policy development for the empowerment of African American single mothers and, subsequently, their families, the African American community, and the larger society. By undertaking this task, they provide African American single mothers, scholar-activists, policy makers, and practitioners information that can foster policy transformations that improve the quality of lives.

A CLOSING INVITATION

This is certainly not the first publication to challenge conventional views on African American single mothers and their families, but no one book can possibly address all the topics that should be examined. We invite others to join in the exciting production of *new* thought, research, and action. What is "new" is based on that which is actually very old. In that regard, it is really *renewed* in the sense that it is based on the contemporary thoughtful reflections that evolve from old works that, regrettably, most people still have not been exposed to. But if we are not to allow history to repeat itself, with books and articles turning yellow with age and gathering dust on shelves from nonuse, we must continue to update, expand, and refine this renewed knowledge and then put it into constant practice until it is absorbed into the "ordinary" knowledge base of all.

REFERENCES

Anderson, E. (1989). Sex codes and family life among poor inner-city youths. *Annals of the American Academy of Political and Social Science, 501*, 59-78.

Asante, M. K. (1990). *Kemet, afrocentricity, and knowledge.* Trenton, NJ: Africa World Press.

Billingsley, A. (1990). Understanding African-American family diversity. In J. Dewart (Ed.), *The state of Black America 1990* (pp. 85-108). New York: National Urban League.

Billingsley, A. (1992). *Climbing Jacob's ladder: The enduring legacy of African-American families.* New York: Simon & Schuster.

Brewer, R. M. (1988). Black women in poverty: Some comments on female-headed families. *Signs: A Journal of Women in Culture and Society, 13*(2), 331-339.

Brewer, R. M. (1993). Theorizing race, gender, and class. In S. M. James & A. P. Busia (Eds.), *Theorizing Black feminisms* (pp. 13-30). New York: Routledge.

Collins, P. H. (1990). *Black feminist thought.* Boston: Unwin Hyman.

Davies, C. B., & Graves, A. A. (Eds.). (1986). *Ngambika: Studies of women in literature.* Trenton, NJ: Africa World Press.

Edelman, M. W. (1987). *Families in peril: An agenda for social change.* Cambridge, MA: Harvard University Press.

Edelman, M. W. (1994, May 8). I feel I am the luckiest child in the world. *Parade Magazine,* pp. 4-6.

Green, C. (1993, January-February). Slave women, family and property. *Against the Current,* pp. 29-36.

Hyman, H. H., & Reed, J. S. (1971). Black matriarchy reconsidered: Evidence from secondary analysis of sample surveys. In J. H. Bracey, A. Meier, & E. Rudwick (Eds.), *Black matriarchy: Myth or reality?* (pp. 186-193). Belmont, CA: Wadsworth.

Jackson, J. S. (Ed.). (1991). *Life in Black America.* Newbury Park, CA: Sage.

Johnson, J. M. (1988). *The endangered Black male/the "new bald eagle": Community planning perspectives.* Silver Spring, MD: Management Plus Consulting and Training Services.

Kershaw, T. (1992). Afrocentrism and the Afrocentric method. *Western Journal of Black Studies, 16,* 160-168.

King, D. (1986). Multiple jeopardy, multiple consciousness: The context of Black feminist ideology. *Signs, 14,* 42-72.

King, J. E., & Mitchell, C. A. (1990). *Black mothers to sons: Juxtaposing African American literature with social practice.* New York: Peter Lang.

Ladner, J. A. (1972). *Tomorrow's tomorrow: The Black woman.* Garden City, NY: Anchor.

Lewis, O. (1946). *Anthropological essays.* New York: Random House.

McGhee, J. (1984). A profile of the Black single female-headed households. In J. Williams (Ed.), *The state of Black America 1984* (pp. 43-67). New York: National Urban League.

McGhee, J. (1985). The Black family today and tomorrow. In J. Williams (Ed.), *The state of Black America 1985* (pp. 1-20). New York: National Urban League.

Moynihan, D. P. (1965). *The Negro family: The case for national action.* Washington, DC: U.S. Government Printing Office.

Moynihan, D. P. (1971). The Negro family: The case for national action. In J. H. Bracey, A. Meier, & E. Rudwick (Eds.), *Black matriarchy: Myth or reality?* (pp. 126-159). Belmont, CA: Wadsworth.

National Center for Health Statistics. (1989). *Monthly Vital Statistics Report, 38*(3). Advance report of final natality statistics, 1987. Washington, DC: U.S. Government Printing Office.

Skolnick, A. S., & Skolnick, J. H. (Ed.). (1989). *Family in transition* (6th ed.). Glenview, IL: Scott, Foresman.

Stack, C. B. (1974). *All our kin: Strategies for survival in a Black community.* New York: Harper & Row.

Steady, F. C. (1981). *The Black woman cross-culturally.* Cambridge, MA: Schenkman.

Terkel, S. (1992). *Race: How Blacks and Whites think and feel about the American obsession.* New York: New Press.

U.S. Bureau of the Census. (1989a). *Changes in American family life* (Current Population Reports, Special Studies, Series P-23, No. 163). Washington, DC: U.S. Government Printing Office.

U.S. Bureau of the Census. (1989b). *Characteristics of persons receiving benefits from major assistance programs* (Current Population Reports, Series P-70, No. 14). Washington, DC: U.S. Government Printing Office.

U.S. Bureau of the Census. (1989c). *Households, families, marital status and living arrangements: March 1989 advance report* (Current Population Reports, Series P-20, No. 441). Washington, DC: U.S. Government Printing Office.

U.S. Bureau of the Census. (1989d). *The Black population in the United States: March 1988* (Current Population Reports, Series P-20, No. 442). Washington, DC: U.S. Government Printing Office.

U.S. Bureau of the Census. (1990). *Money, income and poverty status in the United States* (Current Population Reports, Series P-60, No. 168, advance data from the March 1990 current population survey). Washington, DC: U.S. Government Printing Office.

U.S. Bureau of the Census. (1991). *Marital status and living arrangements: March 1990* (Current Population Reports, Series P-20, No. 450). Washington, DC: U.S. Government Printing Office.

Wei, J. L. (1982). Historical continuities in the Afro-American family. *The Research News, 33*(5), 18-23.

Wilson, W. J. (1980). *The declining significance of race.* Chicago: University of Chicago Press.

Wilson, W. J. (1987). *The truly disadvantaged.* Chicago: University of Chicago Press.

Zinn, M. B., & Eitzen, S. (1990). *Diversity in families* (2nd ed.). New York: HarperCollins.

Acknowledgments

Many people contributed, knowingly and unknowingly, to the mental, emotional, spiritual and physical strengths that I relied on during the life of this anthology project. I want to thank everyone that crossed my path leaving behind positive, uplifting memories that helped sustain my spirit. I am grateful to my greatest source of inspiration, my mother, Rosa Anthony Dickerson. Her unwavering confidence in me was a constant source of reinforcement and I turned to her often for the necessary "stroking" that only a mother can give. Special thanks to John Stanfield, editor of the **Sage Series on Race and Ethnic Relations**, who believed in me and allowed me to learn so much from him over the course of this my first book project. Thanks also to Diana E. Axelsen, who provided excellent assistance throughout the process of book production at Sage. And I want to express appreciation to each contributing author for her invaluable offering to the whole. The words of Sister Sledge best capture the relationship that developed among us as we shared the pleasures and pains of this project: "We are Family! I've got all my sisters with me!"

I should also like to thank all of my colleagues, friends and students at The American University for their constant encouragement and support even during the times when I may not have given my usual 150% effort. I am especially grateful to Evita Bynum, Hugh Wesley Carrington, and Philipia Hillman, graduate students that devoted much of their time and attention to this project. They have earned my utmost admiration and respect for their reflective insights, meticulous attention to detail, awesome organizational abilities, and seemingly boundless energy.

Thanks to everyone in my extended kin network, including Lou Taylor for carefully reviewing and generously commenting on early manuscript drafts; Shani Yejide for always being there when I needed to brainstorm new ideas or when I needed to talk about something *besides* the book; Regina Huggins for demonstrating her caring friendship by delivering many delicious home-cooked meals to my door during the demandingly long days and nights; and James Banks for always doing everything he possibly could to help make all the other aspects of my life easier.

Finally, I am deeply indebted to the countless African American women whose inner strength and commitment to the survival of their families, against all odds, caused this book to be.

1

Centering Studies of African American Single Mothers and Their Families

Bette J. Dickerson

When I define myself, the place in which I am not like you,
I am not excluding you from the joining, but broadening the joining.

—Audre Lorde
(Quoted in Bereano, 1993, p. 10)

The central premise of this chapter is that human phenomena must be understood and interpreted within their specific historical and cultural contexts to increase the scope and ensure the quality and accuracy of the knowledge gained. It is also argued that this "centered" knowledge should be proactive toward empowerment and effective social change. For African American single mothers and their families, in particular, a centered approach is essential for their empowerment because the accumulation of "knowledge for knowledge's sake" by outsiders has been particularly damaging. They are victims of others' attitudes, paradigms, and concepts, resulting in a state of dislocation, or social and psychological marginality. Their experiences must be relocated from the margins of others' experiences to the centrality of their own experiences. However, the approaches commonly used to gather information about this group have tended to denigrate, and even deny, their experiences.

Studies of the African American family usually adhere to one of the following ideological perspectives: the *cultural deviant,* the *cultural equivalent,* or the *cultural variant* approach. The cultural deviant approach views the African American family as abnormal and dysfunctional. The cultural equivalent approach that views African American families as normal as long as they adhere to society's traditional image of family life was based on ideals of the dominant culture: a nuclear unit composed of a mother-father-child configuration, with the man heading the home and the woman bearing children within the institution of marriage, caring for them, and maintaining the home. The cultural variant approach views African American families as culturally distinct functional forms (Allen, cited in Staples & Mirande, 1989).

Past definitions, perspectives, and assessments of the African American family in general, and single mothers in particular, have more often been undertaken from either the cultural deviant or the cultural equivalent approach. These approaches define *family* as being based on conjugality and nuclearity. The conjugal nuclear family, then, is the model to which all should conform, ignoring diversity, consanguinity, and extended patterns that are essential elements of many African American families. Using these false perceptions in assessing African American single mothers and their families has led to inaccurate questions and insubstantial explanations that serve to support the *deficit model.* This has contributed to the labeling of such families as "pathological" aberrations and social problems to be eradicated.

CULTURAL DEVIANT AND CULTURAL EQUIVALENT APPROACHES

Within the area of study focusing on the family, that of African American female-headed families has most often been mired in a cultural deviant paradigm that has not allowed fair, holistic interpretations of the data. The cultural deviant approach has been used most often in studying African American families (Staples & Mirande, 1989). Typically, this form of scholarship is pursued in terms of Eurocentric models and theories, which have resulted in many distortions, myths, and stereotypes. A Eurocentric perspective of society tends to consider the Western system of values, norms, and behaviors as universal and as the only route to societal stability and harmony. Thus it often supports—implicitly or explicitly—the valorization of Western society and rationalizes the Western position as the only reasonable one. By using criteria and measures reflective of the dominant "ingroup" culture, negative qualities are often conferred when evaluating "outgroup" cultures. Outgroup cultures are denigrated through the refusal to recognize the validity of their very existence. They are cast as either deviant, "invisible," unimportant, or irrelevant. Research conducted in this cultural deviant tradition does not render the reality constructed by those studied but, rather, realities conceived of by those who did the studying.

This approach casts the African American family in the stereotypical role of an unstable, deficient, deviant form. As a result of its "deficits," the family has been labeled the primary source of the social problems facing African Americans (Moynihan, 1965). This stereotype evolved largely from the historic premise that slavery destroyed Africa's influence on African American family life (Frazier, 1939/1966). The assumption was that the slavery system broke up families, removing fathers from family life. The result was thought to be a matriarchal unit in which all power and authority belonged to a strong, domineering woman. Most social problems were blamed on this stereotypical matriarchal family form:

> The widespread disorganization of family life among Negroes has affected practically every phase of their community life and adjustments to the larger white world. Because of the absence of stability in family life, there is a lack of traditions. Life among a large portion of the urban Negro population is casual, precarious, and fragmented. (Frazier, 1939/1966, p. 636)

Deviant ways of living were then thought to be passed down through the generations causing the so-called culture of poverty (Frazier, 1939/1966).

Perhaps the best known document associated with the cultural deviant approach is Moynihan's (1965) controversial report. The report actually contained relatively little new information, relying heavily on information presented in Frazier's (1939/1966) earlier work and taking much of it out of context (Platt, 1991). However, because it was produced by a federal government agency, it officially labeled the African American female-headed family inferior, nonproductive, pathological, and dysfunctional. This portrayal mirrored and served to perpetuate the racial stereotypes prevalent in American society. The thesis of the Moynihan report was that family disintegration continued from slavery into the 20th century as African American families remained locked in a "tangle of pathology." The resultant "deviant model" attributed most of the problems of Black families to internal shortcomings and pathologies. Although the initial furor caused by the Moynihan report has subsided, the report's thesis still influences contemporary attitudes, scholarship, and policies about African American single mothers and, perhaps even more important, the women themselves. Gloria Naylor states, "The myth of the matriarch robs a woman caught in such circumstances of her individuality and her humanity" (cited in Dickerson & Barras, 1989, p. 31).

Studies conducted through the relatively noncontroversial cultural equivalent approach delineate and legitimate the normative form and role functions of African American families based on the assimilationist ideals of the dominant European American culture. Generally speaking, assimilation means that family forms and functions of subordinate groups have no marked differences from the dominant group. Basically, a "normal" African American family would forsake its own cultural values and traditions, family forms, and functions. Thus the family inadvertently becomes an important socialization agent in promoting the dominant culture and in minimizing, if not eradicating, cultural differences. This treatment of one family form as universal and all others as anomalies has led to faulty interpretations of findings related to female-headed family structures and extended support systems. Some of the best examples of this approach are found in such early works as those by Drake and Cayton (1945/1962), Johnson (1934, 1941/1967), and Dollard (1937).

The adequacy of the assumptions underlying these commonly applied conceptual models has been increasingly called into question. A major problem has been that class-specific, Western-biased models are grafted onto differing socioeconomic, historical, and cultural realities. Billingsley (1992) cautions that "if we concentrate on the similarities and differences Black families have in comparison with White families, we risk missing the more important distinctions among Black families themselves" (p. 64). To illustrate, throughout history there has been some type of sexual division of labor. However, the depiction of the role of the man as patriarchal "breadwinner" relates to the shift from agricultural-based economies to industrial economies and the onset of the "family wage" and is quite contemporary, particularly for the American descendants of enslaved Africans. At the household level, for many in the dominant culture the family has become equal or secondary to the rewards of individual achievement in the workplace. In contrast, the strongest and most fundamental allegiance of African American women is to home and family (Collins, 1990).

For African American single mothers, the perpetuation of such faulty conceptualizations, myths, biases, and stereotypes has resulted in

- Negative portrayals depicted by others rather than positive self-definitions, both as a group and as unique individuals
- Self-fulfilling prophecies, those false predictions that influence behavior in such a way that the predictions come true
- Vacuums in research literature that prevent enlightenment regarding the range of causes and opportunities, as well as challenges, related to single parenting.

Through the imposition of the cultural deviant and cultural equivalent approaches the following also occur:

1. *Projection,* the conferring of negative qualities on others and, therefore, evaluating them by criteria and measures derived from a standpoint that is not their own. This conceals diversity and imposes an epistemological perspective contrary to the unique attributes of the group under study.
2. *Rationalization,* the assumption that the dominant group's own standpoint is the only reasonable one for all other groups and, thereby, limiting real communication.
3. *Denigration,* the refusal to recognize the very existence of the nondominant group's standpoint, thereby relegating it to a state of invisibility, unimportance, and irrelevance. (Karenga, 1989)

CULTURAL VARIANT APPROACH

The fundamental deficiencies in the cultural deviant and cultural equivalent approaches have not detracted from their popularity. In the 1970s, however, a shift to the cultural variant approach began, partially in reaction to the angry responses to the Moynihan Report. It was acknowledged that the faulty orientations failed "to incorporate numerous new research findings and programmatic insights produced over the past two decades concerning black families—many of which contradict basic tenets of the deficit model" (Hill et al., 1989, p. 2). Much of that "new" research was undertaken with the cultural variant approach. The use of "new" has a hint of irony because knowledge has been continually produced using the cultural variant approach since long before "the past two decades" but has never been given the attention, legitimation, or validation it deserves. Insightful studies, both old and new, on the complexities and variance of the experiences surrounding African American single mothers and their families are available (Du Bois, 1908/1969; Herskovits, 1958; Nobles, 1974; Sudarkasa, 1981). This body of literature, demonstrating how a people and a culture resist and survive in spite of institutionalized oppression and exploitation, has long been in existence. Its findings help to put into context, to reevaluate, and even to revise earlier distorted conceptions from the cultural deviant approach and to expand the limitations of the cultural equivalent approach. Using the cultural variant approach, scholars have taught much about what is and is not going on and have introduced a sense of pragmatic realism into the discussions, definitions, and images concerning these families.

Agreement among those who apply the cultural variant approach may vary regarding the extent of African influences on the African American culture and family, but there is little debate over the fallacy of Frazier's (1939/1966) argument that family organization was obliterated and *all* Africanisms lost during slavery (Billingsley, 1968; Gutman, 1976; Karenga, 1989; McAdoo, 1981). Many scholars dismiss the notion of the pathological African American family (Billingsley, 1968; Staples, 1991). They describe the strengths of African Americans in maintaining a value-centered family that serves to overcome or accommodate realities of societal deprivations (Billingsley, 1992).

There are grounded objections to the matriarchal (female-dominated) depiction of the African American family (Collins, 1990; Rodgers-Rose, 1980; Sudarkasa, 1987, 1988). A more accurate and preferred term is "matrifocal" (centered on the woman). A matrifocal system is usually held together by the extended line of female kin: mother, daughters, and their children pooling resources and often sharing a household. In addition, the emphasis on consanguineous relations in African American families must be understood. Sudarkasa (1981) suggests that most African Americans emphasize consanguineal relationships—kinship based on blood ties. Historically among African Americans the concept of "family" means first and foremost relationships created by "blood" rather than marriage. The extended family, therefore, is of extreme importance. Furthermore, fictive kinship networks, those family-type relationships based on friendship rather than biological or marital relationships, are significant, particularly to single mothers (Stack, 1974).

Research on the matrifocal, consanguineous family system has primarily taken two directions. One points to the strengths of the matrifocal, consanguineous pattern in maintaining generational continuity, providing services to kin, and resisting the negative impact of pressures outside the family (Ladner, 1992; Stack, 1974; Sudarkasa, 1981). The second details the outside pressures: lack of employment, low pay, assignment to demeaning tasks, residential segregation, and other institutionalized patterns of discrimination (Brewer, 1988). In both views, the matrifocal, consanguineous family is a functional response to, rather than the cause of, structural conditions.

These contrasting approaches to the study of the African American family represent forces engaged in an ideological battle. The outcome of this battle will determine whether the distortions of single mothers, which are instrumental in limiting lives, will be maintained or whether these distortions will be replaced with empowering knowledge. To better understand human phenomena, a *centered* theoretical framework best determines the questions to be asked, the methods to use to obtain answers, and the analytical conclusions to reach. In the past, "off center" theories have led to wrong questions about female-headed households that resulted in wrong conclusions. The need for *centeredness* is recognized as a necessary step in the journey toward self-empowerment and positive social transformation.

CENTERED STANDPOINTS

Centrism encompasses the view that a group must be understood in terms of its own cultural meanings, attitudes, and values. In contrast to ethnocentrism, or the belief that one's own culture is superior to all others, a centered approach places a group's own culture alongside those of other groups, thus creating a culturally relative pluralist structure without hierarchy or hegemony. The methodology consists of grounding observations and analyses in the subjects' own historical and cultural experiences, redefining concepts, paradigms, and theories and reconstructing methods, if necessary, to make them relevant and centered (Asante, 1990).

Centered methodologies attempt to gather information *from* rather than *on* the perspective or *standpoint* of the group being studied. Exploitation through racism, sexism, and classism has created an intersecting system that has insidiously oppressed African American women in general and single mothers in particular. As a result of the multiplicative effects of race, gender, and class oppression, African American women have a distinct, unique perspective, or standpoint, on life experiences not available to other groups (Collins, 1990; King, 1986).

The works of proponents of the cultural variant approach demonstrate that clearer understandings of African American women and their life experiences exist when viewed from their own standpoint. Collins (1990) states that "one way of addressing the definitional tensions . . . is to specify the relationship between a Black woman's standpoint—those experiences and ideas shared by African American women that provide a unique angle of vision on self, community and society and theories that interpret these experiences" (p. 22). Because the public discourse around single motherhood is so often shaped by prejudices and stereotypes, it is even more imperative to listen to what such mothers have to say about their everyday life experiences. With the continual onslaught of racism, sexism, and class inequality, African American women who are single mothers have had to find new mechanisms for managing everyday life. Their standpoint is exemplified by the self-reliant strategies that emphasize resiliency, innovation, and survival in the face of the intersection of race, class, and gender oppression. But their voices are silenced and their experiences analyzed and interpreted by scholars and practitioners whose observations are too often restricted by the cultural deviant or cultural equivalent perspective. Objectifying their identity enables those who have power to justify race, class, and gender oppression. This process of objectification negates the subjective nature of African American women and renders them powerless to define their own realities (Collins, 1990).

AFROCENTRICITY:
ONE TYPE OF CENTRISM

Eurocentric domination of knowledge and social thought has consisted not only of marginalizing other cultures' approaches but also of devaluing and limiting information about them. In contrast, Afrocentricity, one form of centrism, is a paradigm (a specific way of looking at the world) that does not detract from human universality because it acknowledges that there are certain basic functions that all cultures share. However, it recognizes and affirms the culturally diverse ways and means of carrying out those functions (Abraham, 1962; Asante, 1987). Afrocentrism stands beside other centrisms without hierarchy, without seeking hegemony. It has to do with the perspective from which one collects and assesses data on African people rather than the race/ethnicity of the researcher. (Asante, 1990).

Afrocentrism is an interactive approach that includes sociohistorical and cultural immersion, rejecting social distancing, or the separation of investigator/subject relationship. It is based on the view that human actions cannot be fully understood apart from the emotions, attitudes, and cultural meanings of given social contexts. It is based on the premise that the determination of one's life chances is based on how one constructs reality, one's place in it, and the way one validates knowledge (Harris, 1992). Kershaw (1992) posits the following assumptions held by Afrocentric scholars:

1. The experiences of people of African descent are worthy of intellectual pursuit.
2. The knowledge gained about human relations from the study of the historical and contemporary experiences of people of African descent is instructive to *all.*
3. The culture, history, and contemporary experiences of people of African descent are unique.
4. The scholarly work produced generates knowledge, resources, and the necessary tools for people of African descent to make, pursue, and achieve informed life choices.

Studies on African Americans have suffered from ahistoricism in that they rarely, if ever, take into account experiences prior to the Reconstruction or, at best, the slavery era. Proponents of Afrocentricity see African history and cultures as critical dimensions of the African American experience. Afrocentric-generated knowledge focuses on the life experiences of people of African descent, examining the phenomena, events, and ideas based on the centrality of Africa (Asante, 1988, 1990). It encompasses locating African ideals and values at the center of inquiry, taking into account the subjects on their own terms, their "place," location, or space. It includes acknowledgment of, grounding in, and use of African origins as the starting point for studies of African peoples. This provides the baseline framework for examining African social phenomena (Asante, 1990).

The intent of Afrocentricity is not to minimize the particular cultures or histories of other groups. Rather, it is "the study of an African phenomenon from the position of African people in the world as subject, rather than as an object. We are not a victim, and we are not on the margins of anyone's culture" (Asante, 1990, p. 1). It applies African ideals to the study of people of African heritage. By exposing parochial approaches to knowledge and cultural standards of behavior, new ways of knowing a multicultural society are suggested (Asante, 1987).

According to Harris (1992), all Afrocentric thought and activity is an attempt to achieve "freedom" and "literacy." *Freedom* is defined as "the ability to conceptualize the world in ways continuous with one's history" (Harris, 1992, p. 155). Self-discovery is freedom, the ability to conceptualize the world in ways continuous with one's history and culture. For African Americans, it is derived from the historical knowledge that provides a basis for consciously merging the best traditions in African and African American cultures. Freedom encompasses how people of African descent define themselves and the extent to which they are able to implement their self-definition. It does not consist in merely discovering or determining self-identity but in also rebelling against the old definitions, categories, and classifications (Foucault, 1980).

Within the Afrocentric paradigm, familiarity with the history and culture of the people under study is essential because history and culture hold fundamental roles in self-definition and empowerment. Therefore immersion in history and culture is encouraged at a level and in a way that marries the individual biography and worldview to precedent. Methods evolve from specific historical and cultural foundations and the issues or subjects are centered rather than objectified.

Literacy is the "application of historical knowledge as the confluence between personality and situation dictates" (Harris, 1992, p. 155). It is the practical dimension of freedom and encompasses the stubbornness of Africanness that creates people who refuse to succumb to any number of limiting phenomena. Literacy is the implementation of freedom and the increasing ability of African Americans to implement freedom that will lead to empowerment.

Kershaw (1992) posits a central question that must be raised for Afrocentric knowledge to be generated:

> Is the knowledge being generated with the purpose of describing analyzing and evaluating Black life experiences and articulated by Black people, with the specific purpose of identifying negative social conditions and helping to develop the tools to change the negative into positive forces as they impact on Black life chances? (p. 164)

Rather than merely explaining and interpreting the condition of the subjects of the exploration to more accurately "predict" their responses to stimuli, concrete, corrective actions should be proposed that lead to freedom through the lessening of contradictions, false perceptions, and oppression (Karenga, 1989). Afrocentric scholarship merges theory and practice into active self- and communal knowledge that leads to positive social change. Use of this intellectually liberating paradigm that *critiques the status quo* and *empowers the researched* fosters a "pedagogy for the oppressed" that implies a redistribution of power in what and how knowledge gets produced, transmitted, and put into practice.

THE CENTRALITY OF AFRICA

Viewing the female-headed family from the American vantage point alone is myopic. There is much in the history and culture of African Americans that has helped them survive in the face of impossible conditions and contributed to the production of a strong, resilient, and adaptive people. Recognizing the need to establish a valid frame of reference for collecting and analyzing contemporary African-centered data, Afrocentricity focuses on the clarification, not "victimization," of the traditional African history and culture (Asante, 1987, 1988, 1990).

Enslaved Africans were brought to America from various countries and from many different tribes along the west coast of Africa, which meant they had diverse cultures and languages. However, the idea of a unified African culture should not be considered totally unrealistic. Each specific tribe had distinct differences but also shared many similarities (Abraham, 1962; Soyinka, 1990). According to Sudarkasa (cited in Wei, 1982), generally shared values included deference to elders, respect for and care of aged parents, mutual aid and companionship among relatives, and the right of women to equal status with men (complementarity).

African American knowledge is cumulative from the enslaved African ancestors that practiced many of the methods of survival and resistance against oppression that they learned from their blood and fictive kin. However, the enslaved Africans brought to North America are more often portrayed as having "been reduced to an element of an oppressor's creation and changed into something defined by another as being useful for the oppressor's purposes, thereby losing one's own material and creative terms" (Asante, 1990, p. 191). The "slave" culture was considered marginal to the dominant society, but it was not peripheral in terms of the psychological and cultural caring that took place within the powerful context of the consanguineal extended family.

The Afrocentric perspective recognizes that enslaved Africans were influenced not only by their immediate circumstances but also by the kinship beliefs and survival behaviors of their African heritage (Asante, 1987, 1988). This approach is in stark contrast to the commonly held assumption that the enslaved Africans, who evolved into today's African Americans, were stripped of their culture, values, and belief systems (Frazier, 1939/1966). Peoples of the African diaspora are sometimes referred to as "composite Africans" with "bleeding cultures," lacking a specific discrete African orientation that would then mean specific ethnic identification (i.e., Yoruba, Ibo), but whose African ancestry is openly, consciously acknowledged, despite the distance from the continent or the time of outmigration. Rather than studying African Americans as "made-in-America Negroes" with no historical or cultural depth beyond the boundaries of the United States, their Africanness must be taken into account along with their Americanness. If not, one discounts thousands of years of history and traditions and ends up with an analytically unsound end product (Asante, 1990).

A central component of Afrocentric study is the examination of statuses, roles, and empowering responses that African women have had in the survival and liberation of Africans and others from oppression, exploitation, and marginalization and in economic and political empowerment. Attention is given to common concerns and situations despite the diversity stemming from the global dispersal. There are a number of historical and cultural gender-defined experiences that women of African heritage from diverse societies share, including the tendency to care and nurture others, to be communal and nonhierarchical, and to emphasize expressive aspects of relationships, value wisdom and spirituality, economic exploitation and marginality, negative literary and mass media images, self-reliance, creation of survival imperatives, less antagonistic feminism, and complementary gender roles (Steady, 1981).

Some scholars have discounted the possibility of the retention of any Africanisms among people of African descent in the United States. Enslaved Africans were thought to exist in a cultural vacuum as if they were incapable of maintaining any aspects of their own cultures or had entered the Americas completely cultureless. Little or no credence is given to the effects of African origination on the subsequent development of the African American family. In fact, the origins of the African American family are thought to begin with the institution of slavery (Dollard, 1937; Frazier, 1939/1966; Johnson, 1934). Enslaved Africans and their American descendants were considered to have little or no control over their personal lives. They were viewed as being totally dependent on the slave owners "for guidance and control in almost all phases of life" (Johnson, 1934, p. 3). Yet vestiges of African heritage have indeed been found to exist in the family lives of African Americans (Gutman, 1976; McAdoo, 1981; Sudarkasa, 1987). According to Nobles, "African American families are African by nature and American by nurture " (cited in Kershaw, 1992, p. 164).

There are particular aspects of the African cultural background of African American people that have helped to shape both the structure and the functions of their families. Family life, based on a network of kinship obligations, is the center of African civilization. One of the strongest cultural connections found has been between the family as it existed among the tribes of West Africa during the time of the European slave trade (Adeokun, 1983). In traditional Africa, *family* is a large group of relatives, related by descent or marriage, sharing a residential unit called a compound. Individuals may come and go, but the family compound continues. Families spread across several households and tend to be transresidential networks (Hammond, 1959; Wolfe, 1959). Marital bonds might break, but family bonds are permanent. Therefore, neither marital bonds nor household stability is the primary criterion for measuring family stability.

The nuclear family, composed of a husband and wife and their children, is largely a Eurocentric concept. In contrast to the conjugal unit or married couple, the structural core of the traditional West African family is a consanguineal unit based on unilineal descent traced through the mother's or father's side but not both. "Family" has a number of configurations, such as a woman with her daughters and/or grandchildren, a woman with her siblings and their children and grandchildren, or adult males with their sisters and all of their children. More often, ingroup solidarity and functions define an extended family rather than actual biological relationships or the number of generations (Sudarkasa, 1981; Wolfe, 1959).

Matrifocal families did not develop merely as adaptations to enslaved life in America. Writings on African societies and cultures indicate that women hold a central role within their families (Abraham, 1962; Ottenberg, 1983; Steady, 1981; Sudarkasa, 1981). Women are recognized as the "primary providers" for their children. Brothers and other adult male kin play an important economic and social role in the lives of women and children (Abraham, 1962; Dickerson & Barras, 1989). Women are valued for childbearing and much of their self-esteem centers on the role of mother. One of their primary sources of power lies in having children, reproducing the lineage and the society (Bisilliat, 1983). According to

Sudarkasa, who is well known for her studies of Yoruba women, "The Yoruba wife kneels before the husband but the husband prostrates himself before the mother" (cited in Wei, 1982, p. 22).

African children recognize their direct descent from their biological parents but also realize that they are members of an extended family and belong to the clan. They belong not just to their respective father and mother but, rather, to the wider kinship group. Close ties exist among siblings, but children reared in an extended family compound have relations between cousins similar to those among siblings. Likewise, aunts, uncles, and grandparents are very close to all the children of the extended family. "Illegitimate" child is a concept that is alien to traditional African society, where one of the greatest misfortunes to befall one is having no kin (Wei, 1982).

In all West African societies, whether patrilineal, matrilineal, or unilineal, the relationship between mother and child is particularly strong, endures for a lifetime, and extends beyond death (Bisilliat, 1983; Ottenberg, 1983). The following describes the strong attachment to the mother held by the matrilineal Ashanti:

> Throughout her life, a woman's foremost attachment is to her mother, who will always protect and help her. A woman grows up in daily and unbroken intimacy with her mother, learns all feminine skills from her, and above all, derives her character from her. . . . For a man, his mother is his most trusted confidante, especially in intimate personal matters. A man's first ambition is to gain enough money to be able to build a house for his mother if she does not own one. To be mistress of her own home, with her children and daughters' children around her, is the highest dignity an ordinary woman aspires to. (Fortes, cited in Billingsley, 1968, p. 45)

One of the most important functions of the African "mother" role is to ensure the well-being of her family members, particularly the children. For example, there is nothing that a Yoruba mother will not do for her children. In fact, her stature increases with the amount of sacrifice she makes for them (Adeokun, 1983).

COMING TO AMERICA

It was enroute to America that the seeds of the legacy of struggle, oppression, and exploitation were planted and, upon arrival, flourished enough to reshape the enslaved African females' "woman" and "mother" roles. The diverse social positions of the scores of women who immigrated to the United States, voluntarily and involuntarily, consisted of strikingly different marital, familial, and work roles. Enslaved African women were just as diverse but were forced to assume one role, that of forced laborers. They were brought to this society with the intent of being permanently racially subjugated, not to assimilate but to toil in unfree, unskilled labor systems that were ruthlessly controlled. They were not allowed membership in the "Cult of True Womanhood" (Collins, 1990; Zinn & Eitzen, 1990).

For those in the first shipment of enslaved Africans, enslavement meant physical and social displacement, both structural causes of the basic lack of connectedness experienced by those in bondage. The meaning of African female and male sexuality was also restructured and regulated for economically and politically oppressive ends. In 1662, the first U.S. law was passed that declared slavery hereditary. As a result, all children would follow the status of their slave mothers, thereby making female slaves a prime commodity and elevating their long-term status in relation to male slaves (Asante & Mattson, 1991). Furthermore, slave marriages had no legal standing, and slave couples had no legal rights to their children. It was all but impossible for the emasculated men in the slave family to establish positions of authority outside the family (Asante & Mattson, 1991; Gonzales, 1992). In the process, women lost the real and symbolic power of motherhood that had allowed them to carry out their reproductive roles with the dignity required for their role as primary socializing agents. They were highly prized for the reproductive role of their mother status without the power and privilege that had traditionally accompanied it (Bisilliat, 1983).

Rather than a family form that developed solely as an enforced reaction to the institution of slavery, African American single motherhood was proactive and involved conscious choices. As Omolade (1986) succinctly states,

> In opting to have children rather than abort or kill them, in resisting the slavemaster's attempts to breed slaves like animals and force families apart, Black women consciously chose to nurture those children, either with the support of their mates or, when necessary, without, but always in a supportive slave community. Black slaves struggled for the right to a family centered on an African-like broad network of kin. (pp. 2-3)

It took immeasurable fortitude and innumerable strengths for enslaved Africans to survive in that dangerous, life-threatening era. Today, many African Americans and their families are once again at "a point of maximum danger" and must have that same determination and rely on those same foundations to move into the 21st century and beyond. It may be the most treacherous passage for African peoples since the Middle Passage. Yet the critical problems facing single mothers and their families are far better known than those historic strengths. As Billingsley (1992) states, "True reform must come from within people themselves. And no true reform can be based on a people's weakness; it must be based on their strengths" (p. 21). It is these strengths that must be acknowledged and called on to effect the real micro- and macrolevel reforms that are required.

CONCLUSION

Invaluable knowledge regarding functional, affective values, roles, customs, and traditions applicable to the present can emerge from careful cultural variant analyses. As early as 1898, Du Bois insisted that it is not possible to adequately understand issues affecting the quality of Black life in America without systematically assessing the influence of historical, cultural, social, economic, and political forces. He stated, "We should seek to know and measure carefully all the forces and conditions that go to make up these different problems, to trace the historical development of these conditions and discover as far as possible the probable trend of further development" (cited in Billingsley, 1992, p. 64). In the United States with its diverse population and kinship systems, the relationship between the condition of African American single mothers and that of their families needs further careful exploration from culturally specific centered perspectives (i.e., Afrocentricity). Given the disastrous results of inaccurate analyses, the importance of relocating the historic and cultural centrality of African American motherhood cannot be overemphasized.

The importance of the family is succinctly captured in the Ashanti proverb that the ruin of a nation begins in the homes of its people. The family, in all its configurations, is the entity in which the production and reproduction of social life are carried out. For women, the status of "mother" is a most important challenging and rewarding calling and must be understood in all its historic and cultural complexity. It is also essential that the various dimensions of the lives of African American women who are single mothers be explored from their own standpoint. Voice must be given to this standpoint that has not traditionally been heard in the academic, policy and program milieu. Providing a centered understanding of this standpoint would constructively advance public discourse on the related roles, statuses, and needs of African American single mothers and their families. Such informed understandings are essential to the amelioration of the very real race, gender, and class inequities they encounter daily.

REFERENCES

Abraham, W. E. (1962). *The mind of Africa.* Chicago: University of Chicago Press.

Adeokun, L. A. (1983). Marital sexuality and birth-spacing among the Yoruba. In C. Oppong (Ed.), *Female and male in West Africa* (pp. 127-137). Boston: Allen & Unwin.

Asante, M. K. (1987). *The Afrocentric idea.* Philadelphia: Temple University Press.

Asante, M. K. (1988). *Afrocentricity.* Trenton, NJ: Africa World Press.

Asante, M. K. (1990). *Kemet, Afrocentricity, and knowledge.* Trenton, NJ: Africa World Press.

Asante, M. K., & Mattson, M. T. (1991). *The historical and cultural atlas of African Americans.* New York: Macmillan.

Bereano, N. K. (1993). Introduction. In A. Lorde, Sister outsider (pp. 7-12; 3-volume collection, *Zami, Sister Outsider, Undersong*). New York: Book of the Month Club, Inc.

Billingsley, A. (1968). *Black families in White America.* Englewood Cliffs, NJ: Prentice Hall.

Billingsley, A. (1992). *Climbing Jacob's ladder: The enduring legacy of African-American families.* New York: Simon & Schuster.

Bisilliat, J. (1983). The feminine sphere in institutions of the Songhay-Zarma. In C. Oppong (Ed.), *Female and male in West Africa* (pp. 99-106). Boston: Allen & Unwin.

Brewer, R. M. (1988). Black women in poverty: Some comments on female-headed families. *Signs: Journal of Women in Culture and Society, 13*(2), 331-339.

Collins, P. H. (1990). *Black feminist thought: Knowledge, consciousness, and the politics of empowerment.* Boston: Unwin Hyman.

Dickerson, B. J., & Barras, J. R. (1989, Summer). Single parenting: A global perspective. *Sisters,* pp. 31-36.

Dollard, J. (1937). *Caste and class in a southern town.* New Haven, CT: Yale University Press.

Drake, S. C., & Cayton, H. R. (1962). *Black metropolis: A study of Negro life in a northern city* (Vol. 2). New York: Harper Torchbooks. (Original work published 1945)

Du Bois, W. E. B. (1969). *The Negro American family.* New York: New American Library. (Original work published 1908)

Foucault, M. (1980). *Power/knowledge: Selected interviews and other writing, 1972-1977.* New York: Pantheon.

Frazier, E. F. (1966). *The Negro family in the United States.* Chicago: University of Chicago Press. (Original work published 1939)

Gonzales, J. L., Jr. (1992). *Racial and ethnic families in America.* Dubuque, IA: Kendall/ Hunt.

Gutman, H. (1976). *The Black family in slavery and freedom: 1750-1925.* New York: Random House.

Hammond, P. B. (1959). Economic change and Mossi acculturation. In W. R. Bascom & M. J. Herskovits (Eds.), *Continuity and change in African cultures* (pp. 238-256). Chicago: University of Chicago Press.

Harris, N. (1992). A philosophical basis for an Afrocentric orientation. *Western Journal of Black Studies, 16,* 154-159.

Herskovits, M. J. (1958). *The myth of the Negro past.* Boston: Beacon. (Original work published 1941)

Hill, R. B., Billingsley, A., Ingram, E., Malson, M. R., Rubin, R. H., Stack, C. B., Stewart, J. B., & Teele, J. E. (1989). *Research on African-American families: A holistic perspective.* Boston: University of Massachusetts, William Monroe Trotter Institute.

Johnson, C. S. (1934). *Shadow of the plantation.* Chicago: University of Chicago Press.

Johnson, C. S. (1967). *Growing up in the Black belt: Negro youth in the rural South.* New York: Schocken. (Original work published 1941)

Karenga, M. (1989). *Introduction to Black studies.* Los Angeles: University of Sankore Press.

Kershaw, T. (1992). Afrocentrism and the Afrocentric method. *Western Journal of Black Studies, 16,* 160-168.

King, D. (1986). Multiple jeopardy, multiple consciousness: The context of Black feminist ideology. *Signs, 14,* 42-72.

Ladner, J. A. (1992). *Tomorrow's tomorrow: The Black woman.* Garden City, NY: Doubleday.

McAdoo, H. P. (Ed.). (1981). *Black families.* Beverly Hills, CA: Sage.

McAdoo, H. P. (Ed.). (1988). (2nd ed.) *Black families.* Newbury Park, CA: Sage.

Moynihan, D. P. (1965). *The Negro family: The case for national action.* Washington, DC: U.S. Government Printing Office.

Nobles, W. (1974). Africanity: Its role in Black families. *Black Scholar, 9,* 10-17.

Omolade, B. (1986). *It's a family affair: The real lives of Black single mothers.* Lanthan, NY: Kitchen Table: Women of Color Press.

Ottenberg, S. (1983). Artistic and sex roles in a Limba chiefdom. In C. Oppong (Ed.), *Female and male in West Africa* (pp. 76-90). Boston: Allen & Unwin.

Platt, A. (1991). *E. Franklin Frazier reconsidered.* New Brunswick, NJ: Rutgers University Press.

Rodgers-Rose, L. F. (Ed.). (1980). *The Black woman.* Beverly Hills, CA: Sage.

Soyinka, W. (1990). The African world and the ethnocultural debate. In M. K. Asante & K. W. Asante (Eds.), *African culture: The rhythms of unity* (pp.13-38). Trenton, NJ: Africa World Press.

Stack, C. (1974). *All our kin: Strategies for survival in a Black community.* New York: Harper & Row.

Staples, R. (Ed.). (1991). *The Black family: Essays and studies* (4th ed.). San Francisco: University of California Press.

Staples, R., & Mirande A. (1989). Racial and cultural variations among American families: A decennial review of the literature on minority families. In A. S. Skolnick & J. H. Skolnick (Eds.), *Family in transition* (pp. 480-503). Glenview, IL: Scott, Foresman.

Steady, F. C. (1981). *The Black woman cross-culturally.* Cambridge, MA: Schenkman.

Sudarkasa, N. (1981). Interpreting the African heritage in Afro-American family organization. In H. P. McAdoo (Ed.), *Black families* (pp. 37-53). Beverly Hills, CA: Sage.

Sudarkasa, N. (1987). The status of women in indigenous African societies. In R. Terborg-Penn, S. Harley, & A. B. Rushings (Eds.), *Women in Africa and the African diaspora* (pp. 25-41). Washington, DC: Howard University Press.

Sudarkasa, N. (1988). Reassessing the Black family: Dispelling the myths, reaffirming the values. *Sisters,* pp. 22-23, 38-39.

Wei, J. L. (1982). Historical continuities in the Afro-American family. *Research News, 33*(5), 18-23.

Wolfe, A. W. (1959). The dynamics of the Ngombe segmentary system. In W. R. Bascom & M. J. Herskovits, (Eds.), *Continuity and change in African cultures* (pp. 168-186). Chicago: University of Chicago Press.

Zinn, M. B., & Eitzen, D. S. (1990). *Diversity in families* (2nd ed.). New York: Harper-Collins.

SUGGESTED READINGS

Asante, M. K., & Asante, K. W. (Eds.). (1990). *African culture: The rhythms of unity.* Trenton, NJ: Africa World Press.

Bascom, W. R., & Herskovits, M. J. (Eds.). (1959). *Continuity and change in African cultures.* Chicago: University of Chicago Press.

Bianchi, S. M., & Seltzer, J. A. (1986). Life without father. *American Demographics, 8,* 43-44.

Davis, A. (1981). *Women, race and class.* New York: Vintage.

French, Howard W. (1987, March 7). Report cites fewer men in Black neighborhoods. *The New York Times,* p. 31.

Lystad, R. A. (1959). Marriage and kinship among the Ashanti and the Agni: A study of differential acculturation. In W. R. Bascom & M. J. Herskovits (Eds.), *Continuity and change in African cultures* (pp. 187-204). Chicago: University of Chicago Press.

Ottenberg, P.V. (1959). The changing economic position of women among the Afikpo Ibo. In W. R. Bascom & M. J. Herskovits (Eds.), *Continuity and change in African cultures* (pp. 205-223). Chicago: University of Chicago Press.

Oyebade, B. (1990). African studies and the Afrocentric paradigm: A critique. *Journal of Black Studies, 21,* 223-238.

Rawlings, S. W. (1989). Single parents and their children. In U.S. Bureau of the Census, *Studies in marriage and the family* (Current Population Reports, Series P-23, No. 162, pp. 13-26). Washington, DC: U.S. Government Printing Office.

Skolnick, A. S., & Skolnick, J. H. (Eds.). (1989). *Family in transition* (6th ed.). Glenview, IL: Scott, Foresman.

Willie, C. V. (1988). *A new look at Black families* (3rd ed.). Dix Hills, NY: General Hall.

Wilson, W. J. (1978). *The declining significance of race.* Chicago: University of Chicago Press.

Wilson, W. J. (1987). *The truly disadvantaged: The inner city, the underclass, and public policy.* Chicago: University of Chicago Press.

Yansane, A. Y. (1990). Cultural, political, and economic universals in West Africa. In M. K. Asante & K. W. Asante (Eds.), *African culture: The rhythms of unity* (pp. 39-68). Trenton, NJ: Africa World Press.

2

Female-Headed Households in Sociohistorical Perspective

Norma J. Burgess

> We seldom study the condition of the Negro today honestly and
> carefully. It is so much easier to assume that we know it all. Or perhaps,
> having already reached conclusions in our own minds, we are loath to
> have them disturbed by facts. And yet how little we really know of these
> millions—of their daily lives and longings.
>
> W. E. B. Du Bois (1903/1990, p. 101)

> It is not because Negro Americans are Africans, or because we can trace
> an unbroken social history from Africa but because there is a distinct
> nexus between Africa and America, which though broken and perverted,
> is nevertheless not to be neglected by the careful student.
>
> W. E. B. Du Bois (1908/1969, p. 9)

Although these words by Du Bois were penned decades ago, the context
continues to characterize research on African Americans and thus forms
the basis for persistent investigations regarding one of the largest populations in the United States.

Family structures are an example of narrowly focused research topics
with little attention to diversity within subpopulations in the United

AUTHOR'S NOTE: The author gratefully acknowledges the support given by the
National Science Foundation and the Center for Research on Women. Neither the
Foundation nor the Center accepts responsibility for the contents herein.

States. Female-headed households are a common family structure among contemporary African American families. Despite scholarly efforts, evidence is still inconclusive regarding the origin of this family type (African or American adaptative roots) and the consequences of this structure in the community and in society. The female-headed family has been the target of poverty-related issues (blaming the victim for economic status while not acknowledging the role of social structure and accompanying inequalities); descriptions such as the antimale matriarch and welfare chasers are often used to characterize these family structures. Without adequate attention to the underlying causes of the disadvantages faced by African American women who head families, contemporary descriptions presented by the media and technical reports add little to our understanding of the female-headed family.

Female-headed households became common structures in the African American community from emancipation onward. Large numbers of children were not regularly found in such households. For example, in 1800, women between 30 and 49 years of age usually had one or two children younger than 18. Additionally, a sizable portion of the female heads in this same time period were more likely to be widowed (Gutman, 1975). Women did not live alone with complete responsibility for their children. Many were assisted by older women in the community and were quite different from the characterization used to describe the contemporary female-headed household.

Prior to 1790, it was difficult to determine how many Africans were slaves and how many were free. Nor is it clear how many Africans were imported as slaves. By 1808, there were approximately 340,000. Others believe that there could have been as many as 400,000. Some of the Africans who were reported early as slaves never had such a status. At least a few of the first Africans brought to this country were indentured servants like White persons of this class imported here during the beginning of the colonies (Woodson, 1925). Strong ties existed between free Blacks and slaves throughout areas where both existed (Fields, 1985). A special feature of Maryland's colonial history reflects the interconnection of the worlds of free Black people and slaves. This relationship between slave and free Black populations meant that free Blacks moved largely within the limits that slavery placed on them.

Recent attention to female-headed families reveals a bias toward African American families that continues to grow and is often cited as support for the now defunct Moynihanian thesis. Moynihan's (1965) controversial report relied heavily on the work of Frazier (1939/1966). Moynihan interpreted the characterization of African American families as disorganized, pathological, and matrifocal and provided support for ethnocentric notions about family structures, namely, that the majority were nuclear and father headed. As a result, when family groupings did not meet the two-parent criteria, they were labeled deviant. When Black-White comparisons were made, little effort was given to include the diversity present among Black family structures, which was later revealed primarily in the work of Billingsley (1968, 1992) and updated by Staples (1987). Billingsley outlined specific complements to the narrowly defined nuclear family among African Americans. His categories included children who were reared primarily by their grandmothers, single parents who lived within their parents' houses with their children, and families without children as a general overview of family structures that were different from Western society's "nuclear family." The perception of destruction and instability of the African American family based on the Frazerian model of matriarchy did not reflect the complexity and variety of issues inherent in social explanations of African American family structure.

PURPOSE

This chapter focuses on the much maligned female-headed household using a sociohistorical perspective. By incorporating the historical development of African American families in the United States, the development of multiple family forms emerged as a complementary alternative to the traditionally defined nuclear family.

The majority of families of African descent included two parents for longer than contemporary society acknowledges, although adaptations and absorption within family structures occurred to ensure safety for children born to single mothers (Billingsley, 1968, 1992). Fictive kin, other mothers, grandmothers, and community members provided support in the place of absent or ineffective fathers (Collins, 1990).

The presence of culture, values, and belief systems in other ethnic and racial groups within the United States allows a similar assumption to be made about the family structures of enslaved Africans with variations. It is widely known that many adjustments were made in the family life of Africans who came to America to assist in its building. Many enslaved Africans and their families adapted to European-oriented culture out of the need to survive. These adaptations were not, however, a precursor to the family structures that eventually characterized the enslaved Africans. Although families adopted some aspects of European culture, remnants of African family patterns remained a part of their lives (Holloway, 1990; McDaniel, 1990). What evolved was a familial pattern and behavior pattern with both African and European origins. This process of acculturation allowed some degree of retention among Africans who were enslaved in America.

The development of the female-headed household within the United States among African Americans is examined here from an Africa-centered perspective. This approach places family structures within a contextual framework that deviates from the Frazerian philosophy and acknowledges the role of African culture and environment in familial development. An Africa-centered perspective recognizes the fact that enslaved persons were influenced not only by their immediate circumstances but that they also relied on the strength of the African heritage regarding kinship and survival behavior (Asante, 1987, 1988; Holloway, 1990). Such an approach is contrary to the notion of annihilation—that few, if any, remnants of African family structures, beliefs, values, and culture remain. The annihilationist perspective has characterized most of the past research on African American families.

Contributions to the continuing debate regarding the presence of Africanisms among contemporary African American families (Herskovits, 1958/1990; Holloway, 1990; McDaniel, 1990) remain a valid, yet persistent issue that commands critical examination. The necessary synthesis between Africanisms and environment surfaces; one cannot dispute the influence that slavery and Africanisms had on enslaved African families within the United States. The idea of complete annihilation or disappearance of the African family is an issue that warrants additional documentation and validation as an alternative model; this model is one that early family scholars accepted at face value.

Enslaved Africans took on the responsibility of the slave community to ensure survival of the group:

> The family, while it had no legal existence in slavery, was in actuality one of the most important survival mechanisms for the slave. . . . In his family he found companionship, love, sexual gratification, sympathetic understanding of his sufferings . . . learned how to avoid punishment, to cooperate with other blacks, and to maintain his self esteem. (Blassingame, 1972, pp. 78-79)

The well-being of the children in families (both two-parent and single-parent) was also the responsibility of the community. As a result, persons who were not related by blood were treated as relatives and given the same social position (aunts, cousins, mothers, etc.) as blood relatives (see Collins, 1990; Davis, 1981).

The family structure among enslaved Africans did not mirror the dominant culture. Fathers often lived on other plantations and were frequently sold away. Without regard for inherent strengths of enslaved families, few allowances were made for kin (fictive or real) relationships to develop in the absence of blood relatives.[1] Similarities in culture, irrespective of the African state of origin, provided ample opportunity for the enslaved persons to bind together for survival. This notion is contradictory to previously held assumptions about the disparity of African origins and the dissimilarity of language as primary difficulties in communication among the enslaved persons (Levine, 1977).

The majority of published research on African American families rests on the assumption that Africans were either void of or stripped of their culture, values, and belief systems during the enslavement period. The works of Billingsley (1968), McAdoo (1988), Asante (1987, 1988), Collins (1990), and the republished work of Herskovits (1958/1990) are examples of works that encompass African American women's feminist thought, Afrocentricism, and relevant ingredients contributing to theory building in the examination of female-headed households. Combining interdisciplinary scholarship on African Americans provides greater opportunities for explanation. Frequently, the unidisciplinary approach to research encourages explanations of limited utility that lack depth in explaining multifaceted phenomena.

Ethnocentric biases regarding nontraditional family structures have also characterized research efforts on African Americans. Many scholars adhered to the philosophy that slavery annihilated the African family structures, including culture, heritage, beliefs, and value systems. What was present was a hybrid of White behavior and adaptations. Biases about family structures led to actions that resulted in the absent father syndrome (social policies and programs that provide assistance to families whose fathers or husbands were not present in the home). This effort provided new meaning and definition to the female-headed household. Because of financial implications, women were forced to either live with males who were barely self-sufficient due to numerous structural factors or accept the contributions provided by the government. The result is an increasingly common family form where single mothers as heads of households live with their children.

Although Africans recognize the mother-child dyad as the primary social and affective unit, it is erroneous to characterize this as a separate nuclear family within the African extended family. Such a formulation has no explanatory value as none of the normal functions of a family were traditionally performed by this unit in isolation. It was not a unit of socialization alone, nor was it a unit of economic production or consumption alone; it was not an isolated unit of emotional support or mutual aid. It obviously was not a procreative unit (Sudarkasa, 1980).

It is an undeniable fact that in all societies, including those of Africa, the procreative unit is normally a male and a female. This unit together with its offspring can be isolated for study or analysis. Sudarkasa (1980) also challenged the notion of the nuclear family as the building block for families in every society where it is found. Labeling the father-mother-child unit the "nuclear family" does not make it invariably so. In many African societies, the nuclear unit within the extended family is not the nuclear family of the West, nor is it the minimal unit into which, for analytical purposes, the extended family can be divided.

Unlike White families, structures for Blacks included other relatives and nonrelatives who played significant roles; some form of adaptation occurred during the time of slavery, and the result was not necessarily a negative one. Unfounded generalizations about adaptive family structures among African Americans resulted from lack of knowledge of traditional African culture and family structure.

FEMALE-HEADED HOUSEHOLDS:
A LEGACY OF SLAVERY
OR AFRICAN HERITAGE?

Enslaved women who had their first children out of wedlock usually did not set up independent households but continued to live with their parents. Most of them subsequently married and began residing neolocally with their husbands. Further, Degler (1980) suggested that the early pregnancies of slave women were largely explained by the nature of slavery itself. Slave masters had an interest in encouraging offspring, an interest that could easily be translated into the earlier the better. Slave women could count on their children being supported as their masters assets. Black women in 1890 had a considerably higher rate of prenuptial pregnancy (defined as a child born less than 8 months after marriage) than did other native- or foreign-born urban or rural Whites.

At one time, sociologists and historians alike assumed that slavery was the source of the female-headed household among Blacks occurring after emancipation. Frazier suggested that the development of conditions that arose during slavery allowed the development of female-headed households in the context of urbanization in later periods (Frazier, 1939/1966). Gutman's (1976) analysis weakened the notion of early beginnings of female-headed families through the use of plantation registers. His findings clearly supported the presence of two-parent families in the majority. Gutman suggested that female-headed households developed mainly in one of two situations. First, a woman whose husband died or was sold off the plantation might head a household composed of her children and perhaps grandchildren born to an unmarried daughter. Second, a woman who did not marry after having one or two children out of wedlock but continued to have children might have her own cabin built for her. Sudarkasa (1988) suggested the importance of distinguishing the two types of female-headed households, the first as a phase in the developmental cycle of a conjugally headed household and the second as a case of neolocal residence by an unmarried female. Most unmarried mothers in Black communities continued to live in households headed by other adults (Sudarkasa, 1988). Living arrangements other than traditional nuclear families were not central in Gutman's focus. The presence of competing interests (the enslaved and slave owners) may have played a critical role in the development of husband/wife families or "family"-headed families.

Gutman's work acknowledged and confirmed the presence of the nuclear family among early African American family structures in the United States and emerged as a priori "proof" that the nuclear family existed to dispute the idea of matrifocal families as the dominant type. The effect of both seminal works is the exclusion of serendipitous or latent functions among the enslaved Africans (Gutman) and early contemporary families (Frazier) that may have reflected adaptive kin interrelationships including various types of female-headed households and residences. Gutman (1976) and Degler (1980) noted confidently that the model of family development exhibited by most slaves was nuclear in form and resembled those of their White owners, including seeking permission for courtship and eventual marriage.

Enslaved persons had to obtain permission from their owners to marry, although such marriages were not legally recognized. Slaves created their own ritual, "jumping the broomstick," to seal their vows. Perhaps this symbolic ritual was an adaptation of other activities present in African cultures that carried over to the new surroundings. In spite of efforts on the part of the slave owners, marriage did not guarantee that one spouse would not be sold away from the other. Slave masters terminated more than one third of the marriages, about one half by death of a spouse, and only about one tenth by mutual consent or desertion (Degler, 1980).

The majority of slave women married, but a substantial minority lived as single women and mothers. Single mothers were not penalized economically or socially relative to married couples. Slave masters welcomed out-of-wedlock children like all offspring of enslaved Africans. Children inexpensively increased wealth for the slaveholder. Their families accepted them as they had in Africa whether they were fathered by husbands or by the owners themselves. Legitimation through the presence of a father was not a requirement. Slave communities continued African extended family systems, even augmenting them with fictive or chosen kin (Amott & Matthaei, 1991; Sudarkasa, 1988). Extended family relations provided a community of parents for the children of single mothers, similar to community support networks present in contemporary society (Collins, 1990).

Gutman rarely addressed the issue of rape and unlimited access of the slave owners to enslaved African females during his lengthy discussion of out-of-wedlock births. Such behaviors were often overlooked by dominant scholars who based their writings on the unsupported *assumption* that African women were naturally promiscuous. Notions of promiscuity in sexual behavior among Africans received their beginning support along with other polygynous societies when early observers noted the presence of multiple partners. Unbeknown to these observers, the practice of polygyny also carried significant responsibility for the married persons in addition to sexual behavior. Gutman noted that many slave women customarily had intercourse with someone other than their resulting husbands before they "settled in" to a permanent relationship. On all the plantations investigated by Gutman, there were some single women who had children by unknown fathers or by different fathers. African American women usually had their first child much earlier than did free White women, even those of the poorer classes.

Apparently during slavery, many Black women lived alone with their children; many fathers were slaves who often lived on nearby farms or plantations. Once slavery was abolished, those families with absent fathers were reestablished along with the abrupt rise in two-parent households (Ricketts, 1988). Similar shifts did not occur in free states (Degler, 1980). Since slavery, the proportion of female-headed households among Blacks has usually been greater than among other Americans. The differences between Blacks and other ethnic groups has continued into the 20th century.

HOUSEHOLD COMPOSITION

Historically, large numbers of children were not present in female-headed households. In 1880, for example, female-headed households among women aged 30-49 usually had one or two children younger than 18. Furthermore, the overall age distribution of all female household heads studied in 1880 suggested that a substantial portion of them were heads only because their husbands had died. Between 23% and 30% of the households studied in each rural and urban area had as its head a woman of at least age 50 (Gutman, 1975). Black women between the age of 15 and 40 far outnumbered males in the same age group. This imbalance was not nearly as marked in the southern rural areas as it was in the southern cities where it was substantially larger.

Differences in the numbers of female-headed households between Blacks and Whites diminish sharply under conditions of economic parity (Furstenberg, Hershberg, & Modell, 1975). Furstenberg et al. (1975) found that female-headed households varied inversely with wealth among urban populations. They were found far less often among families with property valued at more than $500 than among propertyless families.

As with the 1870 federal census, female-headed households and property holdings were negatively related. Significantly, this negative relationship is visible for sums of less than $100, so that in 1838, for example, Black families with $50 to $99 of property were only about three fourths as likely to be female headed as were families with less than $50. Differential wealth accounted for the observed disparity between Philadelphia's Blacks and Whites in family composition (Furstenberg et al., 1975).

Black urban households had readily identifiable structural characteristics following the Reconstruction. These included relatively high proportions of female-headed families, women in the paid labor force, widows, and fewer family members. The majority of households consisted of both a father and a mother within the core family, but a significant minority did not. The percentage of female heads varied in cities throughout the South, but generally, from 25% to 30% of all urban Black families lacked a father or husband in the home at any one time between 1880 and 1915 (Jones, 1985).

As a rule, households headed by women were most common among economically disadvantaged groups and among those with an imbalanced sex ratio in favor of females—two characteristics of the Black population in southern cities (Furstenberg et al., 1975; Jones, 1985). This finding has caused many to question the position that variations in family composition can be traced to divergent subcultural standards. Structural inequalities, then, may offer a better explanation than cultural variation.

In many respects, the argument that the roots of the Black matrifocal family are to be found in slavery represents an extension of the subcultural argument, and the same criticisms that pertain to the subcultural explanation can be applied historically (Furstenberg et al., 1975). What would have been the consequences if fathers had not been sold away? Would the number of female-headed families be similar? In countries where slavery occurred in some form, was this the trend among other persons of African descent, or was this strictly a phenomenon characteristic of Africans in the United States?

New historical studies provide compelling reasons to question the destructive impact that slavery allegedly had on Black family structures (Davis, 1981; Jones, 1985; White, 1985). One major conclusion is that the slave family was undeniably stronger than is often portrayed. Gutman's (1976) data supported the fact that the vast majority of Black families were headed by both parents. The data convincingly contradict the view that slavery "destroyed" the Black family. On the other hand, Gutman's research prepares and tempts the reader to develop a culturally deviant family form when other structures are present. The notion that should be evident in the scholarly mind should revolve around the fact that the destruction hypothesis surfaced within one generation removed from Africa. The destruction was either quite effective or conceptual frameworks and theoretical explanations lacked adequate substance. The viability of complete destruction is not likely, although scholars have treated the concept of family among African Americans as if it were destroyed and is gradually being strengthened and rebuilt. It is far more likely, however, that theories and conceptual frameworks used to explain families were undeniably flawed. Remnants of the African heritage and culture logically remained within the consciousness of the enslaved people. Familiar practices were altered for fear of retaliation. Visible examples of culture, then, cannot be used in isolation as indicators of Africanisms following emancipation. Additionally, because neither Whites nor early family scholars were well versed with the culture of African peoples, it is unlikely that remaining patterns of culture would have been recognized and acknowledged by them.

The negative portrayal of Africa has influenced the worldview of its customs, culture, and beliefs. Characteristic of ethnocentric tendencies permeating research outside the United States, scholars and laypersons alike assumed numerous descriptors of the enslaved Africans and their behaviors. Because much of their everyday life in practice was much different from that of Whites, little attention was given to substantiating that the traditionally conceived family had been destroyed during slavery or that any other form existed.

Free Blacks and Female-Headed Households

Single mother families were as common among free Blacks as among slaves. In some cities, single headedness characterized the majority of free Black families. In 1820, 58% of all free Black households in Petersburg, Virginia, were maintained by single women. These households contained over half of the free Black population and 57% of the children under age 14. In the 1850s, 61% of all free Black family units in Charleston, South Carolina, were maintained by single women. A significant imbalance in the sex ratio among free Blacks in Petersburg and Charleston contributed to the lack of marriageable men. Laws prohibited Black women from marrying slaves or free Whites (Amott & Matthaei, 1991, p. 151).

FEMALE-HEADED HOUSEHOLDS: SOME EXPLANATIONS

Several explanations for female-headed families have been offered. Darity and Myers (1984) suggested that the female age distribution and the female to male ratio were significant factors that contributed to the contemporary incidence of female-headed households. Higher mortality rates among males of all ages affecting the sex ratio also contributed to larger numbers of households headed by single parents. Social policy commentators in the 1960s characterized one fourth of Black families headed by females as irrefutable confirmation that Blacks are caught in a "tangle of pathology" (Jewell, 1988). Mounting evidence showed that more than 40% of Black families are female headed and that these families are overwhelmingly poor. Contemporary studies consistently highlight the fact that the number of families headed by women continues to rise. Invariably, the consequences are higher levels of poverty that these families are likely to endure but not necessarily instability and destruction of their families.

The argument that Black female headship is an economically motivated phenomenon has a long history. For some, it was the fragile economic position of the Black male that compounded the difficulty of Black women in finding marriage partners.

According to Gutman (1975), Frazier failed to use careful methods in developing a historical explanation for the condition of the Black family in the 1920s and the 1930s. The scholarly climate of the day did not allow for discourse on the issue of humanity associated with African Americans and their families, although some scholars such as Du Bois and Herskovits insisted that the link existed and had not been destroyed during slavery. Frazier (1939/1966) read the current state of the African American condition back into the past and linked it directly to the nineteenth century slave experience (Platt, 1991). It is not difficult to dispute, as Frazier (1939/1966) wrote, that "the maternal family organization, a heritage from slavery . . . continued on a fairly large scale" because this critical assertion rested more on opinion than on historical evidence (quoted in Gutman, 1976, p. 633).[2] Despite the lack of evidence, Frazier's arguments about the matriarchy gained widespread acceptance during the mid-1900s, culminating with Moynihan's highly controversial interpretation in the 1960s: that the deterioration of the family itself was a root cause of the pathological nature of the Black family.

CONCLUSION

Much of the speculation about the origins of the matrifocal family has been uninformed by systematic historical investigation. In recent years, historians have begun to correct this situation. With each new study, misconceptions about the past have resulted in similar misconceptions of the present. An ever present problem is the lack of interdisciplinary approaches to the study of families. Scholars for whom the family is not a substantive area of specialization sometimes fail to pay careful attention to diversity within family structures and make erroneous generalizations, definitions, and assumptions about families, race, and ethnic relations and view the structural effects of the "race problem" but fail to include the direct effects on the family and its members. Policy analysts assume one type of family structure and make recommendations toward that end. Granted, the roles of the changing family are acknowledged. Within society, legislators and governmental bodies on an individual basis recognize the need for changes in the development of policies directly related to family policies and structure.

Economic status affects the structure of the family because Black males suffered extremely high mortality and women with children faced difficulties remarrying. To the extent that the number of neolocally resided female-headed families increased during the 1940s and 1950s, the structure intensified not as a legacy of slavery but as a result of northern urban life and the struggle with other immigrants for equal wages and opportunity (Blackburn & Richards, 1981).

The instability of the Black family based on female-headed households has not received empirical support. As survival mechanisms, community networks in the form of "other mothers" and fictive kin often assist single-parent-family efforts (Collins 1990). The most pressing issue, then, is not the family structure itself but the accompanying poverty. For decades, households have been headed by females. The phenomenon is not new, nor does the structure itself command such radical behaviors to encourage marriages to abandon this family structure.

Irrespective of the diverse backgrounds of the Africans enslaved in America, there was a commonality in the familial patterns known to them. Because most enslaved Africans were descended from tribes residing in central and western Africa, language and culture were similar enough so that communication and understanding were easily facilitated. In addition to adjusting to tribal differences, the presence of a European-oriented culture coupled with an alien land provided challenges (Levine, 1977). The enslaved Africans' shared nationalism enabled them to create recognizably African patterns where they lived, which were observable to the careful researcher (Herskovits, 1958/1990). Adaptations were made to their particular circumstance. In some instances, lack of conformity meant life or death decisions. Varying presentations of the self by enslaved Africans to enhance survival are well documented.[3] However, this did not obliterate the fact of their origin. If Israelites enslaved in Egypt for centuries could remain Israelites, if diverse European peoples in the 20th century can still acknowledge cultural survivals from ancient Greece and Rome, it is not so preposterous that Africans, only a few generations removed from their homelands, would show evidence of their cultural roots (Sudarkasa, 1980).

Among African Americans, households that revolve around consanguineal relatives have as much legitimacy and in most communities as much respectability as *family units* as do households centered around conjugal unions. It becomes clear as this fact is understood that the stability of conjugal relations cannot be taken as the sole measure of stability of the family. The conjugal unit is not taken as a necessary indicator of the prevalence of nuclear families of the Western type. African American households and family systems were exceedingly complex following their departure from their native land and in the aftermath of emancipation; this characteristic continues to be exhibited in contemporary society. Arrangements within them continue to vary greatly, but "chaos and disorder" are not useful concepts in understanding African American families (Ricketts, 1988).

NOTES

1. Sudarkasa (1980) examines the relationship between Africans and African American family structures and highlights many differences as well as similarities.

2. For a balanced assessment of Frazier's work on the family, see Gutman (1975).

3. Levine (1977) and Herskovits (1958/1990) offer detailed discussion of behavior in the presence of Whites and behavior in the presence of Blacks as survival skills. Dill (1988) also offers insight into the domestic worker-employer relationship, which suggests similar sorts of contemporary behavior resembling efficient coping strategies for economic survival in the African American community.

REFERENCES

Amott, J., & Matthaei, T. L. (1991). *Race, gender, and work: A multicultural economic history of women in the United States.* Boston: South End Press.

Asante, M. K. (1987). *The Afrocentric idea.* Philadelphia: Temple University Press.

Asante, M. K. (1988). *Afrocentricity.* Trenton, NJ: Africa World Press.

Billingsley, A. (1968). *Black families in White America.* Englewood Cliffs, NJ: Prentice Hall.

Billingsley, A. (1992). *Climbing Jacob's ladder: The enduring legacy of African-American families.* New York: Simon & Schuster.

Blackburn, G., & Richards, S. L. (1981). The mother headed family among free Negroes in Charleston, South Carolina, 1850-1860. *Phylon, 42*(1), 11-25.

Blassingame, J. W. (1972). *The slave community: Plantation life in the antebellum South.* New York: Oxford University Press.

Collins, P. H. (1990). *Black feminist thought: Knowledge, consciousness, and the politics of empowerment.* Boston: Unwin Hyman.

Darity, W. A., Jr., & Myers, S. L., Jr. (1984, November). Does welfare dependency cause female headship? The case of the Black family. *Journal of Marriage and the Family, 46,* 765-779.

Davis, A. Y. (1981). *Women, race and class.* New York: Vintage.

Dill, B. T. (1988). Our mother's grief: Racial ethnic women and the maintenance of families. *Journal of Family History, 13*(4), 415-431.

Degler, C. N. (1980). *At odds: Women and the family in America from the revolution to the present.* New York: Oxford University Press.

Du Bois, W. E. B. (1969). *The Negro American family.* New York: Negro University Press. (Original work published 1908)

Du Bois, W. E. B. (1990). *The souls of Black folk.* New York: Vintage. (Forethought first published 1903)

Fields, B. J. (1985). *Slavery and freedom on the middle ground: Maryland during the 19th century.* New Haven, CT: Yale University Press.

Frazier, E. F. (1966). *The Negro family in the United States.* Chicago: University of Chicago Press. (Original work published 1939)

Furstenberg, F. F., Jr., Hershberg, T., & Modell, J. (1975). The origins of the female headed Black family: The impact of the urban experience. *Journal of Interdisciplinary History, 2,* 211-233.

Gutman, H. (1975). Persistent myths about the Afro-American family. *Journal of Interdisciplinary History, 2,* 181-210.

Gutman, H. (1976). *The Black family in slavery and freedom: 1750-1925.* New York: Pantheon.

Herskovits, M. J. (1990). *The myth of the Negro past.* Boston: Beacon. (Original work published 1958)

Holloway, J. E. (1990). *Africanisms in American culture.* Bloomington: Indiana University Press.

Jewell, K. S. (1988). *Survival in the Black family: The institutional impact of U.S. social policy.* New York: Praeger.

Jones, J. (1985). *Labor of love, labor of sorrow: Women, work, and the family, from slavery to the present.* New York: Vintage.

Levine, L. (1977). *Black culture and Black consciousness.* New York: Oxford University Press.

McAdoo, H. P. (Ed.) (1988). (2nd ed.). *Black families.* Newbury Park, CA: Sage.

McDaniel, A. (1990). The power of culture: A review of the idea of Africa's influence on family structure in antebellum America. *Journal of Family History, 15,* 225-238.

Moynihan, D. P. (1965). *The Negro family: The case for national action.* Washington, DC: U.S. Government Printing Office.

Platt, A. (1991). *E. Franklin Frazier reconsidered.* New Brunswick, NJ: Rutgers University Press.

Ricketts, E. (1988). The origin of Black female headed families. *Focus*, pp. 32-36 (University of Wisconsin Poverty Series).

Staples, R. (1987). Social structure and Black family life: An analysis of current trends. *Journal of Black Studies, 17,* 267-286.

Sudarkasa, N. (1980, November/December). African and Afro-American family structure: A comparison. *Black Scholar,* pp. 37-60.

Sudarkasa, N. (1988). Interpreting the African heritage in Afro-American family organization. In H. P. McAdoo (Ed.), *Black families* (pp. 27-43). Newbury Park, CA: Sage.

White, D. G. (1985). *Ar'n't I a woman? Female slaves in the plantation South.* New York: Norton.

Woodson, C. G. (1925). *Free Negro heads of families in the United States in 1830.* Washington, DC: Association for the Study of Negro Life and History.

3

Women's Life-Affirming Morals and the Cultural Unity of African Peoples

Annie Ruth Leslie

This chapter builds on a previous work in which I investigated the Black woman's traditional view that unwed motherhood was a mistake but not a sin (Leslie, 1994a). I observed that Western Christian morals, in which the "sin of unwed motherhood" was regarded as an intrinsically "corrupt" aspect of human sexuality, influenced the sociological view that Black women's "indifference" to this sin equaled acceptance. As a result, this sexual outlook was associated with deviance and with poor Black women's matrifocal family structure and welfare status (Frazier, 1939/1966; Moynihan, 1965).

Although I found no significant relationship between low-income Black women's single-parent family structure and their indifference to the "sin of unwed motherhood," my findings showed a strong relationship between this attitude and their participation in certain *life-affirming* Black religious and folkloric traditions. This association led me to argue that their sexual outlook was misunderstood and that to assess it properly one must understand first that it was not a condoning of unwed motherhood. Rather, it was an expression of a normative Black morality in which views of sexuality as absolutely corrupt are avoided. Indeed, many of the Black women I studied, both single and married, felt that unwed motherhood was a wrongdoing but was not corrupt. Although these women sometimes used the words "sin" and "wrongdoing" interchangeably, their interpretations indicate that the idea that there is an inherent corruption or taint associated with human sexuality and the human essence was absent.

Western Christian morality holds that behavior such as unwed motherhood, premarital sex, and adultery is intrinsically bad, or a sin. The "original sin" lies in the absolute corruption of human sexuality and the human essence (Bullough & Brundage, 1982; Staples, 1994; Walton, 1972). From the sociological perspective, the absolutism of sin contributed to a negative image of human sexuality (Andersen, 1988) and created rigid dichotomies between good and bad, sacred and secular, as well as between other general oppositions (Bullough & Brundage, 1982; Calvin, 1536/1957; Walton, 1972).

In contrast, Black morality does not consider undesirable acts as intrinsic aspects of people and behavior (Frankfort, 1948; Genovese, 1974; Herskovits, 1941; Leslie, 1994a; Tempels, 1952). Instead, the wrongdoing of unwed motherhood is understood in terms of a mistake theme in which the undesirable aspect of this behavior is external to the behavior (see Blassingame, 1972; Ladner, 1971; Leslie, 1994a). In in-depth interviews with 41 poor Black mothers, both single and married, I found that they generally rejected the view that unwed motherhood was corrupt. As stated above, they did not interpret it as a sin but as a mistake. To them, the mistake meant that a good and natural act, not a sinful act, had occurred in an undesirable way; that is, the necessary father role was excluded from the family unit.

The women also rejected absolute negative definitions of other behavior. They believed that trickery, a vice of the rabbit-hero in the Black American Brer Rabbit tales, was undesirable but not an assault on Christian-sanctioned morals, as claimed in the literature. In their storytelling, these women claimed that situationally defined trickery played a progressive role in that it taught children the importance of thinking ahead and behaving justly (Leslie, 1994b). They interpreted rhythmic music and dance, secular instruments such as drums and guitars, and secular joking styles and messages by preachers as integral aspects of sacred, "good" church worship.

My specific contribution in this chapter lies in explaining how low-income Black women's flexible ways of integrating, not separating, sacred and secular themes in religious institutions and themes of virtue and vice in the Brer Rabbit stories, taken together with their interpretations of unwed motherhood as a mistake, not a sin, constitute a Black morality or a *pragmatic unity ethic,* in which oppositions are harmonized, not dichotomized, so as to affirm the group.

This chapter moves beyond the examination of low-income African American women's life-affirming morals, in light of the larger African and African American moral tradition, to compare this morality with a similar moral orientation among certain poor African Americans and in various traditional African Bantu, Egyptian, Sudanese, and Yoruba groups. Unlike many Christian groups who adhere to moral codes based on sin, these groups reject the notion of sin (Frankfort, 1948; Genovese, 1974; Neimark, 1993; Stuckey, 1987; Tempels, 1952; Wood, 1990). Like African American women's affirmative moral stances, however, this rejection neither promotes nor supports single-parent families or wrongdoing. Quite the contrary: It includes both father's and mother's positions in family units and integrates, not separates, sacred and secular and virtue and vice themes in human institutions (Leslie, 1994c).

My purpose in studying moral similarities between selected African groups and certain poor African American groups is threefold. First, it allows me to situate poor Black women's sexual ethos within their larger African religiocultural context and to label these more accurately as Afrocentric morals. Second, it enables me to describe more comprehensively how Afrocentric morality differs from Eurocentric morality. Third, and most important, it provides me with a normative moral framework in which I can pose new and important questions regarding how Afrocentric morals empower women.

I begin by discussing two important religious traditions—the Western Christian and the African pragmatic—and describing how the African tradition has influenced a particular moral orientation among certain working-class Southern Baptist Black groups and women. Then I present new questions regarding Afrocentric morals and the empowerment of women that should be investigated in future research.

WESTERN CHRISTIAN AND AFRICAN PRAGMATIC RELIGIOUS SYSTEMS

The Christian Tradition

In pointing out how White American men used the concept "Christian" to distinguish Whites from enslaved Blacks, Jordan (1968) observed not only that Christianity was defined in different ways but also that these definitions had "lost any connection with explicit religious difference" (p. 94). Similarly, in advocating the femaleness of Jesus Christ as well as a rejection of marriage, Christian groups such as the United Society of Believers in the Second Coming of Christ (Shakers) demonstrated the remarkable elasticity of Christianity (Kephart & Zelner, 1991). Christianity also was interpreted in different ways by Old World Orthodox Roman Catholic, Coptic, Manichean, and Nestorian Christian groups (Bullough & Brundage, 1982) as well as by more recent New World Baptist, Methodist, and Holiness groups, such as the Father Divine Movement of Washington, D.C. (Frazier, 1963/1974). Even so, Cambridge scholars Mackinnon, Williams, Vidler, and Bezzant (1963) wrote that Christian groups generally agreed that "abstinence" from premarital sexual relations constitutes Christian moral behavior. Mackinnon et al. objected to Christian morals regarding abstinence not because abstinence was necessarily a bad thing but because they believed that the Christian values surrounding it "failed to present adequate positive images of human life" (p. 9). That is, as the founding church fathers interpreted "original sin," abstinence was associated with man's tainted sexual nature. When Calvin (1536/1957) wrote about "original sin," he stated succinctly, "To remove all uncertainty and misunderstanding on the subject of original sin . . . appears to be a hereditary depravity and corruption of our nature, diffuse through all parts of the soul" (p. 42).

As for the medieval church's view of sexual practices, Bullough and Brundage (1982) wrote that "in much of Christian thought, sex has been regarded as sinful, except for procreation" (p. ix). Although they observed that this view was crucial in shaping sin-centered attitudes about sexuality, they admitted that the Bible is somewhat ambiguous about sex. They explained, however, that "in the sex field . . . what we call Christian attitudes are really Augustinian attitudes" (p. xi). In regard to these attitudes, Schopenhauer (1819/1958) observed that Saint Augustine and other founding church fathers, such as the Apostle Paul and John Calvin, equated sexuality with "original sin." Although Paul taught that man's true essence is tainted by human sexuality (Romans 3: 21), Schopenhauer observed that both Paul and Augustine felt this taint could be transformed only through regeneration in Jesus Christ—hence the Immaculate Conception.

Calvin (1536/1957) suggested that original sin had an impact beyond the sexual, namely, influencing the development of absolutist moral stances: "The works that proceed thence, such as adulteries, fornication, thefts, hatreds, murder, revelings, he [Paul] calls in the same manner, 'fruits of sin' " (p. 42). Although Bullough and Brundage (1982) observed that Saint Paul did not believe that sex in marriage was sinful, they noted that he believed married people had "trouble in the flesh" (p. 3). Schopenhauer (1819/1958), however, asserted boldly that "in Christianity proper, marriage is regarded as a compromise with man's sinful nature, a concession" (p. 617). Likewise, Nietzsche (1886/1968) criticized Western Christian sin-centered morals because he claimed they impeded the life process itself.

Although Bullough and Brundage (1982) fell short of labeling Saint Paul's pronouncements misogynistic, they observed that his teachings affected women adversely in that the sins of premarital sex, unwed motherhood, and adultery were associated primarily with women. The 18th-century feminist Mary Wollstonecraft (1792/1992) attacked Western Christian values that equated women's honor solely with chastity because she believed they were evidence of a superficial moral system that impeded genuine virtue and morality. Similarly, feminist Mary Daly (1973) criticized Christian morals for both their denial of self-actualization to women and stifling of honesty in men. From a sociological viewpoint, Andersen (1988) explained that certain Christian myths, which define women as bad, provided people—in the Durkheimian sense—with the "collective" strength needed to live up to certain group responsibilities (p. 213).

Whether Western Christian sinful morals were evident of a moral system that impeded or advanced the individual's ability to carry out group goals, many sociologists observe that many African Americans, including Christians, were indifferent to absolute corrupt views of people and behavior. For instance, Walton (1972) observed that many Blacks rejected absolute separations of sacred from secular music and forms of worship: they eschewed morals that forbade the inclusion of dance, rhythmic music, and instruments in sacred ceremonies because these were considered sinful. In *Slave Culture,* Stuckey (1987) observed that dance, a sacred act for both Africans and African Americans, was associated with "the continuing cycle of life . . . the divine" (p. 25). Similarly, Genovese (1974) stated in *Roll Jordan Roll* that "blacks accepted Christianity's celebration of the individual soul while simultaneously remaining indifferent to sin" (p. 211). He attributed this to Black Americans' life-affirming African values.

The African Pragmatic Tradition

Because Africa is a continent of diverse ethnic and linguistic groups, researchers continue to ask, in spite of the "African origins" school, whether a unified African cultural experience exists for Africans in Africa and for those in the diaspora (see Appiah, 1992; Asante, 1991; Stuckey, 1987). Although the debate continues, scholars have made several interesting observations about Negroid African religion that shed light on African Americans' apparent indifference to the concept of sin. First, in spite of ethnic differences, sin appears to be foreign to many traditional Black African religious systems. Second, this absence is associated with the peoples' beliefs in a benevolent God who creates primarily the good. Third, these two points taken together explain why many Africans harmonize rather than dichotomize good and bad, sacred and secular, and other oppositions including the masculine and the feminine (Asante, 1991; Frankfort, 1948; Herskovits, 1941; Jahn, 1961; Neimark, 1993; Tempels, 1952). That is, because life is viewed as primarily good, the seemingly undesirable elements logically must be explained in terms of how they counterbalance the good. In this sense, the functional role of undesirable elements in African moral systems differs from Durkheim's (1893/1960) functional outlook in that the African one does not support particular social institutions so much as a natural social order that one comes to understand through observation and study (Frankfort, 1948; Herskovits, 1941). Moreover, where sexuality is concerned, the good is thought to be embodied in a procreative, feminine, life-giving principle (Jahn, 1961; Neimark, 1993). In discussing Ifa, for instance, the religious philosophy of the Nigerian Yoruba people, Neimark (1993) recounted how Yoruba women and men believe that the sexual enticement of Ogun, one of their principal gods, by the goddess Osun explains why "life for people on earth would once again progress" (p. 91). Osun's sensuousness, unlike Eve's, forwards woman's and man's growth and development.

Father Placide Tempels, a Belgian priest working in the Congo among various Bantu-speaking peoples, claimed that their positive view of procreation was paralleled by no other people. He attributed this view to certain *lifeforce* principles. Here, lifeforce referred to Bantu beliefs that *being,* the highest good, is a godly energy realized in procreative functions. As Tempels (1952) wrote, "Force, the potent life, vital energy are the objects of prayers and invocations to God, to the spirits and to the dead" (p. 31). In this system, ancestors are exalted inasmuch as they are procreative founders of the human race and thus propagators of the divine vital human strength. The dead, too, are esteemed "to the extent to which they increase and perpetuate their vital force in their progeny" (p. 31). Tempels claimed that these lifeforce principles presented a positive image of the life process and explained why Bantus "reject as foreign . . . the dualism of good and evil as two forces" (p. 36).

Writing about Bantu lifeforce principles in a note to Father Tempels, Herskovits asserted, "I am interested that so many of the ideas that Father Tempels exposes as coming from the Belgian Congo are so close to those that I have found of the Sudanese peoples of the Guinea coast areas. . . . They are the same ideas . . . found in such areas as Haiti and Brazil and Suriname and the New World" (cited in Tempels, 1952, p. 26). In another note to Tempels, Egyptologist Jean Capart recounted how similar progressive human images characterized ancient Egyptian morals (cited in Tempels, 1952, p. 26).

Egyptologist Henri Frankfort believed that the ancient Egyptians' rejection of sin was explained by their view that the lifeforce was basically good. Frankfort (1948) contrasted the Egyptians' moral values with those of the Mesopotamians, whose prevailing mood was uncertainty, and with those of the Hebrews, who believed that the individual's laxity could not be reformed (p. 60). Comparing this view of sin with the biblical view, Frankfort claimed that ancient Egyptians believed that bad was not intrinsic to people or to social institutions; rather, "evil had its appointed place, counterbalanced by good" (p. 73). Ancient Egyptians did not believe that good and bad formed a dialectic; rather, wrote Frankfort, "the Egyptian viewed his misdeeds not as sins but as aberrations. . . . They disturbed his harmonious integration with the existing world" (p. 73). Similarly, Blassingame (1972), Genovese (1974), Mitchell (1975), and Stuckey (1987) concluded that many enslaved fieldhands and low-income Black Americans from traditional backgrounds reject wrongdoing as an intrinsic aspect of the existing social order.

African American Religious Communalism

Although African Americans' social experience in the United States has not been monolithic, an indifference to the idea of sin resembling that of ancient Egyptian, Sudanese, Bantu, and Yoruba peoples has been widely observed (Genovese, 1974; Herskovits, 1941; West, 1988; Wood, 1990). As in the African tradition, this indifference is associated with flexible ways of integrating, not separating, oppositions in human institutions. For instance, in *The Myth of the Negro Past,* Herskovits (1941) observed that African Americans view good and evil as integrally related. He wrote that "of all Africanisms, this element of belief has most persisted in the mores of Negro life everywhere in the New World" (p. 74). Genovese (1974) claimed that when enslaved Africans "accepted Christianity's celebration of the individual soul while simultaneously remaining indifferent to sin" (p. 211), they did so because of their life-affirming African values.

West (1988) associated the life-affirming tradition with Black Americans' communal church service and wrote, "Black people do not attend church to find God, but rather to share and expand together the rich heritage they have inherited" (p. 163). He associated this heritage with rhythmic singing and preaching church styles, which expressed "existential freedom" or a "mode of being in the world that resists dread and despair, embodying an ecstatic celebration of human existence without affirming prevailing reality" (p. 162). Smith (1976) reasoned that "one of the hallmarks of the Black religious experience is a recognition of a natural synthesis of 'sense and soul.' . . . Fact and feeling are not seen as antithetical" (p. 7). Stuckey (1987) asserted that dance, another hallmark of this experience, was to Africans and African Americans a means of establishing contact with ancestors and with the gods (p. 25).

Like Stuckey, Walton (1972) and Levine (1977) observed that the Black Americans' syncretization of secular and sacred music was due to their affirmation of the unity of God, man, and nature. Although Levine discussed how some Blacks objected to this syncretization and characterized secular styles such as the blues as "devil" music, he noted that a unity emerged for most individuals. Blassingame (1972) and Genovese (1974) claimed that enslaved Blacks never internalized morals that denigrated the goodness of the human essence, and Stuckey (1987) observed that New World African peoples demonstrated their reverence for life in the counterclockwise ring ceremonies they performed to commemorate ancestors.

Concerning enslaved women specifically, Wood (1990) summarized other writers' observations about them by stating that they were "without awareness that sex is sin. . . . [There was] no hypocrisy, no frustration, no guilt; and no Augustinian association of shame with a natural act" (p. 203). In spite of the views of scholars such as E. Franklin Frazier, who associated Black women's outlook on unwed motherhood with deviance and matrifocality, Gutman (1976) observed that enslaved and rural Black women both preferred and established marital unions whenever possible during and after slavery. Similarly, I found, as did Ladner (1971) in her ground-breaking study, that regardless of sexual outlook, poor urban Black women preferred motherhood in marriage (Leslie, 1994a).

THE EMERGENCE OF AFRICAN
MORALS IN THE UNITED STATES

Class, Regional, and Religious Differences

American slavery produced at least three major classes of African peoples in the United States: a large, dominant group of field workers, a smaller but significant group of service workers, and a very small stratum of free Blacks. On a continuum between the Western Christian and the African pragmatic, African values thrived most among the field worker majority, whereas certain middle-class, northern, Methodist and Episcopalian groups adopted Christian values (Blassingame, 1972; Pitts, 1982; Stuckey, 1987).

Pitts (1982) observed that the house servant/field worker division led to stratification among enslaved Africans; the leverage and benefits available to house servants encouraged their adoption of Christian morals. In this atmosphere of unequal status and opportunity, the field worker majority received little, if any, incentive to adopt Christian values and relied chiefly on their pragmatic African morals. Retaining significant aspects of their African worldview provided the enslaved with alternative explanations for their enslaved status (Gutman, 1976; Sobel, 1979). Genovese (1974) claimed that field workers adhered to their African values because these stressed the goodness of the natural order, thus affirming their lives in spite of obstacles and providing them with the stamina needed to endure harsh field work and social conditions.

Free Black families were closer to Christian than to African moral traditions (Blassingame, 1972). Composed chiefly of the fair-skinned children of slave owners and/or descendants of freedmen, this stratum generally was better educated than the enslaved groups, and their education supported Western Christian moral orientations. Pitts (1982) claimed that the place of free Blacks in American society was contingent largely on their adoption of Western Christian values.

Just as class differences encouraged the field workers' reliance on African values (Blassingame, 1972), certain Baptist churches achieved success in this area as well. Bremer (1924) noticed how effective Methodist missionaries were in instilling Christian values among enslaved Blacks. Although this success is evident in the actions of Methodist bishops such as Daniel Alexander Payne, who traveled throughout the South preaching that Blacks should desist from practicing their African beliefs and rituals, Stuckey (1987) claimed that some of these Blacks still conducted African religious dances, such as the ring shout, in their church services.

Even though Blacks did not join established White Methodist or Baptist churches in large numbers until the coming of missionaries some 200 years after Africans arrived in the New World, Frazier (1963/1974) noted that many free Blacks attended established Methodist churches, which thus hastened their internalization of Christian morals. Frazier observed that the established church failed to make inroads among many field workers, who continued their African ways of thinking and behaving in the "invisible" church.

After emancipation, when former free and recently freed Blacks joined together in the first organized Black Baptist and Methodist churches, differences in their African-Christian outlooks led some Baptist churches to maintain African cultural traits more strongly than others. Often, the African tradition continued in the southern Black Baptist and urban storefront churches frequented by former sharecroppers and field day workers. Black participants in the established Methodist churches tended to be self-employed and skilled or semiskilled workers, some of whom were descendants of freedmen and service workers (Frazier, 1963/1974).

During Reconstruction, when Blacks held political office and attended schools in larger numbers than ever before, many were encouraged further to assimilate mainstream American values. Even so, the economic status of post-Civil War field hands, now called sharecroppers, remained low (Pitts, 1982). Because of their continuing exploited status, sharecroppers had few resources to support their participation in American schools. Sharecroppers' children had to pick cotton while White children and higher-status Blacks were in classrooms or at home. In this way, as in slavery, sharecroppers and other low-income Blacks remained outside mainstream American culture while middle-class Blacks embraced it.

As World War I seriously disrupted the agricultural system, large numbers of sharecroppers migrated to northern cities in search of jobs and better living conditions. In the cities, these families were segregated into poor neighborhoods with limited economic resources. Although the city limited the migrants' economic opportunities, it fostered the continuation of indigenous African values and an Afrocentric worldview (Collins, 1990; Sobel, 1979; Sudarkasa, 1981). Patterns of residential segregation and discrimination led to the establishment of Black neighborhoods and Black Baptist and Pentecostal storefront churches; these expanded with increased discrimination and with the influx of rural southern migrants (Drake & Cayton, 1945). These storefront and small Baptist churches accommodated many former sharecroppers and other groups of Blacks who generally supported indigenous Black morals. Poor Blacks now had access to each other in numbers greater than ever before. In this way, African morals, rather than disappearing, were reinforced.

THE SOCIALIZATION OF
AFRICAN PRAGMATIC VALUES

Today, many urban Blacks are first- and second-generation descendants of southern, working-class migrants (Hannertz, 1969). Because of their shared social experiences at home and in Black Baptist churches in particular, they are influenced continually by morals that eschew absolutist stances. The women I studied, for instance, made clear distinctions between acknowledging unwed motherhood as a mistake and rejecting it as a sin; they viewed these as two separate things (Leslie, 1994a). In this regard, the comments of one mother were typical: "I always looked at unwed mothers as people who had made mistakes. I didn't think of them as sinners or bad people unless they had done something else bad." Another mother said, "It's not like they've [unwed mothers] done something good people don't do. How can they be bad people? They just made a mistake, that's all." When queried about the mistake, a typical comment was made by one mother who said, "I sometimes hear a lot of Black women say unwed mothers are sinners and I have used that word too, but what I mean by this and what I think a lot of other Black women mean by it is that girls make a mistake in getting pregnant without having a husband to help them raise the child." Another said, "It's not like having a baby . . . was a sin, but you don't have a husband to help you raise your child. A child, especially a boy, needs a father to teach him how to behave." Another mother's comments were typical: "I don't think unwed motherhood is sinful, but if you don't have your child's father around, then the family will not be as strong as it could be if both are there." Another said, "It's hard for me, trying to raise my children without a father, because not only do I have to make enough money to raise them but I have to discipline them by myself." She appeared to be comforted by the fact that "at least I have my older brother, who helps me a lot, so hopefully, I do a good job."

Among the women I interviewed who considered unwed motherhood a mistake, many attended traditional Black Baptist churches and associated "good" church worship with certain rhythmic and secular behaviors and teachings. As with the "mistake" versus the "sin" idea of unwed motherhood, these women made few distinctions between sacred and rhythmic music; they associated the rhythmic with an affirmation of the religious community. As one woman put it, "The church should be a place where you can express yourself and not feel that you have to always sit up straight if you don't want to." In this regard, the comments of one woman were typical: "I don't think that dancing or singing soulful music in church is bad. It all depends on what's in your heart when you do it." When queried about this, she replied, "Whether you mean good or bad by it."

These women felt that the church and rhythmic music were supportive and validating. As one said, "In our church, you can do almost anything the spirit makes you feel like doing." She added, "Music in the church is real important. When you can have a church where there is good music, then a lot of people will come to that church." Another said, "I like music in church that makes you want to shout and dance. It's like the spirit of God being manifested in you." Yet another described what she felt was the correctness of rhythmic music: "The way Black people sing and shout in church lets you know this is acceptable in the eyesight of God." Still another said, "I prefer worship in my church because the music gives you the strength to keep on going. It makes you feel that in spite of all your ups and downs, a better day is coming."

These women associated *good* church worship with the preacher's behavior and teachings. Here again, a secular style predominated: Preachers sing, dance, shout, groan, moan, and tell jokes. One woman commented, "What I like about the church I go to is that my preacher is a good minister because he knows how to 'get down' and shout and make a joyful noise unto the Lord." Another said, "I think what we all like about our pastor is he's not afraid to let himself go. . . . He doesn't just tell you about the word of God, he demonstrates it." Yet another said, "Our preacher doesn't just talk his sermon, he tries to relate what he says to everyday life. He tells jokes about people and about other preachers' bad points and about everyday things."

The secular joking style of preachers that many of these women mentioned is reflected in the story of a Black preacher who did not believe in the existence of Hell. He proved his point by telling his congregants, "Oh no, my friends! The Lord would not repeat himself by making a place called Hell when he already had a place called Georgia!" (Leslie, 1994a).

The women I studied preferred preachers who joked and who, as one woman said, "know how to make people laugh about the things we all do but don't want others to know about." Another woman commented, "My pastor can really make you feel happy by the way he shouts and sings in church." Still another said that good preaching occurred when women "start to shouting and dancing in church and letting the spirit in." All of the interviewees associated the preacher's sonorous voice and rhythmic singing style with good church service. As one woman said, "These make you feel the presence of God."

LIFE-AFFIRMING MORALS AND THE CULTURAL UNITY OF AFRICAN PEOPLES

A common theme exists in ancient Egyptian, Bantu, Yoruba, and certain African American peoples' orientations: All posit the basic goodness of sexuality and the human essence. By affirming the integrity of individuals and social groups, this benevolent view influenced the integration of good and bad, sacred and secular, and other generally opposing themes and modes of behavior. Yorubas, for example, rather than associating a "taint" with woman's essence, herald the sexual as the progressive aspect of woman and man in society. Bantu-speaking Africans reject the dualism of good and evil because it contradicts their belief in the good social order. Ancient Egyptians believed that sin was an aberrant, not an intrinsic, aspect of social life; the bad was held in check by the good. Today, many African Americans are indifferent to the idea of sin and generally reject gulfs between sacred institutions and secular preaching styles and rhythmic music. Many African American women, rather than interpreting unwed motherhood as sinful, transfer the undesirable aspects of this behavior outside the act itself—hence the view that it is a mistake, not a sin.

Taken together, these characteristics point to a morality that rejects values supporting *absolute* badness or evil, as well as values supporting dichotomies in social institutions. Conditioned by strong elements of African pragmatism and realism, the Black American moral orientation appears to be associated not merely with a sexual ethos but with an entire philosophy about the nature of social reality itself.

In the United States, women's indifference to the "sin of unwed motherhood" appears rooted in a normative African, not pathological, tradition. In this normative tradition, principles reflecting the "taint" associated with life and sexuality in the Eurocentric Christian tradition are rejected in favor of pragmatic life-affirming principles, according to which women put life and the living process at the center of their moral pronouncements.

CONCLUSION

I have argued here that the absence of "sin" among various African peoples not only helps explain poor Black women's indifference to the sin of unwed motherhood but also illustrates the cultural unity of many African peoples. By "cultural unity" I do not imply that all African and African American people or churches participate equally, or even at all, in this moral tradition. My discussion of class, regional, and religious differences points to unequal moral participation among African Americans.

My theroretical discussion does not include specific information about Black morals among middle-class Black women. Yet the mainstreaming of Black morals, although removed from their traditional meaning and context, has implications for middle-class women, both Black and White. Beginning at least as early as the 1960s, one aspect of the Black moral orientation—the view that human sexuality is good, not tainted—entered the mainstream among White Americans. This outlook coincided with and influenced the sexual revolution and the women's movement. In addition, as Staples (1991) observes, the sexual revolution led even middle-class Black women to question Christian positions on sexual morality and equality. Today, in fact, both Black and White feminists raise questions about the nature of Eurocentric ethics in general (see Collins, 1991; Frazer, Hornsby, & Lovibond, 1992; Gilligan, 1982; Grimshaw, 1986; Shiva, 1989). Moreover, this questioning has created an atmosphere in which Black morals can be examined in healthy dialogue. They are no longer interpreted by some Whites as a Black moral position and thus as deviant and pathological (although most poor Blacks never interpreted their morals this way).

Yet in spite of this dialogue, one important task remains for researchers: They must study the implications of women's life-affirming morals for women's empowerment. That is, in light of the "dialectics" perspective proposed by Dill (1979), sociologists need to investigate the importance of Black morals for women's continuing survival and empowerment in contemporary American capitalist society. For instance, if traditional Black morals include principles that reject the idea of sin, and if "good" and "bad" are integrally related in ways that affirm life and promote the group, how might this situation empower women? Equally important, if traditional Black morals support principles that include a father role in the family not as a concession to the Western Christian tradition (as some people interpret it) but, rather, as a counterbalancing role originating from the pragmatic unity ethic, how does such an ethic encourage males and females to come together and stay together to raise children? How do other economic and social variables interact with these cultural ones so as to impede or strengthen males and females coming together to raise children? When these and other relevant questions are answered, we will understand more clearly the role of morals in human institutions.

REFERENCES

Andersen, M. (1988). *Thinking about women.* New York: Macmillan.

Appiah, K. (1992). *In my father's house.* Oxford: Oxford University Press.

Asante, M. (1991). *Afrocentricity.* Trenton, NJ: Africa World Press.

Blassingame, J. (1972). *The slave community.* Oxford: Oxford University Press.

Bremer, F. (1924). *America of the fifties: Letters of Fredrika Bremer.* New York: Oxford University Press.

Bullough, V., & Brundage, J. (1982). *Sexual practices in the medieval church.* New York: Prometheus.

Calvin, J. (1957). *On the Christian faith.* New York: Liberal Arts Press. (Original work published 1536)

Collins, P. (1991). *Black feminist thought: Knowledge consciousness and the politics of empowerment.* New York: Routledge.

Daly, M. (1973). *Beyond God the father: Toward a philosophy of women's liberation.* Boston: Beacon.

Dill, B. (1979). The dialectics of Black womanhood. *Signs: Journal of Women in Culture and Society, 4*(3), 543-555.

Drake, S. C., & Cayton, H. R. (1945). *Black metropolis.* New York: Harcourt, Brace.

Durkheim, E. (1960). *The division of labor in society.* New York: Free Press. (Original work published 1893)

Frankfort, H. (1948). *Ancient Egyptian religion.* New York: Columbia University Press.

Frazer, E., Hornsby, J., & Lovibond, S. (1992). *Ethics: A feminist reader.* Oxford: Blackwell.

Frazier, E. F. (1966). *The Black family in America.* Chicago: University of Chicago Press. (Original work published 1939)

Frazier, E. F. (1974). *The Negro church in America.* New York: Schocken. (Original work published 1963)

Genovese, E. (1974). *Roll Jordan roll: The world the slaves made.* New York: Vintage.

Gilligan, C. (1982). *In a different voice: Psychological theory and women's development.* Cambridge, MA: Harvard University Press.

Grimshaw, J. (1986). *Philosophy and feminist thinking.* Minneapolis: University of Minnesota Press.

Gutman, H. (1976). *The Black family in slavery and freedom.* New York: Vintage.

Hannertz, U. (1969). *Soulside: Inquiries into ghetto culture and community.* New York: Columbia University Press.

Herskovits, M. (1941). *The myth of the Negro past.* Boston: Beacon.

Jahn, J. (1961). *Muntu: An outline of neo-African culture.* London: Faber & Faber.

Jordan, W. (1968). *White over Black: American attitudes toward the Negro, 1550-1812.* New York: Norton.

Kephart, W., & Zelner, W. (1991). *Extraordinary groups.* New York: St. Martin's.

Ladner, J. (1971). *Tomorrow's tomorrow.* New York: Doubleday.

Leslie, A. (1994a). *Sexual ethics and the single Black mother.* Manuscript submitted for publication.

Leslie, A. (1994b). *Women's moral teachings and socialization of Black children.* Manuscript submitted for publication.

Leslie, A. (1994c). *Afrocentric morality and the empowerment of women.* Unpublished manuscript.

Levine, L. (1977). *Black culture and Black consciousness.* Oxford: Oxford University Press.

Mackinnon, D., Williams, H., Vidler, A., & Bezzant, J. (1963). *Objections to Christian beliefs.* Philadelphia: Lippincott.

Mitchell, H. (1975). *Black beliefs.* New York: Harper.

Moynihan, D. (1965). *The Negro family: The case for national action.* Washington, DC: U.S. Department of Labor.

Neimark, P. (1993). *The way of the orisa.* New York: HarperCollins.

Nietzsche, F. (1968). *Beyond good and evil.* New York: Random House. (Original work published 1886)

Pitts, J. (1982). The Afro-American experience: Changing modes of integration and race consciousness. In A. Dworkin & R. Dworkin (Eds.), *The minority report* (pp. 141-167). New York: Holt, Rinehart & Winston.

Schopenhauer, A. (1958). *The world as will and representation.* New York: Falcon Wing Press. (Original work published 1819)

Shiva, V. (1989). *Staying alive.* London: Zed.

Smith, J. (1976). *Outstanding Black sermons.* Valley Forge, NY: Judson Press.

Sobel, M. (1979). *Trabelin' on: The slave journey to an Afro-Baptist faith.* Princeton, NJ: Princeton University Press.

Staples, R. (1991). The sexual revolution and the Black middle class. In R. Staples (Ed.), *The Black family: Essays and studies* (pp. 88-91). Belmont, CA: Wadsworth.

Staples, R. (1994). *The Black family: Essays and studies.* Belmont, CA: Wadsworth.

Stuckey, S. (1987). *Slave culture.* Oxford: Oxford University Press.

Sudarkasa, N. (1981). Interpreting the African heritage in Afro-American family organization. In H. McAdoo (Ed.), *Black families* (pp. 37-53). Beverly Hills, CA: Sage.

Tempels, P. (1952). *Bantu philosophy.* Paris: Presence Africaine.

Walton, O. (1972). *Music: Black, White, and blue.* New York: Morrow.

West, C. (1988). *Prophetic fragments.* Trenton, NJ: Africa World Press.

Wollstonecraft, M. (1992). Morality undermined by sexual notions of the importance of a good reputation. In E. Frazer, J. Hornsby, & S. Lovibond (Eds.), *Ethics: A feminist reader* (pp. 23-34). Oxford: Blackwell. (Original work by Wollstonecraft published 1792)

Wood, F. (1990). *The arrogance of faith: Christianity and race in America from the colonial era to the twentieth century.* Boston: Northeastern University Press.

4

Teenaged Mothers:
A Sense of Self

Sharon Elise

White people look at us, at Blacks, like we are the ones always to have the babies and be bad. . . . We're always bad and the White folks, they never do anything.

—"Annie"

People treat you like garbage if you let them. . . . The older White women are the worst 'cause they act like it's only Black girls get pregnant and like their race doesn't.

—"Sally"

A Eurocentric bias has guided our understanding of teenage mothering. Well-established discrimination in the media, governing, and educational institutions that are the purveyors of ideology has prevented the acceptance of existent alternative perspectives. One alternative is found in Black feminist frameworks (cf. Collins, 1989), which would reveal the race, class, and gender organization of teenaged mothering. Such alternatives are significant for furthering our understanding of Black teenaged mothers not only because they can bring forward alternative Black community perceptions of teenaged motherhood but also because they give validity to Black teenaged mothers' agency as well as to structural constraints disaffecting young Black women. Examining *agency* requires that we examine the choices and actions of individual subjects, whereas examining *structural constraints* requires that we have an understanding of how the larger social structure—a racist, patriarchal, capitalist system—affects those individuals and the choices available to them.

Black feminist frameworks have developed within the context of a critical Afrocentricity that called into question universalistic notions of gender and gender relations. A critical Afrocentric approach moves the analysis of families headed by Black mothers forward by decentering the standard Eurocentric approach and recentering the analysis within an African ethos. Furthermore, this approach uses the standpoints of Black people to make sense of social arrangements in diverse Black communities. *Critical* Afrocentric approaches include analyses of gender, class, and other important divisions among Black people. Such a framework reaches beyond the stereotypes that have resulted from the European "yardstick" most often used to measure or evaluate Black lives. The subject of teenaged mothering is one particularly fraught with stereotypes.

Seldom does the public hear the stories of Black teenaged mothers, who are more often objects of inquiry than subjects articulating their own perspectives. In this chapter, I examine both the social construction of teenaged motherhood and an articulation of a "sense of self" by Black teenaged mothers drawn from my own studies of teenaged mothers and those of other scholars.

In my 1990 cross-cultural study of teenaged mothers, a community-based analysis was used to examine the macrolevel structures and conditions facing teenaged mothers in Black ($n = 4$), Native American ($n = 9$), and White ($n = 9$) communities in the Northwest and to assess the community's strategies for supporting teenaged mothers. This was accompanied by observations of 75 teenaged mothers in group settings and by in-depth interviews, lasting 2 to 3 hours, of 22 teenaged mothers.

The results of this study suggest that, although race plays an important role in structuring limited opportunities for young women of color, gender relations characterized by varying forms of male dominance pervade all racial groups, presenting motherhood as a viable route to adult status for girls. Furthermore, differences in cultural proscriptions related to sexuality and motherhood result in different levels of acceptance of teenaged motherhood. Blacks in this and other studies presented the most conservative views toward sexuality, yet maintain the greatest family support for teenaged mothers. Blacks also maintain an alternative social construction of motherhood that does not require marriage as the foundation for motherhood. In so doing, Blacks reject the dominant culture's designation of single motherhood as deviant, even when it occurs among teenagers.

BACKGROUND

Nearly 1 million teenagers become pregnant each year in the United States, which has the highest teenaged fertility rates among developed nations (Westoff, 1988). Among U.S. teenaged girls, Blacks have the highest rates of both premarital sexual activity and out-of-wedlock births (Moore, 1988). In the sequence of events leading to teenaged motherhood, including onset of sexual activity, contraceptive failure, pregnancy, and birth, Black teenaged girls are the most likely to choose alternatives that result in early parenthood (Moore, Simms, & Betsy, 1986).

Many in academe, public policy, and the media have highlighted the issue of teenaged mothering as a growing social problem. Although the social consequences of teenaged motherhood are highly debated, most scholars agree that there are clear health implications for the children of teenaged mothers. For example, the lack of prenatal care for teenaged mothers results in low-birth-weight babies, contributing to high infant mortality rates that are more than twice that in the White population.

According to Moore et al. (1986), the negative consequences of teenaged motherhood have been documented to include the following: low birth weights and other health problems, larger families, risk of marital disruption, fewer earners, lower income, more children to support, poverty, and welfare dependency. These problems can be mitigated, however, when school-based programs provide prenatal courses in both parenting and nutrition and, particularly, when family members provide emotional and material support to their pregnant daughters throughout their pregnancy, childbirth, and postpartum adjustment (Furstenberg & Crawford, 1978).

PROBLEMATIZING
TEENAGED MOTHERHOOD

If, as in the case of teenaged motherhood, childbearing takes place under circumstances deemed inappropriate, it is often characterized as deviant because it falls outside the norms for a socially constructed ideal path to motherhood. Once teenaged childbearing is thus problematized, strategies and solutions to teenaged motherhood are proposed with the goal of *normalizing* those who fall in these deviant ranks and preventing others from joining them. Teenaged mothers are those mothers who are too young, too poor, not educated, not married, and not employed. Thus teenaged mothers are defined *from a deficit perspective* by their distance from the "normal" or ideal mother who is the right age, the right class, and is mothering under the right circumstances, which include heterosexual marriage.

Once a case has been labeled deviant, the problem becomes one of measuring its distance from the ideal, often by undertaking research studies of the behavior of the deviant mother to understand how and why she became deviant and then closing that distance by way of employing various strategies to *change the behavior of the deviant.* The goal is to limit the pool of potential deviants, in this case, of course, teenaged mothers—those young, promiscuous, wayward girls whose evidence of their precocious sexual activity is immoral, whose irresponsibility as *mothers* too horrendous to imagine.

Implicit in the characterization of teenaged motherhood as deviant is the assumption that the fertility behavior of teenaged mothers is "bad" and therefore must be controlled. Also implicit is the *belief* that there is an ideal path to motherhood and that deviations from the ideal pose problems to society at large. Ultimately, then, the practice is to challenge the individual deviants themselves to change their behavior.

We forget, because our society has so long been organized by age classifications and the social meanings we ascribe to them, that there is no innate meaning packaged with "babies," "toddlers," "children," "preteens," and "teenagers." If we grant that we have constructed motherhood, it makes sense that we have constructed childhood as well. According to the French historian Philippe Aries (1962), the history of childhood in Europe begins in the modern era. In other words, childhood is a newly created concept, a newly constructed category of being. And prior to the construction of childhood in the American colonial period, children were miniature adults by the time they were 7 years old. There was no special protection of children; there was no childhood (Demos, 1970). With the construction of childhood comes the construction of different types of children. Platt (1974) discusses the "invention of delinquency" in which the children of the lower races—at the time Southern European and Irish immigrants—were seen as a threat to the racial sovereignty of the "native" White U.S. population, whose birth rates were low in comparison to the "hordes" of immigrants with their many children. Those delinquent children were removed from their homes and resocialized on midwestern farms to receive the proper WASP values.

Given this background, it is not surprising that normative standards remain that idealize a particular notion of childhood. Under the prevailing norms, teenaged mothers are deviant because the dominant society has extended the age of childhood, first to 18 when young people graduate from high school and more recently to 22 when they leave college. It appears that this is related to the amount of time we want them to stay out of the labor market. So, if these young people are considered "children" up to 21 or 22 years of age, we can more readily dismiss soaring rates of teenagers' unemployment because, after all, they must be someone's dependents. This notion of childhood falls outside the reach of Black children, who must take alternative paths to adulthood because they are so often denied the normative paths—through education and labor force status—provided by dominant cultural proscriptions.

Another reason why we define teenaged motherhood as problematic is because it is associated with Blacks, and Blacks are associated with poverty. Black poverty, however, is not a *regular* poverty that could happen to anyone but a poverty that is *pathological,* that *cycles* through families and communities, and that is endemic to the *culture* of Blacks.

Lewis's (1946) concept of a *culture of poverty* lays the foundation for the conceptualization of *cycles* of poverty. According to Lewis, "The crucial thing about the subculture of poverty is that it represents both a reaction and an adaptation of the poor to their marginality and helplessness in the larger society" (p. x). The subculture of poverty is specific to capitalist societies, in which the marginalized, illiterate, slum-dwelling poor develop "a way of life which is passed down from generation to generation along family lines" (p. 68). Although this subculture of poverty may *begin* as an adaptation to the harsh conditions of poverty, it *becomes a culture* with a life of its own due to the socialization of children:

> Once it comes into existence, it tends to perpetuate itself from generation to generation because of its effect on the children. By the time slum children are six or seven years old they usually have absorbed the basic values and attitudes of their subculture and are not psychologically geared to take full advantage of changing conditions or increased opportunities which may occur in their lifetime. (p. 69)

It is important to note that, within this conceptualization of the culture of poverty, the poor become complicit in perpetuating their life conditions to the point that when opportunity comes knocking they cannot or will not open the door! The irony is that, in class society, opportunity does not knock at the door of the poor. Rather, it is the lack of opportunity that is a standard feature of poverty. Therefore, this is one of the major points of Lewis's concept that draws fire from critics concerned with the development of victim-blaming analyses of oppressed people.

Lewis's conceptualization of the culture of poverty includes a characterization of family life. He sees the standard traits of families in a culture of poverty as including a shortened period of childhood, early sexual activity, cohabitation, female- or mother-centered families, greater development of maternal extended family ties, belief in male superiority, fatalism, and a failure to plan ahead (pp. 72-73). It is difficult to support Lewis's contention that these traits are specific to the poor. For instance, the national statistics on sexual activity show that across race and class lines girls are becoming sexually active at young ages (Hofferth, Kahn, & Baldwin, 1987). Furthermore, rates of premarital sexual activity are increasing for White teenagers even as the poverty rates for Whites are dropping, whereas similar rates of sexual activity are declining among Blacks even as poverty is increasing (Hofferth et al., 1987).

Another flaw in Lewis's (1946) conceptualization of family life under a culture of poverty lies in his characterization of those families as both mother centered *and* authoritarian *and* carrying strong beliefs of male superiority. It would seem that if these families are indeed more authoritarian and supportive of male supremacy than others, we would see male dominance within the family as well. It is difficult to support his contentions that there is more male dominance among the poor—as he points out in terms of male abandonment of women and children. Given that men across class lines refuse to pay child support and/or alimony, neglect and abandonment of women and children is more a feature of capitalistic patriarchal cultures than of cultures of poverty.

Lewis contends that it is far easier to get rid of poverty itself than of the *culture* of poverty that produces mechanisms by which it perpetuates itself. Despite the flaws in Lewis's culture of poverty thesis, it has become a foundation for policy and popular cultural analyses of unwed motherhood as a mechanism that reproduces poverty. Although Lewis took care not to racialize the culture of poverty thesis by extending it to cover poor southern Whites as well as all the racial minority groups, the concept of this culture of poverty regenerating itself through the socialization of children in poor mother-headed households became synonymous with Blackness in America.

Moynihan (1965/1967) can be credited with the *racialization* of the culture of poverty thesis through his infamous publication, *The Negro Family: A Case for National Action,* which linked the entrenched poverty of Blacks to cycles of poverty, regenerated by the "tangle of pathology" that was the family structure of Blacks. The dependence of Moynihan's thesis on Lewis's concept of the culture of poverty is clear: Just as Lewis argued in 1946 that poverty was more easily abolished than the culture of poverty, so Moynihan (1965/1967) argued that

> unless we work to strengthen the family, to create conditions under which most parents will stay together—all the rest: schools and playgrounds, public assistance and private concern, will never be enough to cut completely the circle of despair and deprivation. (p. 130)

These arguments follow the ideological thrust of neo-Malthusianism; unwed motherhood—synonymous with early, continuous fertility—is a characteristic of the poor that prevents their socioeconomic development. However, Moynihan takes this further, racializing the thesis, by crediting Black family construction—particularly unwed-mother-headed families— for the malaise of the Black community. In so doing, his work lays the basis for the racialization of teenaged motherhood.

This ideological thrust is also apparent in the "family values" debate of the 1980s and 1990s. The "family values" proponents believe that "dysfunctional" families are the cause at the core of social problems such as criminality and poverty. Most succinctly stated by then Vice President Dan Quayle, who even lashed out at fictional television character "Murphy Brown" when she was depicted as choosing to become a single mother, the conservative position was that single-mother-headed families are intrinsically dysfunctional. By implication, any endorsement of single-mother-headed families signaled the demise of "family values," which are held critical to maintenance of the social and moral order of American society. The racialist implications of such a position are clear when we consider the tremendous rise in single-mother-headed families among Blacks. In fact, there appears to be growing acceptance of female-headed families among affluent White women—perhaps because they are not economically dependent—while Black single mothers are viewed as leeches on the public trust.

RACIALIZING TEENAGED MOTHERHOOD

The cat's out of the bag. We'll name the scandal "The Urban Crisis of
Teenage Childbearing" as reporter Leon Dash of *The Washington Post* does
in the subtitle of his book. Listening to teens tell us how and why they
became pregnant or did the impregnating, we'll be shocked, indignant,
bewildered, fuss a little, wag our heads. Then do nothing because the case
histories brought to our attention occurred in one of Washington's poorest,
blackest neighborhoods. . . . Thus the problem seems a black problem, black
kids birthing black babies, the cycle of poverty perpetuated for another
generation, maybe forever. (Wideman, 1989, p. 37)

Our perceptions of fertility are racially constructed, guided, and motivated. The recently developed concept of "racialization" adds explanatory value to the social construction of teenaged motherhood. Omi and
Winant (1986) explain this process: "We employ the term *racialization* to
signify the extension of racial meaning to a previously racially unclass-
ified relationship, social practice or group. Racialization is an ideological
process, an historically specific one" (p. 64).

Although race has no biological base, race does exist as a real feature
of our society because we created it as a social category affecting the
distribution of social resources; it is therefore part of our sensibilities,
behavior, ideologies, and—most important—our social institutions. Race
must be understood as operating independently in our racially organized
society, not subsumable under ethnicity or class. Its foundations in contemporary American society are historical, derived from the creation of
race as category for political and social methods of sorting groups into
different social locations (cf. Blauner, 1972; Steinberg, 1981). Yet race
still remains *institutionalized* in contemporary society, an ongoing pre-
dictor of life chances, social mobility, and access to social resources.

If we recognize that race and racism are institutionalized in U.S.
society, it follows that the way Americans make sense of human behavior
is racially constructed. This fact is particularly salient in the area of
fertility behavior, for it is predominantly European and European American—read "White"—scholars who are concerned with fertility behavior
and it is predominantly people of color—racial groups—whose fertility
behavior is viewed as troublesome:

Blacks are once again being assaulted by "Moynihanism"—the perceptions
of White scholars and media about the status of Black families and their

children. White America's latest analyses come wrapped in concern for the escalating problem of teenage pregnancy and births by Black girls. As usual White scholars and helping professionals would like to control the diagnosis and prescription for Black adolescent parents and their offspring. (Jones, 1987, p. ix)

According to Omi and Winant (1986), the process of racialization explains an ideological shift in which racial meanings are recomposed to describe what is happening among people of color in society. Thus problems of unemployment and changes in our economic structure that result in severe poverty for Blacks are ignored in favor of explanations based on "defective Black cultural norms" (pp. 65-66).

Scholars have assumed that fertility behavior is economically constructed (Zelnick, Kantner, & Ford, 1981) or that fertility behavior is constructing economic conditions. The response of radical scholars (Mamdani, 1981) has been to assert that there is a separate economic rationale guiding the fertility behavior of "marginalized groups." These arguments fail to address motivations of love, of trying to keep a boyfriend by having a baby "for him," or wanting some love object—where the baby is a desirable "product" for itself—or assisting the progress of the conjugal relationship. Also unaddressed is the issue of *subjectivity* in sexual relations, which is required for responsible sexual behavior. In this sense, an understanding of the racial and patriarchal structuring of conjugal relations is required to open the field of questions to other motivations.

Fertility behavior has generally provided an easy solution for economic problems—reducing social poverty by reducing the poor. Fertility behavior that is defined as aberrant provides a target on which to blame the problems of the poor. Thus the racial reasoning is that "welfare people" are unwed Black mothers who are having babies to get welfare. Conveniently, this reasoning works both ways: They are abusing the system by having babies to get free money and if they wouldn't have so many babies they wouldn't be poor and need welfare.

In the current era of neoconservatism, Omi and Winant (1986) argue that the new discourse is rearticulating racial meanings without using explicit racial terms, thus masking the effects of new policies. Antiwelfare moves, hidden as attempts to prevent building dependency among the poor, represent attacks on state spending for racial minorities and poor Whites. And just as Omi and Winant argue that the " 'semipermanent welfare constituency' is implicitly non-White in the popular public imagination," so too are teenage mothers Black, poor, and on welfare in the popular public imagination (p. 124). This theme is also advanced in a recent work, *Chain Reaction,* in which Edsall and Edsall (1992) argue that "race and taxes have created a new, ideologically coherent coalition by pitting taxpayers against tax recipients" (p. 3). Racial divisions, they claim, are at the heart of tax revolts in which "tax recipients" are racially defined, sparking a refusal to support them.

The so-called problem of the teenaged mother is a cultural invention: As such it is a problem that White society is having with Black society. Sexuality looms in this picture, deeply as it exists in the public psyche, fed historically by the legacy of slavery and the sexual/racial character given to Black women and men. As Omolade (1983) asserts, the European men who first "explored" Africa saw the nakedness of Africans coupled with Blackness: In the European psyche, Blackness was negative in every way; When it was coupled with nudity, they saw it as indicative of an absence of sexual morality in African culture. The expressiveness of African culture in song and dance merely fueled these impressions. As this racialization/sexualization process was born in their minds, attached to Africans as the object, they created a sex/race system predicated on the absence of sexual morality in Black people.

The slave system that the Europeans created allowed them to sexually exploit Black people, creating the conditions they imagined existed in African cultures (Jordan, 1977). The brutality and immorality of this sexual system is detailed by several feminist revisionists who relay accounts of sexual oppression of boys, girls, and women. The sexual oppression of those enslaved included rape, sexual use of "virgins" to cure venereal disease, and general exposure to White male debauchery (hooks, 1981; Omolade, 1983).

The sex/race ideology developed to justify the heinous practices of the enslavers has been reconstituted and applied to Black people. In this social construction, Blacks are defined as oversexed and culturally deficient, leading to excess in fertility coupled with paternal irresponsibility. The ideology, framed by socioeconomic systems that subjugated Blacks, explains their continuing subordination as a product of their own malaise. Its solution is cultural assimilation, requiring Blacks to change their behavior, acculturating on the basis of an Anglo conformity model (Gordon, 1964). Accordingly, Black men should behave like White patriarchs, heading their families and economically providing for them. Black women should defer to their men within the family and should restrain their sexuality. The reality of poverty is ignored, as are structural barriers such as unemployment, White racism, and sexism. Cultural assimilation to an Anglo norm has been heralded as the precursor to structural assimilation, or integration into social institutions. However, the assumption that American society is an open society is erroneous. Hacker (1992) reports that, even when Blacks are successful in assimilative institutions—schools—their "payoff" is considerably less than that of Whites:

> The advice so often offered to blacks, that they should stay in school, seems valid only insofar as it informs them that with additional education they will move ahead of others of their own race. There is little evidence that spending more years in school will improve their positions in relation to whites. . . . Moreover, blacks who do stay in school soon learn there is no assured payoff. Those who finish college have a jobless rate 2.24 times that for whites with diplomas, an even greater gap than that separating black and white high school graduates. (p. 96)

Furthermore, in terms of assimilating, or taking on, the patriarchal norm, Baca Zinn (1987) reports that a two-parent family structure is no guarantee against poverty, particularly for racial minorities: "The long term income of Black children in two-parent families throughout the decade was even lower than the long term income of non-Black children who spent most of the decade in mother-only families" (p. 11). And Ehrenreich (1986) reports that, given the median income for Black males, we would have to add three Black males to a mother-headed family with two children to clear the median U.S. family income and four Black males to enter the middle class.

The sexual aspect of the framework used to examine teenage mothers must be further explored in terms of patriarchy. By patriarchy, I refer to a system of male dominance in which men are granted privilege through the social exploitation of women. For example, typically it is the teenaged *mothers* whose behavior comes under question, and it is often their *unwed* status that generates public concern amid questions of sexual morality and economic well-being. Perhaps this is because unwed motherhood—as a phenomenon associated with Black women—represents an attack by them on, or at least resistance to, the White patriarchal system, which pivots around the organization of male dominance within heterosexual marriage. Johnson (1988) says,

> Heterosexual marriage . . . is another structural regularity. Marriage makes women into wives and gives adult men (not necessarily the biological or

social "fathers" of a woman's child) a measure of control over mothers and children and over women's early primacy in children's lives. . . . The structure of the husband-wife relationship, considered apart from other contravening sources of power, tends to define wives as lesser partners in any marriage. (pp. 4-5)

Johnson also argues that women's mothering represents a source of power for women in which their children are subordinated to them and in which they have the power of shaping their children through socialization, which is primarily provided by the mother. Thus teenaged mothers' behavior defies the social organization of their domestic labor under the dominant race/class/gender system, in which they are to pass from the authority of their fathers to the authority of their husbands. They are expected to give up mothering until they are under male authority in a heterosexual marriage, according to dominant cultural values.

Eurocentric notions of family life as circumscribed within a male-headed family are problematic for most Blacks. As mentioned above, Black men generally lack the economic stability—given their low place in the economy—to function as oligarchs in the family. Despite their economic failure to reap a "family wage" and the authority vested with that, Black men do manifest other aspects of male dominance over women in those areas that are available to them. One such area is sexuality and fatherhood. Gibbs (1988) reports that young Black males view fatherhood as evidence of their virility. This may be due to the constricted options for Black men that include, according to Connor (1988), "mainly entertainment, sports, or street crime" (p. 213).

The patriarchal and capitalist organization of social life fashioned by Europe's descendants defines men by their physical and economic dominance over women and sometimes over other men. When economic dominance is not available to Black men, physical prowess and other expressions of masculinity become important. The source of sexism in Black communities, however, cannot be traced to some dysfunction of the family nor to the supposed emasculation of Black men by Black women. Rather, it is the sexism of the dominant White culture that finds Black families aberrant because of the so-called weak position of Black men within them, even as the racism of that culture finds Black men so threatening that they are disproportionately represented among the incarcerated.

These values that call for a male breadwinner who heads a nuclear family are in contradiction to the social construction of family life by

African Americans, particularly given the cultural heritage they brought with them, as peoples of Africa, to this society.

Although there is tremendous variation in the political and economic organization of the peoples of West Africa historically, there are some common features in the organization and import of family life. These are elaborate lineage systems, the importance of work roles for all family members, the significance of extended family for individuals, and the importance of motherhood, among others. For Blacks drawing on their West African cultural heritage, motherhood has not been circumscribed within marriage per se but within an extended family lineage system with a complex system of obligation and reciprocity. Children have not been the exclusive responsibility of their parents but have been socialized and cared for within a larger extended network of kin, within which siblings are significant caretakers for younger children. The conjugal relationships in marriage between women and men are less important than their position in extended families, which together traditionally formed the larger lineage grouping (Sudarkasa, 1987).

The introduction of chattel slavery defined Africans as property and tore them from the familiar forms of social organization based on family ties. Yet many historians argue that although Africans of varying tribes were plucked away from their family groupings they carried the legacy of family life as they had known it with them to North America. Central to this legacy is a conceptualization of family structure as based on a large kin network rather than a patriarchal, nuclear family structure.

Some new forms of households did emerge under chattel slavery, however, in which women headed households. In some cases, these household heads were women who did not remarry after the death or sale of their husband. In other cases, female-headed households consisted of an unmarried mother and children. Generally, single-mother-headed households among Blacks are now considered to be associated with Blacks in pronounced numbers after the 1950s. Burnham (1985) argues that the increased incidence of Black female-headed households is related to the harsh economic conditions imposed on Black people. Such conditions, in her view, are consistent with a historical attack on Black family life, an attack which, in contemporary times, results in families being reduced to their smallest possible component—a mother and her children.

Only a framework that succinctly addresses the fundamental bases— patriarchal, racial, capitalist—of our social organization can begin to explain teenaged motherhood. Such a framework must seriously present the human agency of teenaged mothers themselves, thus challenging the traditional "top down" or expert perspective with which teenaged motherhood has been examined.

According to Brown (1985), social scientists have assumed that Blacks are sexually permissive and have used that assumption as a yardstick for measuring Whites' premarital sexual permissiveness. This idea was racially constructed and is historically based in the ideologies arising from the colonization and enslavement of Africans by Europeans. Therefore, the assumption that moral codes governing sexuality—including constraints on premarital and extramarital sex—were absent is erroneous (Gutman, 1976; Omolade, 1983). This remains true for contemporary African Americans, although the assumptions of Blacks as sexually loose prevail.

From data based on a nationally representative sample, Brown (1985) finds that there is variance among Blacks in terms of sexual permissiveness. Attitudes toward premarital sexual permissiveness were not found to be related to class—as measured here by income—but were significantly related to the influence of Black religious institutions and the attitudes of Black adolescent female peers. Interestingly, she finds that "factors other than socioeconomic criteria appear to be important to status, lifestyle and belief systems in the black community" (p. 385).

These findings complement Leslie's assessment that African-American women do not feel unwed motherhood is sinful (Chapter 3, this volume). Again, one should not infer that Blacks give approval to teenaged or unwed motherhood. Rather, such attitudes reveal the refusal of Black communities to stigmatize members whose behavior falls outside dominant cultural proscriptions. They further indicate the need for examining Black community members' interpretations of teenaged motherhood. Overall, Black communities appear to maintain an approach that is at odds with the dichotomous logic apparent in Eurocentric thinking, in which motherhood is cast in terms of "ideal" or normal versus "bad" or deviant. Rather, Afrocentric thinking operates out of an inclusive philosophy that embraces, in Leslie's terminology, a *pragmatic unity ethic*. Such an approach is at odds with the dominant one that establishes an ideal—although the process of establishing an ideal motherhood is dynamic, as the recent shift toward social approval for White middle-class mothers who are "single by choice" suggests.

A number of scholars would theorize that cultural norms proscribing premarital sexual behavior are absent among those groups that exhibit high rates of premarital sexual behavior and of unwed parenthood. Abrahamse,

Morrison, and Waite (1988) found that 48% of Blacks, 32% of Hispanics, and 24% of Whites would consider having a child outside marriage. They further found that Blacks voiced a preference to bear their first child before age 20, although the age preferred by married teenagers was older. The major findings of the study were that those young women "who have the most to lose by becoming single mothers are the least likely to say that they would consider having a nonmarital birth" (p. 17). In other words, those for whom pregnancy and motherhood would cause a down-spin in economic or educational opportunities do not voice acceptance of that for themselves. Early motherhood, then, is an option highlighted for those who lack other avenues toward adult status.

On a community level, Zelnick et al. (1981) found that Whites perceive that their communities are intolerant of unwed motherhood. They also perceive similarity in the views of their community and those of the dominant society. In contrast, up to one third of Blacks perceived their neighborhoods as "not condemning" unwed mothers. It is important to note that "not condemning" does not translate into approval for unwed motherhood.

While many in the professional academic community still maintain the view that teenaged childbearing begins or continues a cycle of poverty, teen mothers and their parents do not agree. In a recent study, Henderson (1981) found that

> the teenagers generally agreed that having a child had not substantially changed either their lives or their expectations for the future. Professionals consistently took a more pessimistic viewpoint, citing most of the effects of teenage childbearing that have been reported in the professional literature—greater marital instability, disrupted schooling and greater likelihood of unemployment and dependence upon public assistance, for example. (pp. 81-82)

According to Henderson, this opposing perspective on the effects of teenaged motherhood is not surprising in communities where unemployment and reliance on public assistance are common and the possibility of college attendance continues to be very limited.

Both Henderson's study and Brown's and Leslie's discussions of an alternative cultural framework among Blacks suggest that Black teenaged mothers and their surrounding community apply a different set of meanings to a range of issues related to both determinants and consequences of teenaged motherhood: their sexual mores and behavior, resulting pregnancies and childbirth, and conjugal and extended family relations.

Black girls in my own and other studies admit an awareness of sexual conservatism in their communities. Although their awareness of strictures against premarital sex does not preclude their sexual activity, it does dissuade them from actively taking responsibility for becoming sexual subjects. This can be further compounded in cases where young women's first sexual encounters were abusive and unwanted.

More than half of the women in my study had experienced unwanted sexual assaults ranging from molestation to rape. Although I did not have the foresight to include a question asking about sexual assault in the first phase of interviewing, I did find, in my first set of interviews, that it kept cropping up in the field of questions where I asked about "family background." I then incorporated a question about the nature of their first sexual experience—whether wanted or unwanted—into my interview schedule. It is interesting to note that the Black women in the study had not discussed their unwanted sexual experiences with their mothers, even after admitting they had become sexually active. Unwanted sexual experiences with family members ranging from brothers to uncles to grandfathers were kept secret, according to the Black women, because, as they often put it, "it would kill my mother to know her [relative] did this to me."

This research is not the first to reveal a connection between sexual abuse and teenaged motherhood. In her 1986 incest study based on a random sample of 930 women, Russell found that

> few women made a direct connection between their childhood victimization and later life experiences such as adolescent pregnancy, marital separation or divorce, or repeated sexual victimization. Such experiences, however, were far more common among women who had been incestuously abused than among those who had not. (p. 201)

In her study of 30 Black teenage mothers, Kaplan (1988) also noted that sexual abuse may be significant to their adolescent sexual activity, with pregnancy "allowing sexually abused teenage mothers a way to grow up and get away from their early traumatic experience" (p. 82). She cited a 1987 survey of a random sample of 445 teen mothers in which 60% reported an "unwanted sexual experience"—although not specifically referring to incest. Both these studies, then, support the contention that sexual abuse may be a significant "route to teenaged motherhood" because sexual abuse has such a traumatizing effect on the victim, impacting her sexuality and, perhaps, leading to particular reproductive decisions such as early childbearing.

A more recent study by Moore, Nord, and Peterson (1989) discussed the fact that very little attention has been focused on investigating the extent to which teenage sexual activity is "nonvoluntary." Whereas I was interested in the generalized sexual assaults on my subjects, Moore et al. were only able to establish findings on rape—forcible sexual intercourse—based on the National Survey of Children in 1987. Seven percent of the respondents reported they had been forced to have sex (i.e., raped). Furthermore, this experience was significantly correlated with sex and race, with nearly 13% of White women reporting rape by age 20, compared with 8% of Black women. This is a reversal of the general population figures where women of color are reported as more likely to be victims of sexual assault than White women and sexual assault is generally intraracial (Andersen, 1993).

Because such an assault renders her powerless, it may create a sense of passivity on the part of the young girl that prohibits her from making active decisions about her sexual behavior and contraception. The effects of sexual abuse are not well documented, however, particularly with respect to race and class differences.

Among those who participated in my study, Blacks were particularly shy about discussing sexuality. Whereas a young White girl candidly said, "I had more sex at 14 than a couple on their honeymoon!", the Black girls in the study seemed not to proclaim their sexuality but to accept it as an inevitable aspect of conjugal relations. Patrice (all names are fictitious) noted that her sister had warned her that it would take her a while "to get into it." Sally said that "when it was over" she jumped up to look in the mirror to see if she looked different. And Annie said that she wasn't worried about getting pregnant when her mother found her pills and threw them away because she "wasn't doing it all the time!" All three referred to sex as "it" when discussing their own sexual activity, reflecting the sexual conservatism of their larger community. Sexual conservatism was also revealed, as when Annie had obtained oral contraceptives and her mother had responded to these signs of her daughter's sexual activity by throwing her birth control away, saying that Annie had no use for that. These experiences contrasted sharply with those of some of the non-Black girls in my study, whose sexual activity was acknowledged and condoned by their families. Some were taken to get contraceptives by their mothers, and many were permitted to stay out overnight or even to have boyfriends stay with them overnight.

Although Black girls did not confide in their mothers regarding sexual abuse, becoming sexually active, or the use of contraceptives, none were hesitant about revealing pregnancy to their mothers, although they met with varying reactions. For example, drawing from my study, when Annie told her mother she was pregnant, "she didn't get mad or anything. . . . She just said, 'Well, you have a responsibility now.' " On the other hand, when Sally told her mother, "It was like 'You're a disgrace now.' . . . But after I had her they were all right there and they all wanted to do for her." Patrice did nothing about her pregnancy for several months and when she finally told her mother, "My mother said, 'What are you going to do?' I said, 'I'm going to have an abortion,' and she looked at me like 'What? You're going to do what?' "

Most of the young women I interviewed were opposed to abortion. In addition, some were vehemently opposed to adoption, which was viewed as a "White thing." According to Annie,

> A White person will put up her baby for adoption real quick but whereas a Black person, they won't do that because . . . I don't know, because I see the Black person—maybe they can just cope more with the kids and stuff whereas the White . . . The Black, I see that in our backgrounds about kids because in slavery days they were taking care of the White folks' kids and—look here! [gestures at her White neighbors' child] We're still doing it now!

Annie dismissed adoption and referred to Blacks' enslavement as a metaphor for Blacks' greater ability to "cope" with what life brings, particularly from White people.

Patrice viewed the choices presented to Black pregnant girls as circumscribed by society:

> You gotta face, it when you're Black and you get pregnant you have two choices that society has chose for you, that your mother, your father, your great-grandparents have chose for you—you have an abortion or you keep your baby. You don't give your baby up for adoption, that's what society has chose for you.

It is ironic that Patrice presented these as the two choices available, given that she waited too long to obtain an abortion and then did consider adoption on several occasions before deciding she had to raise her son so that he wouldn't hate her.

In my cross-cultural study, I found that Black girls presented a closer bond with their mothers than did the White or Native American girls, who voiced resentment toward their mothers over a variety of issues, including neglect, abandonment, failure to protect them from sexual abuse, and failure to support them, emotionally or materially, after they had become teenaged mothers. They tended to blame all their problems on these features: Their home life was bad because their mothers let the fathers beat them, because they let the father beat the children, or because the mother drank. Like society, these young women, with several exceptions, were prone to place responsibility for the well-being of their families on their mother and, ultimately, responsibility for the failures of the families as well.

In contrast, the Black teenaged mothers voiced support for and from their mothers. I did not interview mothers (although I did observe inter- actions); so, I have no way of knowing *their* feelings about the extra burdens of grandmothering. Patrice, who has a disabled mother, revealed that after getting pregnant she had moved in with her grandmother to spare her mother, and that she doesn't feel she should burden her mother with herself and her daughter:

> My mom didn't lay and have this baby. . . . My mom can't take care of me *and* my baby. . . . She's on workmen's comp, and I'm saying, how can she care for me, my son, and her?

As in the case of the Black subjects not wanting to burden their mothers with sexual assault by male relatives, Patrice's comment reveals a care and concern of the daughter for the mother. Black daughters, unlike the Native American or White daughters, were more apt to identify with their mothers' struggles for survival than to blame them for their circum- stances. This may explain, in part, why they put less weight on their conjugal relationships than do the White and Native American girls who participated in this study. White and Native American girls devoted much of their interview time to discussing their conjugal relationships. In contrast, Black girls spent much of their time discussing their family backgrounds, their relationships within the family, and their views of their pregnancy and motherhood. This may also be related to the West African cultural norms discussed above, in which conjugal relations take a back- seat to relationships within the lineage system.

The fact that conjugal relations were less significant than extended family relations does not signify that these relations were either positive or negative. Annie discussed a stable, long-term relationship with her "fiancé" but did not appear at all ready to leave her mother's home where she and her baby reside together with several of her other siblings:

> I tried the first time, moving with my baby's father and then we had a little problem 'cause that was my first time moving and I didn't know how to cook—I'm not used to cooking. My mom does all that . . . cleaning . . . and she does me and my baby's laundry, but I know how to do the stuff but she just does it. . . . [My boyfriend] will be 21 in two weeks. . . . He works, he has a full-time job. So, I'll stay here or get my own place . . . 'cause I signed up for the housing.

Sally, however, discussed a conjugal relationship with her baby's father in which she was often battered, leading at one point to her hospitalization. She is resentful of her baby's father, whom she has broken off with now, and feels that he should be helping her parent and provide for her child. Sally's resentment runs particularly deep because she feels her baby's father's neglect is merely a repeat of her father's abandonment of her family. Of her father she said, "He's never really been a daddy." Although he is a successful businessman and parented four children with her mother, they never married and she was never given any child support. Now, Sally feels that her baby's father has ducked out in similar fashion.

Patrice also spoke negatively of the men in her life: her uncle, who molested her throughout her childhood and into her adolescence; her father, whom she never met until she was a teenager—and who then showed up drunk—and her baby's father. When she became pregnant, the baby's father told her she would "just have to grow up." To add to her bitterness, the baby's father's parents refused to acknowledge him as their grandchild.

Despite the contrasts in these conjugal relationships, all three of these young women plan futures that hinge more on their relations with their children than on their conjugal relations. They were clear and precise about their plans for finishing their education, for the careers they wanted, and for housing and child-care arrangements.

Presser (1980) and Furstenberg (1976), studying consequences of child-bearing for urban adolescent mothers, found that many young mothers do return to school at a later date—often facilitated by the availability of public assistance (i.e., economic resources). Pregnant high school girls are now more likely to remain in school during their pregnancies. According to a study by Mott and Maxwell (1981), school attendance by pregnant girls increased to 42% of Whites and 70% of Blacks in 1976, compared with 20% and 45%, respectively, in 1968. Thus they are now more likely to *continue* their education once they become pregnant. After childbirth, 17% of Whites returned to school, compared with 39% of Blacks, up from 5% and 15%, respectively, in 1968. This may be due, in large part, to the Title IX legislative action that ended school expulsion of "unwed mothers" in 1972 (Mott & Maxwell, 1981).

Passage of the educational amendments and the concurrent increase in school attendance during and after pregnancy indicate that faulty reasoning has dictated the adage that young women who become mothers are destined to begin the cycle of poverty or to continue in the cycle begun by their foremothers. It has been assumed that young women drop out of school due to their pregnancy and/or childbearing. At a recent Stanford conference, Kristin Luker, author of *Abortion and the Politics of Motherhood,* suggested that "teens do not, as is conventionally assumed, have children and then drop out of school but are already in the process of dropping out when they get pregnant" (cited in Beyers, 1989, p. 9). Trussell (1988) noted that it is very difficult to determine whether early pregnancy affects education or vice versa (cited in Beyers, 1989, pp. 9-10).

Some of the women who had dropped out spoke of how responsibility for their child made them realize they needed to get an education. According to Patrice,

> I quit school . . . twice. I quit this year because I just wanted to hang out and I knew I could come in January and finish all my stuff and I'm finishing on time. . . . I thought, if I don't finish school my kid's gonna come home and I won't be able to help him with his homework.

She went on to comment on the importance for teenaged mothers to finish school to counteract popular opinion about them: "When they [drop out] they let us down too because they're letting someone that comes up and does statistics just say, 'Well there's another one gone just because she had her baby.' "

Patrice's statement shows, again, how Black teenaged mothers are well aware of the negative forecasts that scholars and the popular media hold for teenaged mothers. They do not want to be viewed as a statistic. They hold alternative views of family life and family construction that are, however, at odds with the dominant culture. These alternative views are rooted, in part, in cultural difference and also in the racialized social organization that leaves young Black women frustrated at the lack of opportunities in their lives. This lack of opportunities does not directly lead to teenaged motherhood, but along with the sexual conservatism of

Black communities and the patriarchal oppression they experience, it leaves them unlikely to accept a responsible role in sexuality and reproduction.

CONCLUSION

In this chapter, I have argued that teenaged motherhood is socially constructed and that the framework for that construction is a racialized and racist, gendered and patriarchal, capitalist society. As a result, understandings of teenaged motherhood have been flawed, and we have been presented a picture of teenaged mothers that casts them as deviants whose behavior is problematic and who are overwhelmingly Black. In contrast, we see that girls who become teenaged mothers, whether they are Native American, Black, or White, do so for a variety of structural and idiosyncratic reasons and that they receive mixed messages from their communities as a consequence of what is deemed *early* parenting. Given this background as well as a historical and cultural understanding of Black families, we can better understand the special circumstances of Black mothers.

The three young Black mothers whose stories deepen our understanding of teenaged motherhood were fortunate to receive housing and/or other material and emotional support from their mothers and grandmothers. However, according to Ladner and Gourdine (1989), many Black extended families in contemporary society are unable to provide such support, particularly when this further burdens young grandmothers beset, as they often are, with their own struggles for survival. Black teenaged motherhood, while not conforming to the deviant status assigned it by the dominant White society, can present yet another burden for communities consistently under siege. Increasingly, Black families are intergenerational, composed of grandmother, young mother, and her children. Such families, given the economic plight of Black women in a racist and sexist economy, are thrust into a "survival mode." Our problem, then, is not to approve or disapprove of teenaged mothers but to move beyond developing theories of Black pathology—as are often applied to teenaged mothers—and move toward creating more avenues for the inclusion and empowerment of young Black women in American society.

One of the first steps toward this empowerment must involve educating them to understand the kind of ideological processes that affect them: racialization and gender ideology as well as false myths of upward mobility. The understanding that would come from such knowledge can help young Black women to prepare realistically for adulthood and alternative paths toward adulthood without succumbing to ideological proscriptions of the dominant culture. Second, young women and men must be adequately educated in sex education and made comfortable with controlling their own sexuality. As a necessary aspect of this education, contraception and dealing with issues or experiences related to sexual abuse must be addressed. The community agencies examined across racial and ethnic boundaries shared one thing in common: a realization that peer counseling and peer education are integral to the empowerment of teenagers. It is primarily within the framework of their peer culture that teens develop their responses to the constraints they face. However, all of these processes must begin early, as Black girls and boys confront the limited roles the larger society has dictated and struggle to envision a brighter future. Furthermore, those involved in education must realize and confront the sexual conservatism that characterizes so many Black communities, despite the persistence of an ideology of oversexed Blacks.

On the whole, however, the "problem" that dominant society has with teenaged mothers will not go away simply by empowering these mothers to deal with society as it is. The ultimate empowerment for Black teenaged girls will come through changing the given hierarchical social arrangment to a horizontal one that does not use race and gender to constrain certain members of society to the bottom rungs of the ladder.

REFERENCES

Abrahamse, A. F., Morrison, P. A., & Waite, L. J. (1988). Teenagers willing to consider single parenthood: Who is at greatest risk? *Family Planning Perspectives, 20*(1), 13-18.

Andersen, M. (1993). *Thinking about women: Sociological perspectives on sex and gender* (3rd ed.). New York: Macmillan.

Aries, P. (1962). *Centuries of childhood: A social history of family life.* New York: Vintage.

Baca Zinn, M. (1987). *Minority families in crisis: The public discussion* (Research Paper No. 6). Memphis, TN: Memphis State University, Center for Research on Women.

Beyers, B. (1989, May 3). Teen pregnancy: Grounds for cautious optimism? *Stanford University Campus Report,* pp. 9-10.

Blauner, R. (1972). *Racial oppression in America.* New York: Harper & Row.

Brown, S. V. (1985). Premarital sexual permissiveness among Black adolescent females. *Social Psychology Quarterly ,48*(4), 381-387.

Burnham, L. (1985). Has poverty been feminized in Black America? *Black Scholar, 16*(2), 14-24.

Collins, P. H. (1989). The social construction of Black feminist thought. *Signs: Journal of Women in Culture and Society, 14*(4), 745-773.

Connor, M. E. (1988). Teenage fatherhood: Issues confronting young Black males. In
    J. Gibbs (Ed.), *Young, Black, and male in America: An endangered species* (pp.
    118-218). Dover, MA: Auburn House.
Demos, J. (1970). *A little commonwealth: Family life in Plymouth Colony.* New York:
    Oxford University Press.
Edsall, T. B., & Edsall, M. D. (1992). *Chain reaction: The impact of race, rights, and
    taxes on American politics.* New York: Norton.
Ehrenreich, B. (1986, July/August). Two, three, many husbands. *Mother Jones,* p. 8.
Furstenberg, F. (1976). *Unplanned parenthood: The social consequences of teenage
    childbearing.* New York: Free Press.
Furstenberg, F., & Crawford, A. G. (1978). Family support: Helping teenage mothers to
    cope. *Family Planning Perspectives, 10*(6), 322-333.
Gibbs, J. (Ed.). (1988). *Young, Black, and male in America: An endangered species.*
    Dover, MA: Auburn House.
Gordon, M. (1964). *Assimilation in American life.* New York: Oxford University Press.
Gutman, H. (1976). *The Black family in slavery and freedom.* New York: Pantheon.
Hacker, A. (1992). *Two nations: Black and White, separate, hostile, unequal.* New York:
    Macmillan.
Hofferth, S., Kahn, J. R., & Baldwin, W. (1987). Premarital sexual activity among U.S.
    teenage women over the past three decades. *Family Planning Perspectives, 19*(4),
    46-53.
hooks, b. (1981). *Ain't I a woman? Black women and feminism.* Boston: South End Press.
Johnson, M. (1988). *Strong mothers, weak wives: The search for gender equality.*
    Berkeley: University of California Press.
Jones, H. (1987). Foreword. In S. F. Battle (Ed.), *The Black adolescent parent* (pp. ix-x).
    New York: Haworth.
Jordan, W. D. (1977). *White over Black: American attitudes toward the Negro, 1550-1812*
    (2nd ed.). New York: Norton.
Kaplan, E. B. (1988, Spring). Where does a Black teenage mother turn? *Feminist Issues,*
    pp. 51-83.
Ladner, J., & Gourdine, R. M. (1984). Intergenerational teenage motherhood: Some
    preliminary findings. *Sage: A Scholarly Journal on Black Women, 1*(2), 22-24.
Lewis, O. (1946). *Anthropological essays.* New York: Random House.
Mamdani, M. (1981). The ideology of population control. In K. Michaelson (Ed.), *And
    the poor get children: Radical perspectives on dynamics* (pp. 39-49). New York:
    Monthly Review Press.
Moore, K. A. (1988). *Facts at a glance.* Unpublished fact sheet, Charles Stewart Mott
    Foundation, Washington, DC.
Moore, K. A., Nord, C., & Peterson, J. L. (1989). Nonvoluntary sexual activity among
    adolescents. *Family Planning Perspectives, 22*(3), 110-114.
Moore, K. A., Simms, M. C., & Betsy, C. L. (1986). *Choice and circumstance: Racial
    differences in adolescent sexuality and fertility.* New Brunswick, NJ: Transaction
    Books.
Mott, F. L., & Maxwell, N. L. (1981). School-age mothers: 1968 and 1979. *Family
    Planning Perspectives, 13*(6), 287-292.
Moynihan, D. P. (1967). The Negro family: The case for national action. In L. Rainwater
    & W. Yancy (Eds.), *The Moynihan report and the politics of controversy* (pp.
    39-124). Cambridge: MIT Press. (Original work by Moynihan published 1965)

Omi, M., & Winant, H. (1986). *Racial formation in the United States*. New York: Routledge & Kegan Paul.

Omolade, B. (1983). Hearts of darkness. In A. Snitow (Ed.), *The powers of desire* (pp. 350-367). New York: Monthly Review Press.

Platt, A. M. (1974). *The childsavers: The invention of delinquency* (2nd ed.). Chicago: University of Chicago Press.

Presser, H. B. (1980). The social consequences of teenage childbearing. In C. Chilman (Ed.), *Adolescent pregnancy and childbearing: Findings from research* (DHHS PHS/NIH Publication No. 81-2077, pp. 249-266). Washington, DC: U.S. Government Printing Office.

Russell, D. (1986). *The secret trauma: Incest in the lives of girls and women*. New York: Basic Books.

Steinberg, S. (1981). *The ethnic myth*. Boston: Beacon.

Sudarkasa, N. (1987). The status of women in indigenous African societies. In R. Terborg-Penn et al. (Eds.), *Women in Africa and the African diaspora*. Washington, DC: Howard University Press.

Teens, parents, officials don't agree on impact of teen motherhood. *Family Planning Perspectives, 13*(2), 81.

Trussell, T. J. (1988). Teenage pregnancy in the United States. *Family Planning Perspectives, 20*(6), 262-272.

Westoff, C. F. (1988). Unintended pregnancy in America and abroad. *Family Planning Perspectives, 20*(6), 251-259.

Wideman, J. E. (1989, March). From child to child: A cycle of perpetual poverty. *The Washington Post National Weekly Editon, 37.* Copyright © 1989, Washington Post Book World, Washington Post Writers Group. Reprinted with permission.

Zelnick, M., & Kantner, J. F. (1980). Sexual and contraceptive experience of young unmarried women in the United States, 1976 and 1971. In C. Chilman (Ed.), *Adolescent pregnancy and childbearing: Findings from research* (DHHS PHS/NIH Publication No. 81-2077, pp. 43-82). Washington, DC: U.S. Government Printing Office.

Zelnick, M., Kantner, J. F., & Ford, K (1981). *Sex and pregnancy in adolescence*. Beverly Hills, CA: Sage.

SUGGESTED READINGS

Bane, M. J. (1986). Household composition and poverty. In S. H. Danziger & D. H. Weinberg (Eds.), *Fighting poverty* (pp. 209-231). Cambridge, MA: Harvard University Press.

Banfield, E. (1974). *The unheavenly city revisited*. Boston: Little, Brown.

Bonjean, L. M., & Rittenmeyer, D. C. (1987). *Teenage parenthood: The school's response*. Bloomington, IN: Phi Delta Kappa Educational Foundation.

Brewer, R. (1988). Black women in poverty: Some comments on female-headed families. *Signs: Journal of Women in Culture and Society, 13*(2), 331-339.

Brown, P. (1986). Foreword. In K. Moore et al. (Eds.), *Choice and circumstance: Racial differences in adolescent sexuality and fertility* (pp. ii-vii). New Brunswick, NJ: Transaction Books.

Butts, J. D. (1981). Adolescent sexuality and teenage pregnancy from a Black perspective. In T. Ooms (Ed.), *Teenage pregnancy in a family context* (pp. 307-325). Philadelphia: Temple University Press.

Campbell, A. A. (1968). The role of family planning in the reduction of poverty. *Journal of Marriage and the Family, 30,* 236-245.

Chilman, C. S. (Ed.). (1980). *Adolescent pregnancy and childbearing: Findings from research* (DHHS PHS/NIH Publication No. 81-2077). Washington, DC: U.S. Government Printing Office.

Dash, L. (1989). *When children want children.* New York: Morrow.

Ehrenreich, B., & Stallard, K. (1982, July/August). The nouveau poor. *Ms.,* pp. 20-28.

Etienne, M., & Leacock, E. B. (Eds.). (1980). *Women and colonization: Anthropological perspectives.* New York: Praeger.

Furstenberg, F. (1980). The social consequences of teenage parenthood. In C. Chilman (Ed.), *Adolescent pregnancy and childbearing: Findings from research* (DHHS PHS/NIH Publication No. 81-2077, pp. 267-308). Washington, DC: U.S. Government Printing Office.

Furstenberg, F. (1981). Implicating the family: Teenage parenthood and kinship involvement. In T. Ooms (Ed.), *Teenage pregnancy in a family context* (pp. 131-164). Philadelphia: Temple University Press.

Furstenberg, F., Brooks-Gunn, J., & Morgan, S. P. (1987). Adolescent mothers and their children in later life. *Family Planning Perspectives, 19*(4), 142-153.

Gordon, L. (1986). Who's afraid of reproductive freedom for women and why? Some historical answers. *Frontiers, 9*(1), 9-26.

Guttmacher, A. (1981). *Teenage pregnancy: The problem that won't go away.* New York: Alan Guttmacher.

Harper, A. L. (1983). Teenage sexuality and public policy: An agenda for gender education. In I. Diamond (Ed.), *Families, politics and public policy: A feminist dialogue on women and the state* (pp. 220-235). New York: Longman.

Hill, M. (1983). Trends in the economic situation of U.S. families and children, 1970-1980. In R. R. Nelson & F. Skidmore (Eds.), *American families and the economy* (pp. 9-53). Washington, DC: National Academic Press.

King, D. (1989). Multiple jeopardy, multiple consciousness: The context of a Black feminist ideology. *Signs: Journal of Women in Culture and Society, 14*(1), 42-72.

Ladner, J. (1970). *Tomorrow's tomorrow: The Black woman.* New York: Doubleday.

Moore, K. A., & Burt, M. (1982). *Private crisis, public cost: Policy perspectives on teenage childbearing.* Washington, DC: Urban Institute.

National Black Women's Health Project. (1982). *Health fact sheet on Black women.* Washington, DC: American Public Health Association.

Rainwater, L., & Yancey, W. (1967). *The Moynihan report and the politics of controversy.* Cambridge: MIT Press.

Taborn, J. M. (1987). The Black adolescent mother: Selected, unique issues. In S. F. Battle (Ed.), *The Black adolescent parent* (pp. 1-13). New York: Haworth.

Trussell, T. J. (1980). The economic consequences of teenage childbearing. In C. Chilman (Ed.), *Adolescent pregnancy and childbearing: Findings from research* (DHHS PHS/NIH Publication No. 81-2077, pp. 221-247). Washington, DC: U.S. Government Printing Office.

U.S. Bureau of the Census. (1989a). *Current population reports, households, families, marital status and living arrangements: March 1989 advance report.* Washington, DC: U.S. Government Printing Office.

U.S. Bureau of the Census. (1989b). *Household economic reports, transitions in income and poverty status: 1984-1985* (Current Population Reports, Series P-23, No. 123). Washington, DC: U.S. Government Printing Office.

U.S. Bureau of the Census. (1989c). *The Black population in the United States: March 1988* (Current Population Reports, Population Characteristics, Series P-20, No. 442). Washington, DC: U.S. Government Printing Office.

Zabin, L. S., & Clark, S. D., Jr. (1981). Why they delay: A study of teenage family planning clinic patients. *Family Planning Perspectives, 13*(5), 205-217.

5

Single Parenting:
A Visual Analysis

Dhyana Ziegler

> It doesn't help matters when primetime TV has Murphy Brown, a
> character who supposedly epitomizes today's intelligent, highly paid,
> professional woman, mocking the importance of fathers by bearing a
> child alone and calling it just another lifestyle choice.
>
> Dan Quayle (in May 19, 1992, speech)

When then Vice President Dan Quayle uttered the above remarks during
a speech, he had no intention of forging a national discourse and debate on
the plight of single parenting in the United States. Nonetheless, the issue of
single parenting and family values catapulted to the forefront of the national
media with a choir of voices joining in, singing its praise and criticisms.

During the *Murphy Brown* television program's 1992 fall season opener,
the network producers and Candice Bergen (who plays the fictional
character) seized the opportunity to use the one-hour time slot to slap back
at Quayle and to boost the show's rating. The season premiere ended with
a speech in response to the vice president's earlier condemnatory remarks.
In essence, the Murphy Brown program struck back at Vice President
Quayle, showing that the nature of families varies greatly, depending on
the circumstances with which each family is confronted. To illustrate this
point, Candice Bergen showed the viewing audience several people who

were single parents, and emphasized that they all were loving people who were committed to their families. In other words, people in single-parent families invest the same time and energy, face the same struggles, and meet the challenges that other families do.

The Dan Quayle/Murphy Brown affair helped to bring the issue of single parenting to the forefront and beyond its focus as a symptom of society but more as an integral pattern in life's quilt, a reflector of society inclusive of all its cultures and ethnic groups. It is ironic that Quayle chose to pick on TV character Murphy Brown, who is portrayed as a single woman with an annual income of more than $50,000 who made the choice to be a single parent, because Murphy does not fit the typical stereotype usually associated with single parenting, primarily and often profiled as an African American female who is on welfare. As a matter of fact, on the evening of the sitcom's 1992 fall premiere where Murphy struck back at the vice president, Quayle selected a group of African American single parents in Washington, DC, to view the program with him to serve as a symbol of his support for single parenting. Unfortunately, Quayle's choice of this racial composition for the audience opened the door for more comments regarding his motives:

> Although he had never explicitly criticized Black single parents—he had insisted his remarks about Murphy were not an attack against single parents at all—the gesture suggested he was sensitive to criticism that his remarks were a coded racial appeal. (Kolbert, 1992, p. A17. Copyright © 1992 by the New York Times Company. Reprinted by permission)

Quayle evidently missed the whole point regarding diversity and families that extends far beyond the issues of race and gender.

The Dan Quayle blunder will probably never go down in history as one of his great moments, but it did stimulate some good dialogue. One could only be hopeful that Quayle and many others learned something from this opportunity: First, that single parents come in all colors, shapes, and sizes and, second, that many single parents are proud to be single parents and their children are proud to be a product of a single-parent household. These are also families with love, strong values, and a host of dreams. It is also important to understand that family values have always been a part of African American traditions and practice. Historically, African Americans have had to struggle for political and economic success; nonetheless, love, ethnic pride, and a sense of community have always been an intricate part of the African American family, single or otherwise. These family values were in existence long before African people were snatched from the continent of Africa and brought to America. And although single parents have existed in America from the time Africans were enslaved, extended kinship networks, both real and fictive, have kept the family strong.

The aim of the following discussion is not to compare and contrast existing research methodologies, literature, and statistics regarding female heads of households (although it is clear to me that there are many socioeconomic factors that impact the issue of single parenting) but, rather, to discuss some of the myths and stereotypes regarding single parenting primarily promoted through television, the medium that has an uncanny ability to set the agenda for society in regard to race, gender, and culture. In addition, the research explores some of the successes and struggles of professional African American female heads of households who are making it against all odds and in some cases choose to do so.

MYTHS AND STEREOTYPES
OF THE AFRICAN AMERICAN FAMILY

Historically, African Americans have been portrayed in the mass media as "symptoms" of society (Ziegler, 1991). Additionally, previous research on African American single parents has produced mixed messages, stereotypical images, and been criticized by many scholars as shortsighted. According to Kilpatrick (1979), earlier works on the Black family can be categorized into two areas: One views the Black family as dysfunctional and the other views it in light of its linkage to African forms of culture. However, the latter view is totally ignored in the works by Frazier (1939/1966) and Moynihan (1965) that had a significant role in the establishment of governmental social policies regarding the Black family. Their findings resulted in negative depictions that "viewed the Black family as unstable, disorganized, and unable to provide its members with the social and psychological support needed for them to be assimilated fully into the American Society," and Moynihan's work, particularly, viewed the Black family as a "tangle of pathology" (Kilpatrick, 1979, p. 347).

Kilpatrick's (1979) succinct description of earlier research suggests the research has been drawn from a limited perspective and is drawn from limited data and therefore is myopic in scope. This criticism has prompted African American social scientists to study the African American family from a more realistic examination of its highlights as well as its shortcomings.

According to Peters (1974), previous research emphasized "concepts of 1) deviancy, 2) pathology, and/or 3) uncontrolled sexuality" (p. 349). Bennett (1990) said there are "scores of misconceptions about Black sexuality and Black kinship networks, but the vast propaganda campaign against the Black family is generally organized around ten major myths" (p. 168):

1. Raw and uncontrolled sex, according to the biggest and most pervasive myth, is at the root of the Black family problem.
2. The root cause of the problem, according to the second most widely disseminated myth, is loose morals.
3. Blacks lack a family tradition and came to America without a sense of morality and a background of stable sexual relationships.
4. The bonds of the Black family were destroyed in slavery.
5. The Black family collapsed after emancipation.
6. The Black family collapsed after the Great Migration to the North.
7. The Black family is a product of White paternalism and government welfare.
8. The Black family has always been a matriarchy characterized by strong and domineering women and weak and absent men.
9. Black men cannot sustain stable relationships.
10. The history of the Black family is a history of fussing and fighting by hard-hearted men and heartless women.

(Reprinted by permission of Ebony Magazine.
© 1990, Johnson Publishing Company, Inc.)

This research indicates the range of extremities, myths, and stereotypes that have been used to describe the African American family.

African Americans are not a monolithic people and therefore should be studied according to their diversity. As in all cultures, some people may fit a certain pattern but not all people can be categorized in the same manner. Unfortunately, some of the research on African American families is so limited that it does not account for differences within a culture. The narrowing of categories to describe an entire ethnic group is very shortsighted. African Americans must be studied from a diverse perspective accounting for intercultural differences, such as economic and class differences.

MOYNIHAN AND MOYERS

Two pieces of work that have created some dissonance regarding the African American family are Daniel Patrick Moynihan's (1965) report, titled *The Negro Family: The Case for National Action,* and Bill Moyers's (1986) documentary, titled *The Vanishing Family: Crisis in Black America.* The titles of both these works connote a negative theme, and both portray the African American family as a "symptom of society" calling for national action and insinuating that the African American family is in a crisis. They create a backdrop that says African Americans have no family values, represent a crisis for America, and need national action and attention. Collins (1989) sums it up when she states that in both reports there is a "shared assumption that white economic privilege is due, in large part, to the superior attitudes and values of white Americans" (p. 876). Because there are few written or visual accounts portraying Whites as "symptoms" of society, there is indeed an unbalanced perspective in regards to White versus African American perspectives of family values based on what has been portrayed through the media. Obviously, there are problems that exist in society in general that can be attributed to *all families.*

Ironically, Moynihan's report surfaced in 1965, one year after the 1964 Civil Rights Act. The timing of the report would seemingly appear to be a strategy, conscious or unconscious, to undermine the African American culture as uncivil, unworthy, or unfitting for mainstream America and therefore not worthy of all the rights and privileges of White America. In his report, Moynihan (1965) concluded that "at the heart of the deterioration of the fabric of Negro society is the deterioration of the Negro family. It is the fundamental source of the weakness of the Negro community at the present time " (p. 5). It would appear that Moynihan had not yet accepted African Americans as a part of the fabric of society as seen in the Eurocentric view of family values. As a matter of fact, he ascribed to the philosophy that African Americans were entangled in pathology, again portrayed as a symptom of society.

Moyers's documentary seems to serve the same underlying purpose as Moynihan's research. Both works wave in front of America the African American family as a banner of disgust and portray African Americans as a race and culture that is self-destructive and out of control—a race that is unworthy of mainstream America. Moyers selected an inner-city neighborhood in Newark, New Jersey, as the model from which to draw upon negative images of African American families. Moyers used this community as an example of African American culture, which in itself was shortsighted.

In addition, Moyers's documentary and Moynihan's report discuss the reversed gender roles that suggest African American women are the power forces in the home and conclude that the families would be stronger if the male was a more dominant force in the household. Thus the "matriarchy" versus "patriarchy" symbol in African American households is one of the factors contributing to the deterioration of the African American family. Both theses appear to predict a future of doom for the African American family and to blame the African American woman as the culprit behind the demise of the family, which suggests a very sexist approach to their research. In any event, these two works helped set an agenda for the cultivation of negative attitudes and views toward the African American family, and the mass media have assisted in the promotion of this imagery.

While these works by Moynihan and Moyers did much to reinforce prejudices, stereotypes, and distortions of the African American family that were welcomed by some Whites, they also stimulated a call for action that generated responses from African American scholars that present a more Afrocentric view of the African American family as opposed to the narrow Eurocentric perspective that had existed previously. The Afrocentric view provides a more realistic approach, in my opinion, to study and draw conclusions pro or con regarding the plight of the African American family.

MASS MEDIA AND THE
AFRICAN AMERICAN FAMILY

Just as the Moynihan and Moyers works present a one-sided view of the African American family, the same shortcomings and misconceptions that exist in research can also be found in the mass media's portrayal of the African American family at large. Mass media have promoted single parenting as a negative plight and have waved the plight of poor African American females in front of America's face. According to Baptiste (1986), "Since its inception American primetime T.V. has presented an unrealistic, pejorative and distorted image of Black families. This unflattering image has served only to ridicule such families" (pp. 41-42). And because so many Americans watch television, unfortunately sometimes what one sees is what one believes.

The primary functions of the mass media (print, broadcast, cable) are to inform, educate, and persuade the public, to entertain, and to transmit culture. The mass media have also been described as the teacher of postindustrial society. The packaging of a message may create some distortions of a particular culture or ethnic group, resulting in a negative image and belief regarding the culture or ethnic group that is described as a negative process of mass media enculturation (Ziegler, 1991). This was evident in the 1968 Kerner Commission's report that criticized the mass media for their negative portrayal of African American race, culture, values, and status in society. To be more specific, the report criticized the mass media as a whole for being "shockingly backward" in their portrayal of minorities and called for immediate reform. The Commission cited the shortcomings of television in two broad areas regarding African Americans: First, visibility of Blacks was generally low, particularly in regard to their routine portrayal as part of society, and second, when Blacks did appear in a program they were presented in stereotyped and demeaning ways, as Whites saw them, not as they saw themselves (*Report on the National Advisory Commission on Civil Disorders,* 1968). Baptiste (1986) uttered the same criticisms 18 years later:

> The negative images of the black family portrayed on T.V. is an offense to black families at every socio-economic level. Not only are these images unrealistic, inaccurate, and stereotypes, they neither represent the diversity of black families in the society nor provide positive models that may be emulated by black people. (p. 60)

Baptiste's conclusions clearly point to the shortcomings of television in its distortions of culture, and he also observed that "class" differences among African Americans are rarely dealt with on television. Baptiste further asserted that television is "undoing much of what professionals in the family field are doing to promote healthy positive behaviors within black families" (p. 60). Baptiste's comments underscore the ability and power of television to create myths and stereotypes. Moreover, the mass media have served to address and promote the White family or Eurocentric culture as the norm or typical nuclear family. This research highlights the shortcomings of research and literature on the African American family that continue to perpetuate the myth and stereotypes discussed earlier.

It is important to examine the content of television and its messages about the African American family in this discussion because television gives society a backdrop to form opinions and ideas regarding race and gender. In terms of the African American female, television has even pushed her as the dominant figure in the household regardless if she is a single parent or a wife. Baptiste (1986) believes that females are portrayed on television in several categories that have a negative effect on male roles. These characterizations are female/maternal dominance, abdication of paternal responsibilities by Black males, and derogation and ridicule of Black men. Furthermore, these roles have had a negative impact on African Americans' position in society. Baptiste asserts that these portrayals are detrimental to the African American family: "By portraying black families as either predominantly maternally dominated, single-parented, or female headed, television is subscribing to a stereotypical belief about black family structure and unwittingly this is reinforcing the myths about black families" (p. 45).

Although some of Baptiste's conclusions may be warranted, single-parent female heads of household are a part of the reality of the American family in general, and in the case of African Americans is not an image that is used to belittle African American males. The race and gender issue, in my opinion, is just a divisive strategy to distract from the main issue, which is that these images and material confirm a lack of balance in programming and research. This lack of balance is also apparent in the media's ability to portray positive images of White families including single-parent female heads of households, but not a balanced perspective of all American families that includes African Americans and other families of color, single parents or otherwise.

PROFESSIONALS WHO
ARE SINGLE PARENTS

According to the National Center for Health Statistics, more than 1.1 million of the 4.1 million babies born in the U.S. in 1990 had an unmarried mother. Twenty-eight percent of all births, 20% of White births, 37% of Hispanic births and 67% of Black births were to single women. The 67% statistic represents a diverse group of single African American women. The National Center for Health Statistics also reported that the number of educated first-time mothers over age 30 rose substantially during the last decade. These are African American women who are not married, are successful in their careers, and have decided to have a child before their biological clock runs out.

Much of the early research and literature on single parents, however, does not account for any kind of demographic variance and has left much to be desired. Maume and Dunaway (1989) report that children who grow up in single-parent households will most likely drop out of school and that daughters will likely become single parents also. However, as a product of a single-parent household I am quite disappointed by these conclusions and would certainly not categorize myself into any of the psychological profiles previously defined in this research or as one who practices deviancy, pathology, and uncontrolled sexuality. In fact, some women have made the choice to be single parents and are quite insulted by these descriptions. Although Murphy Brown is White and middle class, and symbolizes the ascent of the single White mother as a norm not extended to African American women, I believe the show made an attempt to dispel some of the myths and to send a message to the public that single parents "work, they struggle, they hope for the kind of life for their children that we all want for our children" (*Murphy Brown*, 1992). The finale of the Murphy Brown/Dan Quayle episode gave viewers a glimpse of many different types of single parenting (by males, by females, by adoption, and so forth).

Six professional women were interviewed for a documentary on single parenting, titled *Single Parenting: A Woman's Perspective* (Ziegler, 1987).[1] The documentary was produced in response to Bill Moyers's documentary and as a project for the Delta Research and Education Foundation because Moyers's piece is myopic in scope, narrowly focused, and offers few voices and perspectives. *Single Parenting* provides an opportunity for African American women to tell their own story and share the challenges, frustrations, and rewards of being a single parent. Of the six women in the documentary, two were divorced, two made the decision to become a single parent, one decided to adopt a child, and one is a widow. These women collectively provide another perspective on single parenting that is not couched in deviant behavior, pathology, or uncontrolled sexuality. The women present a glimpse of their lives as professional African American women who just happen to be single parents. This is in contrast to the dismal picture presented in Moyers's piece that depicts nothing but despair and the demise of the virtues and values of the African American family.

The African American professional women in the *Single Parenting* documentary share some of the same commonalities and problems as most other single professional mothers as well as two-parent households. The issues and problems are the same: finances, commitment, personal sacrifices, child care, lifestyle adjustments, stress, self-esteem, and other challenges of parental involvement: Even though medical advances in the past decade have made pregnancy over age 30 a more biologically viable option, the personal and professional challenges remain.

These challenges have not deterred professional African American women from becoming mothers, and many who spent earlier years working on their careers decide to become single parents after age 30 and sometimes 40. However, these professional women find they have to be willing to make sacrifices.

Ziegler's (1987) documentary allowed the women to describe their joys and frustrations encountered as a single parent. The documentary highlighted the similarities and differences among the women based on their single-parent status; however, all six discussed the financial burdens of being a single parent. One woman described it this way:

> This whole single parenting experience is a very continuous one. I mean, you're not on solid ground in that you're never in a secure position. There's always that financial burden. There's always this trying to figure out where you're going to get money and you're trying to give your children a middle-class experience so to speak with limited funds.

Even women who are considered financially secure find it difficult to juggle resources as a single parent. In addition to the financial burden, there are great personal sacrifices for the professional woman. She has to make major adjustments in her personal life. For instance, many African American single mothers have little or no time for dating or other social activities. In fact, there is not much time for anything except raising their children.[2]

In the case of a widowed or divorced woman, the sacrifices can seem even greater. As the widowed woman in Ziegler's *Single Parenting* documentary explained,

> My husband was a cooperative parent and tried to share a lot of responsibilities. He worked out of town a lot but when he was in town he tried to

take some of the load off me. If the children were sick we'd usually take
turns being at home and if he knew that he would be out of town, he would
take the most days off so that I would have time to do what I needed to do.

A woman who loses her spouse has to make adjustments in her schedule
that leave little time for herself. She makes the adjustments for her
children because, as this woman put it, "they're number one."

Some divorced women have many more psychological adjustments to
contend with beside raising their children alone. One divorced woman in
the documentary explained the impact of her divorce on her self-esteem:

> You start to question yourself and you have to try and take all the pieces of
> the puzzle that make you and put them together again because they are
> literally torn asunder in a divorce situation. You wonder if you are the type
> person that you think you are, if you have the qualities that you thought you
> had that would be appealing to someone or desirable to someone. . . . You
> begin to wonder and have to work harder to get your self-respect back and
> your self-esteem.

Another women said that the divorce had a negative effect on her person-
ally and her family because divorce was not culturally acceptable in the
Virgin Islands: "I felt as though my family shunned me somehow." In any
case, they have had to struggle to make adjustments in their lives and
sacrifice in order to give their children the best part of themselves.

Sacrifice is the common bond that professional African American
single parents share, regardless of their condition. Of course, it can be
said that all parents make sacrifices, but single mothers have to bear all
the financial as well as emotional support alone. The women who made
the decision to be a single parent or to adopt also had to make lifestyle
adjustments, making their children their priority, and making it alone.
Although all parents make adjustments, the women in the *Single Parenting* documentary collectively spoke of their love and commitment to
parenting and how that love and commitment kept their lives going and
brought them satisfaction and success but not without great sacrifice. One
woman who made the decision to become a single parent explained that
some of the problems that single parents face are the same as those that
two-parent households experience:

> There're problems many two-parent families experience similar to problems
> single parents have except that I think the problems a single parent experi-
> ences are twofold,in that there's only one parent. There's only one parent

that has to feed the child. There's only one parent that has to clothe the child. There's only one parent that has to take care of the medical needs, the school needs, the love, and the nurturing.

As these women vented their fears and frustrations, what clearly stood out was the love and the willingness to do whatever it takes to provide a healthy and nurturing environment for their children. Their shared goal is to provide a loving home. One woman summed it up beautifully: "It is better sometimes to have one parent that you know really loves you than not to have a parent at all."

CONCLUSION

It is evident that Ziegler's (1987) documentary *Single Parenting: A Woman's Perspective* clearly portrayed African American single professional women in a different light in contrast to the earlier works by Moyers (1986) and Moynihan (1965). Allowing the African American women to tell their own story shed a different perspective on the plight of single parenting. Additionally, it appears that more African American scholars are beginning to take up the challenge to rewrite history that has proved to be shortsighted, prejudiced, and culturally unbalanced. There are many successful African American single parents and successful offspring of single-parent households. It is important to view the news media and other visual depictions of the African American family with a critical eye. Dorothy Height (1989), Chief Executive Officer of the National Council of Negro Women, echoes the same conclusion:

> Recent negative portrayals of the black family have made it painfully clear to most African Americans that although much has changed in the national life, much remains the same. The incessant emphasis on the dysfuntioning of black people is simply one more attempt to show that African-Americans do not really fit into the society—that we are "overdependent" and predominantly welfare-oriented. Quite overlooked in this equation is the fact that most black Americans are, on the contrary overwhelmingly among the working poor. (p. 136; reprinted with permission)

These are not the usual pictures we see coming across the airwaves that many people take at face value. It is indeed time to tell the other side of the story through a different vision. It is time to generate another perspective. All single parents are not on welfare or caught up in pathology, deviance, and sexuality. The limitation of earlier research and visual communications has created a cesspool of ignorance that is an insult to African American people who are an integral part of the fabric of this society. The irony is they are rarely portrayed in the media as a "symbol" of society but most often as a "symptom."

The purpose of this research was to shed light on single parenting from a different eye and perspective. The shortcomings of earlier research and depictions are evident. The challenge ahead, however, is for researchers and scholars to create a new viewfinder so that society can see the African American single parent (male or female) through different eyes. This is going to take a new vision, sacrifice, and commitment. And these are the same qualities that single African American women face while raising their children against all odds. As TV's Murphy Brown asserted, "They hope for the kind of life for their children that we all want for our children." It is my hope that researchers and scholars will adjust their viewfinders so that they can see through a new vision that is not narrow and more a reflection of the fabric of society that is indeed couched in the true practice of "family values."

NOTE

1. The documentary *Single Parenting: A Woman's Perspective* was not originally produced for scholarly analysis. The six-person sample was considered adequate for a 30-minute documentary. Although a sample this small may not seem statistically significant, it serves as a pilot sample for this discussion on the various types of single parents.

2. For a discussion of issues confronting African American professional women who want children, see "Racing the Biological Clock: Increasing Numbers."

REFERENCES

Baptiste, D. A. (1986). The image of the Black family portrayed by television: A critical comment. *Marriage and Family Review, 10*(1), 41-63.

Bennett, L., Jr. (1990, November). The 10 biggest myths about the Black family. *Ebony,* pp. 168-175.

Collins, P. H. (1989). A comparison of two works on the Black family life. *Signs, 14*(4), 875-884.

Frazier, E. F. (1966). *The Negro family in the United States* (2nd ed.). Chicago: University of Chicago Press. (Original work published 1939)

Height, D. (1989, July 24/31). Self-help—A Black tradition. *The Nation,* 136-138.

Kilpatrick, A. C. (1979). Future directions for the Black family. *Family Coordinator,* 28(3), 347-352.

Kolbert, E. (1992, September 23). Murphy Brown's feud: When art replaces life. *The New York Times,* p. A17.

Maume, D. J., & Dunaway, G. R. (1989). Determinants of the prevalence of mother only families. *Research in Social Stratification and Mobility, 8,* 313-327.

Moyers, B. (1986). *The vanishing family: Crisis in Black America* [Documentary]. Washington, DC: Corporation for Public Broadcasting.

Moynihan, D. P. (1965). *The Negro family: The case for national action.* Washington, DC: U.S. Government Printing Office.

Murphy Brown (1992, September 21). One-hour season premiere episode aired on Columbia Broadcasting System (CBS) Television Network, 9 p.m. Eastern Standard Time.

Peters, M. F. (1974). The Black family—Perpetuating the myths: An analysis of family sociology textbook treatment of Black Families. *Family Coordinator, 23*(4), 349-357.

Racing the biological clock: Increasing number of single professional women chase motherhood. (1991). *Ebony, 46*(9), 63-67.

Report on the National Advisory Commission on Civil Disorders. (1968). *New York Times* edition. New York: Dutton.

USA TODAY. (1993, February 26). Unmarried moms.

Ziegler, D. (1987, June). *Single parenting: A woman's perspective* [Video documentary]. Knoxville, TN: WSJK-TV. Copyright 1987, Dhyana Ziegler. Quotations used by permission.

Ziegler, D. (1991). Multiculturalism: An opportunity for educators. *FEEDBACK, 32*(3), 2-4.

6

The Impact of the Law on
Single Mothers and the "Innocent"

Willa Mae Hemmons

In discussing the situation of the African American single mother within the context of the law, there is an important sociolegal relationship that must be considered. That relationship impinges heavily on her ability to care for, nurture, provide for, and, in many other ways, generally sustain her family. The legal system supports the prejudices, predilections, arbitrariness, and discrimination of the economic, political, educational, and even religious social institutions. According to Parsons (1951), a religious type of institution is important in this dynamic insofar as it helps to justify and rationalize a society's hierarchies. In short, a religious-type institution helps to legitimize and give credence to those who are deemed worthy in the society. Parsons characterized the legal systems as performing the solidarity and unifying functions of a religious institution. Such a characterization can be validated by the manifestation of the legal system's historical and continuing role in society of officially authorizing and sanctioning the dominant group's values and attitudes.

This chapter describes how recent judicial opinions emanating from the legal system have changed the perpetuators of racial and social injustice into the "innocent." Those who help to maintain the society's differential allocation of goods and services are elevated through the legal system to benign, innocent sufferers. Presumably, this suffering is caused by the malfeasance of the unworthy (e.g., welfare mother or unemployed malingerer). Hopefully, this chapter demonstrates how legal theory—particularly from the body of law known as affirmative action—has been effective in maintaining the economic injustice that preserves the inequities endured by the African American woman. Another important legal manifestation of the role of the "law" is found in the fact that one's very "legitimation" in U.S. society is defined by the status pronounced at birth that is provided by the legal system. A set of married parents is a prerequisite for even a "legitimate" entry into this world. Nearly 30% of all American children are now born to unmarried parents; two thirds of African American children are coming into the world "out of wedlock," compared to one fifth of European American children. (U.S. Bureau of the Census, 1990). This ratio helps to corroborate the view that U.S. society is somewhat deterministic in such initial efforts at institutionalizing second-class status for African Americans. Thus, at this point in time, social, economic, and political forces are serving to form a firmer demarcation line between the "good, the bad, and the ugly" as useful value constructs for future application of differential treatments. The legal system clarifies, reifies, and magnifies this demarcation line.

The traditional sociological paradigm that is probably most valuable is one that acknowledges that the functions and processes of the legal system are reflections of the greater society (Merton, 1954). The legal system mirrors the organizational structure, the interrelationships, and the dynamics of the society that it serves. Without that initial understanding, an adequate comprehension of the impact of the legal/political system on the African American female single parent is impossible. The prejudices, discriminations, punishments, and abuses that characterize the society are sanctioned, implemented, and legitimized by the legal/political system and vice versa.

Use of the term "innocence" in this chapter implies that it is ironic that those victimized by racism and sexism are treated as the perpetuators of wrongdoing (e.g., the Black female single parent). The same sense of irony here makes one wonder at the manner in which those who benefit from the disparities inherent in the undeserved treatment of the former are characterized as *innocent*. It is a strange but societally functional reversal of roles. In other words, the victims are blamed for the pathologies of their predicament (Ryan, 1972).

An underlying theme of this chapter is that there is a transposition of innocence that operates to undermine the effectiveness, the support, the quality of life, and the ability to rear the children of the African American single mother. I outline the legal determinism undergirding the African

American female household head's attempt to conduct her family affairs in an atmosphere of dignity and respect. I also present figures from the economic institution in illustration of the consequences of "lawfully" maintaining the African American female household's financial status quo. The legal system is thereby posited to be one of the most intransigent obstacles to full economic, educational, and social parity. Identification of the Black woman as a culprit camouflages the real "Simon Legrees" (see *Uncle Tom's Cabin* by Harriet Beecher Stowe, circa 1860). Recognition of the role of social institutions in wreaking havoc on the Black family (Billingsley, 1968) also helps to take the onus away from males of African descent (Moynihan, 1965).

The oppressive nature of U.S. law with reference to African Americans is an ironic development when one considers the history of law as a concept. Eurocentric jurisprudence derived its fundamental principles of justice from the Kemet (Egyptian/African) priests Imhotep and Pepi's ideals of proof as a rational interpretation of reality (Asante, 1987). Logical persuasion formed the foundation for decision making and problem solving. Incorporating these strategies into the Eurocentric justice system, the Anglo-Saxons of England went on to develop their court system based on the persuasive abilities of two otherwise presumptively "equal" opponents. Before the introduction of these Kemetian principles, the European sense of justice derived mostly from trial by fire and water types of ordeals. Logic, reason, and justice were incorporated into the European system to form the basis of today's Anglo-Saxon U.S. legal system. Such democratic ideals, however, become distorted and ill fitting when applied to Black single mothers. This is a situation for which the jury model is not an adequate remedy. U.S. courts have awarded millions of dollars to persons harmed as a result of defective vehicles and dangerous toys; but no Black family has ever received such an award to compensate for the effects of racial discrimination.

The problem in what became the United States, of course, is that the African American from his or her onset in the country did not then and does not now hold an equal place in U.S. society. The cases decided by the U.S. Supreme Court—from *Dred Scott v. Sanford* in 1857 (declared that "Negroes" were not citizens of the United States and that Congress did not have the power to prohibit slavery in a federal territory) to *Plessy v. Ferguson* in 1896 (upheld the separate but equal doctrine) to *R.A.V. v. St. Paul* in 1992 (voided ordinance prohibiting crimes of hate, such as cross burning on a Black family's lawn)—suggest that social, economic, and political forces (Billingsley, 1968) predominant in the United States have been reflected in and reinforced by those decisions.

In examining the status, position, and role of the African American woman who is the head of her household, it is necessary to look at the manner in which the interrelationships between social institutions operate (Parsons, 1951). The symbiotic nature of most major social institutions in the United States has been very comprehensive. For instance, in terms of preserving the basic norms and values of U.S. society, the societal institutions have, for the most part, been relatively responsive to one another. In the past, this has been particularly true of the economic and the legal institutions. Sometimes though, usually citing the "American tradition of equality and justice," there have been divergences from the prevailing trend of protecting a predominant European American culture and social organization.

The attempt to give meaning to the Statue of Liberty's request to "give me your hungry, your tired, your poor" and to appease the most powerful ethnic groups in the United States, which are of European genesis, has put a strain on the U.S. socioeconomic-political system of democracy. A discussion of the true fundamental (in the sociological sense) values underlying democracy as practiced in the United States is not complete without consideration of a social theorist whose views informed much of the American "dream," which was based on individualism. That theorist is Herbert Spencer (1904); his Social Darwinist philosophy asserted that the social elite were biologically superior to the rest of the population.

Of course, in using such a framework of analysis, any deficiencies in the African American woman's performance, productivity, or position in society would be attributed to her own inadequacies. Such an analysis could provide the legal underpinnings for a judicial opinion that characterizes the African American woman as an exploitative misfit undeserving of any protection from the courts. From such a viewpoint, any educational or economic (e.g., employment or entrepreneurial) benefit allowing her to overcome past and present discriminatory handicaps would be deemed a windfall. Applicable not only to the legal system's processing of discriminatory treatment claims, Spencerian beliefs help augment caricatures of the African American woman as "Welfare Queen," "Matriarch," and "Happy Hooker" (Angelou, 1986), among others, which are part and parcel of the normative formulations used by European American-dominated welfare state, family, and criminal justice institutions, respectively. In sociological terms, using the "survival of the fittest" rationale, the Supreme Court had by 1990 demolished any concept of affirmative action as an effective mechanism for redressing job-related discrimination against African Americans and women.

Theories propounded by social scientists such as Robert Merton (1954) and Erving Goffman (1963) are ignored as viable explanations of the structural or systemic causes and effects of human behavior. Even though Merton is a macrosociologist and Goffman can best be characterized as focusing on micro levels of human interaction, both emphasize the fact that existing societal forces greatly influence human responses. In other words, degrading and demeaning social conditions and individual situations significantly increase the odds of negative, inappropriate individual reactions. Thus a person of minority or female origin can easily be found to be lacking when the courts presume a more supportive underlying foundation. The lack of merit, then, becomes a self-fulfilling prophesy. Further, the courts rarely take into account unequal positions at the starting gate. For strict constructionists of the U.S. Constitution, social science is felt to be useless as a tool of legal analysis in determining which result should be selected. The courts claim to base their frameworks of analysis on the American value of meritocracy. However, even the typical meritocracy arguments have been challenged by social scientists. Nevertheless, the courts have held fast to them as a way of giving credence to, inspiring faith in (Parsons, 1951), and legitimizing their decisions.

OBSERVATIONS

There are numerous examples of the law's negative impact on the African American female single parent. For example, the law provides stiff criminal penalties against welfare fraud (e.g., *Ohio Revised Code* Sec. 2913.02) while not criminalizing such aberrations as student and farmer loan "defaults." The law, at the same time, provides monthly allotments inadequate for even basic survival. Even the version of "welfare reform" tendered by President Clinton, as reflected in his economic plan, held more punitive components than constructive ones when applied to the Black female-headed family.

Because the Black female-headed family type constitutes approximately 40% of all family types that receive AFDC (Aid to Families with Dependent Children) benefits, much of the animosity directed at welfare has racial overtones. This is probably a very salient reason why it evokes so much hostility from the "innocent" taxpaying public such that any presidential administration receives strong political pressure to reduce both AFDC benefits and the number of AFDC beneficiaries. It is ironic that any Clinton job requirement proposal comes at a time when a job has taken on more the qualities of a *reward* than a punishment. In short, most African Americans on welfare are there because they are effectively excluded from the mainstream of the U.S. "legitimate" job market.

Indeed, more and more, getting (and, in many instances, keeping) a job is becoming an expression of political ingenuity, networking, adeptness, and empowerment even in ostensibly nonpolitical areas. Many "welfare mothers" would welcome the opportunity to enter the now increasingly cherished world of the office worker—particularly if that opportunity were accompanied by adequate health care, child care, and retirement benefits. In a time when such office workers are clinging desperately to such relatively scarce jobs, it would be interesting to see how government and industry could be forced to open their clerical, administrative, and managerial (e.g., "Murphy Brown"; see also Ziegler's chapter in this volume) doors even further to include the welfare mothers. That situation would probably evoke even more fury than the current, more abstract objection to tolerating the systemic repercussions of the welfare state—in short, there would undoubtedly be some more backlash from the "innocent." It is hard to imagine the federal and state governments as presently constituted becoming embroiled in that kind of controversial battle on behalf of welfare mothers when the lowliest of jobs is now often seen as some kind of prize. Although numerically there are more Whites on welfare, Blacks are disproportionately represented. When the "innocent" are scrubbing latrines and collecting garbage, it is unlikely that the government will attempt to displace them with "undeserving" African American welfare mothers.

Despite the presidential administration, however, federal and state welfare law provides for interpretation of welfare eligibility by dispensing a morass of catch-22 regulations, which, by virtue of the inadequate living allocations, are extremely difficult to obey. The African American female single parent on welfare is hence made almost a prima facie criminal violating the legal expectations of millions of *innocent* taxpayers. Unfortunately, it does not necessarily matter that sometimes the players representing the legal institution are African American. For instance, Cornel West (1993) points out how Supreme Court Justice Clarence Thomas derided his sister, Emma Mae, for having been on welfare and even insinuated that she was a welfare cheat. In his discussion, West maintains that Thomas did as great a disservice to Emma Mae as he did to Anita Hill insofar as Thomas, according to West, played "the racial card." Emma Mae and Anita Hill arguably represent two ends of the legal spectrum—as manifested by social class designations. West's point, however, is that Black women are put in degraded positions fostered by society and reinforced by the legal system, and have "the social burden" of bearing and raising their children under these circumstances. Further insights into Supreme Court views on African American women and the "innocent" may be gleaned from the fact that Justice Thomas has generally voted with Justice Antonin Scalia against affirmative action (e.g., *St. Mary's Honor Center et al. v. Melvin Hicks,* 1993) and civil rights.

Other points ominous for affirmative action can be inferred from this behavior. One such point is that it is an inaccurate definition of the concept of Afrocentricity to expand that term to include "any expression by a person of African descent" (cf. Asante, *The Afrocentric Idea,* 1987, or Fanon, *The Wretched of the Earth,* 1965). Afrocentrism and "centrism" help to put in perspective the motives and manners (the whys and hows) of the dominant group's use of the legal system for the preservation of its societal, economic, and political interests. However, Afrogenesis by itself will have little impact upon men or women who have been incorporated into the structural components of an oppressive system and who perceive their livelihood as depending on that system (West, 1993). Such "incorporated" men and women must suppress Afrocentrism such as cooperation, a group orientation, and spiritualism in favor of competition, an individual orientation, and materialism, respectively. In other words, these marginal men (and women) take the risk of rejecting the supports of their Afrocentric heritage for the Eurocentric rewards rooted in commercialism.

The perils of gambling one way or another may sometimes be a choice between the devil and the deep blue sea for "upwardly bound" corporate Blacks. For instance, an African American male corporate manager who had been recently promoted among massive white-collar layoffs was heralded by coworkers as doomed because he told his boss (the vice president of the corporation) that he could not attend an upcoming holiday party because of his Pentecostal-related religious beliefs. As long as the perception exists that, to survive, an Afrogeneric person feels the need to rigidly conform within the context of a systemically oppressive Eurocentric organizational structure, then his or her skin color has minimal impact on that individual's conscious decision making. In other words, the ethnic or racial affinity of those being oppressed has no bearing on the decision making of such an ethnically or racially similar oppressor—unless, of course, it is circumstantially expedient. Having an Afrogeneric supervisor who enforces oppression in a Eurocentric corporate setting is perhaps even worse than having a Eurogeneric supervisor who does so. This is so because the actions of the former are more protected by the courts, which have generally held "Black supervisors cannot discriminate against Black employees." This explains the relative proliferation of Afrogeneric persons in personnel offices—even if their proportion in other areas of the corporate environment is proportionately absent.

A second point is that even with the passage of the 1991 Civil Rights Act, these remarks do not bode well for future decisions regarding affirmative action and protection of "innocent" European American males from African American females. (It is interesting to note here that when Supreme Court Justice Ruth Bader Ginsburg, the second woman in history appointed to that bench, and Justice Thomas sat together on the D.C. Circuit Court of Appeals, both voted the same the majority of the time. Perhaps that will change since Justice Thomas has voted almost 100% of the time with the very anti-affirmative action jurist, Justice Scalia. If Justice Ginsburg aligns with the other female Supreme Court member, Justice Sandra Day O'Connor, then affirmative action outcomes might be more auspicious.)

Another reason for the pessimistic view, however, is that the Supreme Court has been striking down "unreasonable," "unjust," and "ill conceived" legislation since the *Marbury v. Madison* case in 1803. Furthermore, the Court is now led by a Chief Justice (William Rehnquist) who is essentially a "strict constructionist." Strict constructionists believe that if a fundamental right is not patently in the Constitution it should not be imposed by legislation. This means that, the Civil Rights Act of 1991 notwithstanding, the Rehnquist Court, including its African American member, cannot be expected to made decisions that will positively affect the status of Black women and their families; such changes may not be rapidly forthcoming—at least not through the strategy of affirmative action.

Another example of how the legal system perpetuates the derogatory position of the Black woman and hence places increased obstacles in the way of her raising her children in a single-parent forum is in the way the law defines and treats "illegitimates" (the legal definition of children born out of wedlock). For various reasons that the dominant society likes to equate with "morality" (Moynihan, 1965), Black women are significantly more likely than White women to have out-of-wedlock children. The law inflicts an exacerbated penalty on such children (and their mothers) that they carry with them to the grave. Unacknowledged, illegitimate children have virtually no rights of inheritance under the laws of most states. They cannot bring wrongful death lawsuits seeking damages as relates to their paternal parents. They do not have to be recognized by administrators of Workmen's Compensation or Social Security agencies in causes of action relating to their father's death or injury. Hence many African American children are denied valuable sources of support that "legitimate" children have. Despite this situation that relates back to the medieval prioritization of children based on mother-father relations, modern-day law maintains that such illegitimate children do not have an equal protection claim. Such discrimination is thus legal, having been sanctioned and supported by the U.S. Supreme Court. As far as their African American mothers are concerned, it probably would be easier financially for them to wear a scarlet letter A. However, society has labeled Black women, in large part by their color, as disreputable—so embroidery does not have to be invoked to do the stigmatization necessary to separate the haves from the have-nots. As I maintained earlier, the legal system has served to officially institutionalize the subordinate status of the African American female endemic to other social settings such as school, work, and play.

These examples can go on ad infinitum. Hence a major point of this chapter is that the U.S. court system has acted to create the rather incongruous picture of families headed by Whites and males as victims of economic and educational encroachments by those headed by Blacks and females, especially when both the latter two characteristics are contained in one individual family head—a Black female one. Furthermore, this distortion operates to delegitimize, disenfranchise, demean, and diminish the ability of the African American woman who is solely responsible for the rearing of her children.

Although this phenomenon is perhaps most visible in the area of affirmative action, it also has great salience for juvenile and criminal justice, domestic relations, probate, consumer law, and debtor's rights as well as other laws that serve to organize and regulate economic and political relations. In all these legal arenas, the dominant societal mandate of racial and sexual repression is maintained and reinforced. It remains to be seen how far recently passed legal protections relating to sexual harassment will go in emancipating women, Black and White, from constrictive employment and educational situations. Being the sole or primary support of one's children exacerbates the inability of a woman to escape from a situation involving sexual harassment. The law, dominated by men, is probably suspect as an immediately practical tool for persons being terrorized in an unseemly work situation. It is not that having children is an excuse for tolerating such demeaning treatment; it is just that having children gives one a greater incentive for taking such abuse insofar as one has fewer options in "willfully" leaving one's employment.

Similarly, culpability is essentially a matter of societal edict and sociolegal manipulation. The problems that the Black single mother faces have exposed her inordinately to compromising economic situations when, unable to compete successfully in the job market, she has victimized herself or her children by turning to behaviors defined by the law as illegal (for example, by the "victimless" crimes of prostitution, drug abuse, or welfare transgressions). The role of the African American woman, particularly as that role relates to her family, is thus a much maligned (Moynihan, 1965), much disputed one (Billingsley, 1968; Glasgow, 1981; Hill, 1972) in terms of her true social position in America. The influence of the law upon that role and upon the ability of the African American woman to engage in survival strategies for her family acts as a societal albatross. The legal system in America has also been maligned—and, to the victims whose liberties it has infringed, rightfully so. The legal system is founded upon controversy. Dispute resolutions form its raison d'être. The "dispute" regarding the legal system in this treatise, however, centers not so much around its function as a forum for feuding individual parties but, rather, around its ability to provide a foundation for the fair and equitable disposition of matters involving, directly or indirectly, the prospects of the African American female-headed family. This ability is compromised by the fact that recent case law has reconfigured the European American male as a victim—or as an "innocent" in the U.S. legal system. Thus we must review the African American family in the social context within which it exists (Hill, 1972).

LEGAL ANALYSIS OF SPECIFIC COURT DECISIONS

The most grotesque manipulation of the law preventing Black single-parent mothers from equal economic access—and indeed punishing them in an uncanny way—is particularly distorted by the development of the concept known as reverse discrimination. For instance, it is through the construction of White males as innocent victims, with attendant cutbacks in affirmative action, that the "rulers" of the legal system have been instrumental in perpetrating the inequities experienced by the African American woman trying to support herself and her family. It is thus the contention of this chapter that the most debilitating area of law for the Black female household head is affirmative action. That is because as long as she is "the last one hired and the first one fired" she will continue to hold her place as the most economically subordinate category in the United States. Indeed, such workplace discrimination against her and her African American male cohort is a major contributing factor to her "singleness" in the first place. Her role at the bottom of the economic ladder, in turn, helps to keep her in an unequal bargaining position vis-à-vis the other legal areas. These inequities are just as intransigent and just as (or more) disparate as when Carter G. Woodson documented them in 1933 or Jessie Bernard did in 1966 or Billy J. Tidwell did in 1992. According to some, to expect the legal system to eliminate racism is akin to letting the fox watch the hen house (Hutchinson, 1990; Malcolm X & Haley, 1965). In other words, the U.S. legal system perpetrates the types of inequities that support the continued subordination and dehumanization of African Americans, male and married, female and single. For the latter, however, the situation is even more exacerbated, particularly when the African American single female has offspring.

A rather tortured demonstration of the pull and tug between U.S. values and the institutions designed to achieve those values is currently going on in the arena of the check and balance governmental system. The apparent tug of war is in the field of affirmative action and involves the courts versus Congress. It is a most "deliberative" manifestation of the calibration and recalibration of the U.S. system of governmental checks and balances.

As the start of the "war" one might point to the passage of the Voting Rights Act of 1965 and the Civil Rights Act of 1964. During what some fondly term the Civil Rights Era or the Second Reconstruction, not only were the civil rights amendments of 1866 resuscitated but a plethora of new laws and programs were introduced to reinforce the spirit of those original amendments.

The civil rights acts were products of the legislature. Various programs, particularly those embodying what came to be known as affirmative action, were heralded as presenting effective plans for eradicating discriminatory policies and practices. The concept was scarcely a few years old, however, before cries of "reverse discrimination" and "preferential treatment" rang out to debilitate and perhaps ultimately to destroy it. Affirmative action provoked so much hostility after "protecting" minorities and women in the realm of higher education involving a discriminatory admissions policy that it set off a reaction that signaled a dramatic retreat by the Supreme Court. That retreat was inaugurated by the dual decisions of *Regents of the University of California v. Bakke* (1978) and *Kaiser Aluminum & Chemical Corp. v. Weber* (1979). With the encouragement of *Bakke* and *Weber,* time after time an "innocent" European American male came forth to demand that he be treated "equitably" without regard to his color or sex. The *Bakke/Weber* duo undoubtedly sent a sigh of relief to the majority and the male communities, as both cases essentially redefined who the "innocent" victim of discrimination was. Taken together, these two cases institutionalized the term *reverse discrimination* and reformalized the education/employment/economic discrimination victim as the European American male. This startling turn of events alleging that European American males discriminate against themselves on the basis of race and sex was elaborated on by the Supreme Court in subsequent cases during the 1980s (see discussion below).

To try to eliminate the absurd impact of these cases, after much political haggling as well as after the highly publicized Hill-Thomas Senate Judiciary debate in September 1991, Congress passed an updated civil rights law. This most intensive exercise of "seesaw" with the judiciary can be interpreted as seeking to determine who is actually the victim in discrimination cases. It is ironic also that in a struggle to preserve her rights the African American woman herself has had little actual input in either the outcome or the process that preceded it. There are no female African American justices on the Supreme Court. Carolyn Mosely-Braun (D-IL) was the first Black female ever elected to the Senate, and the number of female African Americans is still nominal in the House of Representatives. Although Senator John Danforth inserted a clause in the 1991 Civil Rights Bill that prohibited discrimination against Senate staffers, initially the executive branch of the government was ordered to end race-based hiring; that directive, however, was later rescinded.

Despite the fact that this rationale has been disputed, many observers agree that the primary reason for several of the major changes in the Civil Rights Act, as previously mentioned, was to overcome decisions by the Supreme Court that were detrimental to the achievement of equal rights by women and minorities. This goal received a major blow in the 1993 Supreme Court decision involving a Black male, Melvin Hicks. In *Hicks,* which was appealed from the Eighth U.S. Circuit, Justice Scalia was joined by Chief Justice Rehnquist and Justices O'Connor, Kennedy, and Thomas in a ruling that disallowed relief from job bias even though employers had falsified the reasons for dismissal. The fact that the employer had lied in Hicks's firing was insufficient to support his cause of action under Title VII of the Civil Rights Act of 1964. Although Hicks had sued alleging racial discrimination, the Supreme Court sent the case back to the Eighth Circuit for a consideration as to whether or not Hicks was dismissed based on personality differences or based *specifically* on racial differences.

The major changes sought by passage of the Civil Rights Restoration Act of 1991 revolved specifically around the issues of disparate impact, discrimination and harassment, and reopening old discrimination cases. Led by *Bakke* and *Weber*, in several landmark cases during the 1980s the Supreme Court had set aside important minority and female claims of discrimination. In one case, the Court allowed racial harassment as well as racial and ethnic discrimination in hiring, promotions, demotions, discharges, retaliation, and other employment issues. The employers' burden of proving "exclusionary employment policies or practices are justified by business necessity" was removed in *Wards Cove Packing Company v. Antonio* (1989). Also, the Supreme Court transferred to the employee the burden of proving which exact individual employment practice produced a discriminatory effect. In another case, the Court held that employees did not have to rely on previous civil rights consent decrees and consequently could file an infinite number of reverse discrimination lawsuits. Furthermore, the Court decided that the right of employees to challenge discriminatory seniority systems was not necessary. Keeping to its demolition mission, the Supreme Court eliminated the use of discrimination as one of a number of motivating factors in employment decisions.

Hence, as a balance to the check administered to affirmative action by the Supreme Court, on February 7, 1990, a bill titled the Civil Rights Act of 1990 was introduced in the Senate by Edward Kennedy (D-MA), James Jeffords (R-VT), and 38 other senators, and in the House of Representatives by Augustus Hawkins (D-CA), Hamilton Fish, Jr. (R-NY), and 158 other representatives. In a bipartisan effort, the bill ultimately passed was even called the "Danforth Bill." Congress thus strove to combat what evidently was deemed a serious misinterpretation of congressional intent by the Supreme Court. In other words, the legislative branch of the federal government is trying to redeem the civil rights that the judicial branch had demolished. Moreover, Congress added sexual discrimination to the Civil Rights Act—a move predicted to add to the number of filings under it. Purportedly then, the African American woman is thus dually protected—but is she really?

Through a legislative initiative signed by President Bush in November, 1991, Congress sought to overturn each ruling in the aforementioned cases that denied employment rights of women and minorities. In addition, the legislative enactment expanded the time for filing administrative charges with the Equal Employment Opportunity Commission from 180 days to 2 years. Furthermore, Congress decided to allow discrimination victims to recover compensatory and punitive damages against private employers when intentional discrimination could be proven. Moreover, Congress overturned a serious affirmative action setback rendered by the Supreme Court and allowed prevailing parties to recover their cost for the use of expert witnesses during litigation.

The future socioeconomic well-being of the African American woman, particularly one who is single, depends on the outcome of this "ping-pong" diplomacy process. If, despite congressional efforts, the courts continue to depict the African American woman as the perpetrator of discrimination against "innocent" European American males, her prospects are decidedly more limited. If affirmative action through "affirmative neglect" is allowed to die and not allowed to intervene in bringing African American women closer to parity within the nation's educational, employment, and entrepreneurial systems, she will remain substantially legally impaired in those areas. This has significance for the African American single-parent mother despite her individual socioeconomic status because if she is behind educationally and economically relative to European Americans, her children will continue to suffer due to those deficiencies in their range of resources.

SOCIOECONOMIC ANALYSIS: CUMULATIVE DEMOGRAPHIC EFFECT OF SPECIFIC DECISIONS

The ultimate consequence of economic discrimination executed by the legal institution is that the African American woman who is single is poorer than her cohorts who are European American, male or married. According to the 1990 census (U.S. Bureau of the Census, 1991), the median income of a household headed by an African American single woman is $12,537, which is significantly lower than that earned by others of a different race or sex or, particularly, both. Controlling for gender, a comparison can be made with those who are of like sex but of a different race. A household headed by a woman of European descent has a median income of $20,867. Controlling for race, it must be pointed out that an African American single-male-headed household is supported by a median income of $24,048—a number of even greater statistical significance than that which results when median incomes of the Black woman and the White woman are compared. The median income of a European American male-headed household is $32,869. The disparity between this figure and that for the African American female-headed household speaks for itself as even more significant evidence in the search for "innocence."

In the single-female-headed household category, the ratio of Black to White median income is 60:1. On the other hand, Black single-male-headed households have median incomes that are 73.2% of that of their White counterparts. Revealing the advantage of marriage for African American women, those in a married-couple family situation have a median household income that is 83.8% of that of their European American cohort. Therefore, the single African American woman, despite the legal system, improves her chances of parity with European Americans by more than 23% by being married.

Unfortunately, for economic purposes at least, African American married-couple families are only 33.4% of all Black types of households as opposed to European married-couple families that are 58.1% of all White household types. Thus single-household-head families predominate in the Black community. Furthermore, because such families are a fact of life, strategies are needed to take that fact into consideration in designing methods to enhance the quality of life (e.g., educational attainment, home ownership, environmental safety, level of income, etc.) for the African American woman and her family.

Interestingly, the percentages of Blacks and Whites who live in family versus nonfamily households are almost identical—70.0% and 70.2%, respectively. In terms of all family households, the median income of Blacks is 58% of the median income for Whites. African American female households in a nonfamily situation earn a median income that is 59.2% of that of European Americans. Black male households in a nonfamily situation have a slight advantage over their Black female counterparts in that they have a median income that is 65.0% of that of Whites.

To get a clearer understanding of what the African American *single* female household head has done to the "innocent" European American male of a single-female-headed or a married-couple family household, it is useful to compare the median incomes of those categories. First, remember that the median income for a single African American female-headed family is $12,537, whereas that for the single White male corollary household is $32,869 and that for the White married-couple family household is $40,433. In other words, using strictly single-family household comparisons, the average household income of the White female is more than 1⅔ times that of the Black female, whereas that of the Black male is approximately twice that of his female colleague and that of the White male is almost three times that of his alleged Black female discrimination perpetuator.

These figures really give insight about who is innocent and who is not from an economic standpoint. The unemployment rate for European American men was 5.8%, whereas that for African American men was 11.7%. Women, although earning substantially less, had better luck finding jobs. Still, African American women's unemployment rate of 10.2% was more than twice that for European American women. To sum up, in legal terms African Americans are currently discriminating against European Americans, with the result that the unemployment rate for African Americans is twice as high as for European Americans. This is a truly paradoxical result if one accepts the legal characterization of the African American female as a predator upon *innocent* European American male employment, entrepreneurial, and educational efficacy. In short, such huge gaps in economic viability between Blacks and Whites demonstrate essentially how ludicrous legally based are allegations of an African American female economic displacement. Nonetheless, such court-legitimized allegations continue to hamper the ability of the African American female to provide for a family in which almost 60% of the time she is its head.

One reason for this continued disparate economic result as sanctioned by the law is that the Supreme Court eschews what it labels nonspecific reliance on social statistics such as these. The Supreme Court has a tradition of looking only at the specific case or controversy before it. Cumulative, collective, or national numbers such as these are inappropriate for legal analysis, according to the Supreme Court. This frame of reference should be compared, however, to that of sociologist Patricia Hill Collins (1991). Hill Collins provides two ideas in particular that give insight into the functions of rationales such as that of the Supreme Court. The first is that it takes the specific to explain the universal reality. Thus when the Supreme Court refuses to acknowledge universal truths in deciding specific cases, it is denying the subjugated reality of an African American's and/or a woman's life. Second, knowledge by a dominant or a subject group is selective. Hence, because the former is generally more powerful, unless other factors intervene the "knowledge" of the former will prevail (pp. 233-235).

In the same vein as that of the Supreme Court, it was the purported aversion to numbers (e.g., quotas, goals, etc.) of the Bush administration that endangered the passage of the 1991 Civil Rights Bill. Hopefully, from the African American female perspective, the 1991 Civil Rights Act will restore coverage for racial harassment claims pursued under the 1866 Civil Rights Act (Sec. 1981). Similarly, the provisions of the 1991 Civil Rights Act prohibiting attacks on existing consent decrees by new reverse discrimination litigation will be welcome by many municipalities across the nation. Suits against cities that had already litigated discrimination claims brought by women and/or minorities were threatening to bankrupt the already limited resources of municipal governments. For instance, after the *Martin v. Wilks* (1989) decision, Title VII litigation by nonparties to consent decrees escalated in cities from San Francisco and Oakland (California) to Cincinnati, Cleveland, and Toledo (Ohio) to Gadsden (Alabama), and to Albany (Georgia). Again, the macroscopic has no reality without the microscopic, and specific legal proclamations have the general effect of overall diminished female and minority access.

If the resources of such cities are strained by having to protect "innocent" European American males, they are even less adequate to address pressing urban problems that plague and disproportionately affect African American female household heads. Another example of the consequences of global employment discrimination being protected by "specific" court action lies in the area of occupational mobility. In terms of occupation, as of 1991 for employed men over 16 years of age, 26.9% of all European American males were at the managerial and professional level, but among African American males, only 13.3% were at that level. In comparison, for employed women over 16, 18.6% of African American females were at the managerial/professional level, compared to 27.2% of European American females at that level (U.S. Bureau of Labor Statistics, 1991).

Another arbiter of "innocence" can be found in statistics setting forth poverty-level frequencies. Revealing the propensity for reverse discrimination again—if court edicts are to be given credence,—African American female-headed households with no husband present led the percentage of family types below the poverty line with 48.1%. Female European American households with no husband present had 26.8% of their numbers below the poverty line. For the "innocent" European American males who had households with no wife present, the percentage was 9.9%, whereas that for like African American male-headed households was 20.6%. The percentage of African American married-couple families below the poverty line was 12.6%, compared to 5.1% of European American married-couple families. These numbers, although so far scrupulously ignored by the courts pursuant to the Supreme Court's lead, become even more salient when one considers the fact that 43.8% of African American families are headed by a female, as compared with 12.9% of European American ones. Furthermore, 51.2% of African American children live with their mothers; however, only 16.2% of European American children do so. The impact of the refusal of the courts to take these figures into account in applying law to a specific case means that each individual mother must, on her own, marshal evidence of a specific corporation's or government entity's or school's culpability in denying her employment, entrepreneurial opportunity, or education. The fact that these organizations have become increasingly sophisticated in hiding such evidence and that the resources of such individual mothers have become increasingly limited in finding such evidence is essentially ignored by the courts—and this is done in all "fairness and impartiality" when the underlying presumption is that such burdens of proof rightfully fall upon the individual.

These statistics bring to mind another underlying court phenomenon: the propensity of courts to still hold antiquated views of women's roles and responsibilities—female judges sporadically placed notwithstanding. These numbers show that assumptions about any decreased need for women to succeed in the workplace because of a helpmate are patently false—especially for African American women, whose ability to earn a living is often the only resource they have to provide for their families. Furthermore, their families include as often as not not just their own children but their nieces, nephews, brothers, sisters, cousins, aunts, uncles, and/or elderly parents. Such extended families require more income at a time when the welfare state, regardless of presidential administration, is markedly diminishing. The end of the 20th century also marks a time of intense competition for a few "worthy" jobs and economic opportunities that makes the predilection of the courts for decreased employment, education, and entrepreneurship protection for historically deprived populations that much more ominous. Societal inequality has been expanded and made more entrenched since the civil rights movement.

The aforementioned stress on metropolitan resources is also instructive when it is noted that 40.8% of African American households live inside the central cities of large metropolitan areas. So, the more that "innocent"

European American males sue the cities for reverse discrimination, the less those cities will have to address such concerns as education, social services, crime, safety, drugs, health, economic development, and the myriad other urban issues that help hold the African American woman hostage to a system that blames her as the victim for perpetrating her bondage. The major contribution of the legal system in preserving the processes of its sister institutions is that it continues the inequities embodied in the disparities represented by the above statistics.

CONCLUSION

Economic conditions have been cited here to emphasize the debilitating effects that the affirmative action decisions of the courts have had on the African American female household head's ability to provide for her family. The efforts of Congress in passing the Civil Rights Restoration Act of 1991 notwithstanding, the Supreme Court may at some future time seize upon "legislative intent" to reinterpret what Congress actually meant. For instance, during the Senate debate, Senator Robert Dole asserted that the act was compatible with *Wards Cove*. Essentially, the status quo represents power relationships that currently exist in the society. As such, then, it is probably naive to think that a system representing the legitimate power structure of the society (e.g., authority) can be counted on to make decisions that would result in meaningful changes in the hierarchies represented by that structure. This is why the empowerment of oppressed minorities is made that much more imperative for their survival.

Social institutions, such as the courts, are established ways by which a society addresses its universal needs. The U.S. society, as seen through the above laws and statistics, addresses its universal "status quo" needs in a particularistic, individualized way that selects its treatments by virtue of a person's racial, gender, and socioeconomic characteristics. It is significant in a negative way for the African American female-headed family that the treatment bestowed on its head gives it the lowest economic, political, and educational status of any family type in the United States. The sociological framework that gives the most meaningful insights into the societal situation of the African American sole-parent female and her family is one that allows for that factor. Therefore, it is only by looking at her relative status and the societal forces, as implemented significantly by a legal system that keeps her societally encased vis-à-vis other classes of persons, that predictions of her family's surviv-ability can be made.

The discriminations embedded in the social structure and enforced and reenforced by the legal system work to keep the African American woman and her family in a secondary social status. This is not to say that providing adequate legal and economic remedies to African American women would in any way diminish those available to European American males. It is becoming clearer and clearer that, even in times when resources are reportedly scarce, those in the highest ranges of power and privilege get more while those, Black or White, in the lower ranges receive less. This trend, with the assistance as this examination contends of the legal system, is accentuated for the Black woman (see again the above statistics regard-ing income and poverty levels). So, it might be that the average working-class European American male is "innocent." But the essence of the problem is that of lack of relative access to power and opportunity and the perpetuation of that situation through societally institutionalized use of the law.

The true power elite has put the working classes in the position of fighting over bread crumbs while those at the highest echelons continue to eat cake. As long as this situation exists, antipathy toward affirmative action will be exacerbated and the ability of Black women to raise their children will be correspondingly undermined. As long as the African American woman does not have equal access and opportunity for getting hired and protection from being arbitrarily fired because of her race and gender, being alone with children will mean, for her, an impaired eco-nomic and political status. She will not have the resources to expose her children to the basic requirements of a decent living. Her family will constantly be in a hand-to-mouth situation while living actually and figuratively "on the edge."

The reenforcement of racial disparities in the workforce also means that the probability of her being and remaining single is increased. This is because, contrary to popular fiction, a major reason why Black men are characterized as being irresponsible is that the system, through the same legal machinations as pertain to Black women, denies them, too (Mad-hubuti, 1990). In other words, through its entrenched, institutionalized denial of economic opportunity by virtue of reactionary legal pronounce-ments, Black women and men are denied the opportunity to be with each other in a legitimate context. Unemployment of either makes them both secondary and marginal to society. This is because the basic societal unit of this society is still the family, defined ideally by the power brokers as consisting of a mother *and* a father. Thus if discrimination in the workplace keeps both Black men and women superfluous in a societal context, then both are delegitimized in a societal context. Any other format is deemed by the Eurocentric establishment as being an aberration (Hill Collins, 1991, p. 233). This situation is exacerbated when, because of this discrimination, either is led to make a living through delegitimized means (Quinney, 1977). This keeps the African American single-parent family disabled, distorted, and disenfranchised from the societal perspective (Glasgow, 1981).

The only way to counter such attitudes is to develop in some way a truly educated, enlightened populace that can make sophisticated observations, assessments, conclusions, *and* changes. The only problem with this solution is that, like the legal institution, the education institution is in the hands of the power elite, who, due to these legally sanctioned circumstances affecting the African American mother, remain the same from one generation to the next. This situation will remain unless and until, through *socialization, politicalization,* and *mobilization,* the African American woman becomes effectively empowered. Empowerment of the single Black female parent would mean the end of an isolated, alienated existence as far as the greater society is concerned. It would enable her to have meaningful access to and input in the educational, employment, and economic systems that work in a mutual and reciprocal manner from the context of the legal system to keep her and her family "down." Therefore, empowerment of Black women is a necessary condition precedent to changes in the legal system. Networking, interaction, and continual communication provide the foundations for such a requirement. Each one must teach one. Right now, many Black women are in the church. They are also in the prisons. Some are in 2-year and 4-year institutions of higher learning. Wherever Black women are to be found they must be reached and addressed. Ignorance for the Black woman is not bliss. For her and her family it means ultimate annihilation.

REFERENCES

Angelou, M. (1986). *Poems.* New York: Bantam.
Asante, M. K. (1987). *The afrocentric idea.* Philadelphia: Temple University Press.
Dred Scott v. Sandforth. 60 U.S. 383 (1957).
Billingsley, A. (1968). *Black families in White America.* Englewood Cliffs, NJ: Prentice Hall.

Fanon, F. (1965). *The wretched of the earth.* New York: Grove.

Glasgow, D. G. (1981). *The Black underclass.* New York: Vintage.

Goffman, E. (1963). *Stigma.* Englewood Cliffs, NJ: Prentice Hall.

Hill, R. B. (1972). *The strengths of Black families.* New York: Emerson Hall.

Hill Collins, P. (1991). *Black feminist thought: Knowledge, consciousness, and the politics of empowerment.* New York: Routledge, Chapman & Hall.

Hutchinson, E. (1990). *The mugging of Black America.* Chicago: African-American Images.

Kaiser Aluminum & Chemical Corp. v. Weber, 476 W. 3401 (1979).

Madhubuti, H. R. (1990). *The Black male, obsolete, single, or endangered?* Chicago: Third World Press.

Marbury v. Madison, 1 Cr. 137 (1803).

Martin v. Wilks, 109 S. Ct. 2180 (1989).

Merton, R. K. (1954). *Social theory and social structure.* Glencoe, IL: Free Press.

Moynihan, P. (1965). *The Negro family: The case for national action.* Washington, DC: U.S. Government Printing Office.

Parsons, T. (1951). *The social system.* New York: Free Press.

Plessy v. Ferguson, 163 U.S. 537 (1896).

Quinney, R. (1977). *Class, state and crime: On the theory and function of criminal justice.* New York: David McKay.

Regents of University of California v. Bakke, 438 U.S. 265 (1978).

R. A. V. v. St. Paul, 1125 S. Ct. 2538 (1992).

Ryan, W. (1972). *Blaming the victim.* New York: Vintage.

St. Mary's Honor Center et al. v. Melvin Hicks, 113 S.Ct. 2741 (1993).

Spencer, H. (1904). *The principles of ethics: Vol. 1.* New York: D. Appleton.

U.S. Bureau of the Census. (1990). *Current population survey.* Washington, DC: U.S. Government Printing Office.

U.S. Bureau of the Census. (1991). *Money income of households, families, and persons in the United States: 1990.* Washington, DC: U.S. Government Printing Office.

U.S. Bureau of Labor Statistics. (1991). *Employment and earnings, January 1991.* Washington, DC: U.S. Government Printing Office.

Wards Cove Packing Company v. Antonio, 490 U.S. 642 (1989).

West, C. (1993). The pitfalls of racial reasoning. In C. West, *Race matters* (pp. 23-30). New York: Beacon.

X, M., & Haley, A. (1965). *The autobiography of Malcolm X.* New York: Grove.

SUGGESTED READINGS

Bazelon, D. L. (1978). The hidden politics of American criminology. *The evolution of criminal justice: A guide for practical criminologists.* Beverly Hills, CA: Sage.

Beale, F. (1970). Double jeopardy: To be Black and female. In T. Cade Bambara (Ed.), *The Black woman: An anthology* (pp. 90-100). New York: Signet.

Bynum, V. (1991). *Unruly women: The politics of social and sexual control in the old South.* Chapel Hill: University of North Carolina Press.

Etzioni, A. (1968). *The active society: A theory of societal and political processes.* New York: Free Press.

Gary, L. E., & Brown, L. P. (1975). *Crime and its impact upon the Black community.* Washington, DC: Howard University Press.

Glona v. American Guarantee & Liability Insurance Co., 391 U.S. 73 (1968).

Harrington, M. (1984). *The new American poverty.* New York: Penguin.

Hornsby, A., Jr. (1991). *Chronology of African American history.* Detroit: Gale Research, Inc.

Kunjufu, J. (1984). *Developing positive self images and discipline.* Chicago: African-American Images.

Lawyers Committee for Civil Rights Under Law. (1990). *Annual report: Civil rights in 1989-1990.* Washington, DC: Author.

Levy v. Louisiana, 391 U.S. 68 (1968).

Manegold, C. S. (1991, February 7). After two failed nominations, many women are seething. *The New York Times,* p. A1.

Matthews v. Lucas, 427 U.S. 495 (1976).

Prestage, J. L. (1980). Political behavior of American Black women: An overview. In L. Rose (Ed.), *The Black woman* (pp. 233-245). Beverly Hills, CA: Sage

Rose, L. (Ed.). (1980). *The Black woman.* Beverly Hills, CA: Sage.

Quinney, R. (1975). *Criminology: Analysis and critique of crime in America.* Boston: Little, Brown.

Sennett, R., & Cobb, J. (1973). *The hidden injuries of class.* New York: Vintage.

Silberman, C. E. (1976). *Criminal violence, criminal justice.* New York: Vintage.

Steffensmeir, D., & Kramer, J. H. (1982). Sex-based differences in the sentencing of adult criminal defendants: An empirical test and theoretical overview. *Sociology and Social Research, 66,* 289-304.

Weber v. Aetna Casualty & Surety Co., 406 U.S. 164 (1972).

7

African American Children in Single-Mother Families

Suzanne M. Randolph

It takes a whole village to raise a child.

—African proverb

As of 1990, more than half of all African American children under 18 years of age lived with one parent, usually their mother. This is the first time since these data have been maintained that the single-parent family form is the most prevalent among African Americans. Thus cries of alarm have been sounded over this and similar statistics for other racial/ethnic groups (see Table 7.1). Increasing social problems in the African American community as well as greater acceptance (or tolerance) of a wide range of lifestyles have contributed to the increased percentage of African American children in households headed by a single woman. In most instances, the head of these households is the child's mother (biological or adoptive); in other instances, either a female relative or nonrelative may have responsibility for the care of the child. This range of household and family types results in an intriguing cultural matrix that supports and facilitates children's development. However, the picture that is often painted by research and the media suggests that children in these families are at great risk for detrimental outcomes; although some are, many do well.

Table 7.1   Percentage of Children Under Age 18 Living With One Parent, by
Race/Ethnicity for 1960, 1970, 1980, and 1990

| | Year of Census Data | | | |
Race/Ethnicity	1960	1970	1980	1990
Black	21.9	31.8	45.8	54.8
White	7.1	8.7	15.1	19.2
Latino	N/A	N/A	21.1	30.0

SOURCE: U.S. Bureau of the Census (1991, p. 5).

The problems and strengths of children and their families are discussed
in this chapter. An overview of the problems facing children in single-
mother families is presented along with race-specific findings. An attempt
is made to untangle the cultural matrix that cloaks these children and
protects them from poor developmental outcomes. Adaptive strengths that
have sustained African American families and communities are presented
and discussed as strategies for ensuring optimal development of children
in single-mother families. Specifically, dimensions of the African worldview (Nobles, 1974), such as spirituality, communalism, positivity and
role flexibility, are used to highlight adaptive strengths of African American single-mother families in fostering development in young children.

EFFECTS OF SINGLE-PARENT
STATUS ON CHILDREN:
GENERAL FINDINGS

Research has shown that many children in single mother families are
as successful as children in two-parent families on emotional adjustment
and school achievement (Cashion, 1982). However, in their recent review
of mother-only families, McLanahan and Booth (1991) present a summary of literature that suggests several deleterious effects of single-
mother status on children. According to their review, these children have
poorer academic achievement (boys more so than girls), higher absentee-
ism from school, higher dropout rates at school, lower earnings in young
adulthood, higher rates of poverty, earlier ages at first marriage, children
at younger ages in and out of marriage, higher divorce rates, higher rates
of committing delinquent acts, and higher rates of drug and alcohol use.

A common theory used to explain these deleterious effects has been that these problems are due to the absence of a male in the household (Davidson, 1990). However, other scholars point to alternative factors. For example, some children from single-mother families have lower self-esteem than children in two-parent families, but this has been found to be due to the negative stigma and expectations associated with their status rather than to family structure. There is also within-group variation among children in single-mother families based on the reason for the mother's single status, family income level, age of mother, or the family's life cycle (e.g., presence or absence of preschool children or adolescents). These points are discussed further in the following sections.

Most notable among the explanatory factors is the family income level in single-mother families. Cherlin (1981) has argued for some time that "it seems likely that the most detrimental aspect of the absence of the fathers from one-parent families headed by women is not the lack of a male presence but the lack of a male income" (p. 81). As others have explained in this volume, one third of all single-parent families live in poverty and the figure worsens for families of color, who have the added burden of racism that keeps mothers from gainful employment or decent housing. Over half of single-parent African American families live in poverty. It is less likely that African American single mothers will be awarded child support or receive child support and alimony in cases of divorce or paternal support decrees or will live in a household with a second wage earner (Grossman & Hayghe, 1982; Johnson & Waldman, 1983). These descriptive accounts of the disproportionate representation of African Americans among single-mother families are only suggestive of the impact of poverty on children's outcomes. Another line of inquiry examining economic hardship and the relationship of maternal behavior on adolescents' socioemotional functioning provides a more complex view of developmental implications of mother-only family structures (McLoyd, Jayaratne, Ceballo, & Borquez, 1994).

McLoyd et al. (1994) examined the relationship of economic hardship on adolescent socioemotional functioning in African American single-mother families. Two economic stressors, work interruption and unemployment, were found to affect adolescents' socioemotional functioning indirectly through their impact on mothers' psychological functioning and, in turn, parenting behavior and mother-child relations. Unemployment predicted depressive symptomatology, which predicted more frequent maternal punishment and was mediated by mothers' negative perception of the maternal role. More frequent maternal punishment was associated with the adolescents' cognitive distress and depressive symptoms, and these relations were mediated by the adolescents' perception of the quality of the parent-child relationship. Moreover, both stressors were associated with maternal perceptions of financial strain, which predicted adolescents' perceptions of the family economic hardship. Adolescents who perceived their families as experiencing more severe economic hardship reported higher anxiety, more cognitive distress, and lower self-esteem (McLoyd et al., 1994). Thus there appear to be complex interrelationships among family structure, maternal functioning, family economic experience, and adolescent functioning in African American single-mother families. Also, as in earlier studies of families with infants and young children, McLoyd et al. found that one form of social support (perceived availability of instrumental support) was associated with reduced maternal reports of symptoms of depression, less maternal punishment of adolescents, and more positivity about the maternal role.

Another explanation related to the economic status of the single-mother family centers on the involvement of children in household management and decision making. This relationship is best understood in terms of its implications for the psychological functioning of single mothers and their children. That is, children in single-parent households, as compared with children in two-parent households, generally do more household tasks and are more involved in household management and decision making (Weiss, 1979). Because the children are seen by the mother as having a major responsibility in the household functioning, they also serve as friends and confidants with whom the mother shares her worries and problems, including economic hardships. This may undermine her children's psychological well-being (McLoyd & Wilson, 1990). For example, McLoyd and Wilson (1990) found that economic hardship per se was unrelated to a child's psychological functioning but was positively related to a mother's psychological distress, which in turn was positively related to a child's psychological problems. It should be noted that in this study social networks, which included satisfying contact with family members, were associated with lower psychological distress in the child. Others have also found that, in general, the kin network provides help to buffer poor outcomes in African American single-mother families (Taylor, Chatters, Tucker, & Lewis, 1990). However, it should be noted that because of poverty or near poverty status, some of these families move more and thus may lose friends and social support networks that could help protect children from detrimental outcomes.

ARE BOYS AT GREATER
RISK THAN GIRLS?

The increasing problems of African American boys and men have been presumed to be due to family structures such as those we have been discussing. A major presumption is that the absence of fathers (and thus, presumably, male role models) has led to a lack of parental control that results in aggressive and even self-destructive behavior among African American males. However, a recent study examining mother-only versus father-only family effects on their same-sex children found that among 35 outcome variables same-sex effects were found for only 2: computers in the home and saving for a child's college education. Outcomes such as self-concept, locus of control, achievement, popularity, school behavior, tobacco use, and parental involvement showed no effects. These findings are based on a predominantly White middle-class sample, with mothers' single status due to divorce. In general, there is a paucity of research examining gender-related differences in parent-child relationships and outcomes in African American single-mother families. Thus there is no empirical evidence to date to suggest that the pattern of same-sex findings would differ for African American families. However, factors other than father absence can be examined to explain differential outcomes for African American male children.

The gender role socialization of African American male children is closely tied to the difficult and complex problem of masculine development in the United States generally. Gender-related role expectations intensify around the time of puberty and require accomplishment of specific developmental tasks (Hill & Lynch, 1983). That is, if males are to function successfully in designated adult roles, they are expected to achieve a sense of identity, function independent of their families of origin, and choose an occupation or career (Lloyd, 1985). However, the gendered racism against African American men in the United States makes this an exceptionally challenging task for African American families. That is, post-industrial displacement of unskilled jobs and gender-specific academic problems in public schools have placed African American men (particularly fathers) at alarming risk for chronic joblessness, provider role failure, and familial estrangement (Bowman, 1988).

One well-known gender-based adage about the child-rearing practices of African American mothers is that they "raise their daughters and love their sons." This refers to circumstances in which girls are socialized to take on adult responsibilities at earlier ages than boys and are expected to assist with household maintenance and child rearing, study harder, and be socially responsible, while boys are allowed to "have their way." For example, as early as infancy, gender differences have been shown in the expectations that African American mothers of daughters as compared to mothers of sons have for the age at which they should develop self-help skills; mothers of daughters expect them to develop these skills at earlier ages than do mothers of sons (Rosser & Randolph, 1991).

During the postslavery period, mothers' overprotection of their sons may have been aimed at making them less aggressive and thus less prone to racist attacks. Also, traditionally, even in two-parent, dual-earner families, this may have been so in the industrial era because male children could be expected to get jobs based on their physical strength, whereas the "way out" (of domestic employment in White households) for girls was thought to be through education. During the industrial era this child-rearing strategy may have been viewed as adaptive for African American families, but in the current high-technology and information society, the jobless rate for African American men has been increasing while that for African American women has stabilized or expanded.

Also, the rates of African American women who are never married and divorced with children have been increasing, leaving increasing numbers with primary responsibility for raising both male and female children without regular involvement of their fathers. Thus, although the socialization strategy of the old adage ("loving" sons) may have been adaptive during the industrial era, it may now be less adaptive for African American male children. A growing gender gap in educational preparation has resulted in poorer educational performance and attainment among African American boys as compared to girls at all educational levels, the displacement of unskilled jobs has had more adverse effects on African American boys than girls, and despite increasing acceptance of gender role flexibility, the "provider" and "caretaker" roles still carry differential weights among men and women (Bowman, 1988; Bowman & Saunders, 1988).

Bowman and his colleagues found, for example, that the emotional consequences of failure and success as a provider appear to be especially intense among African American men and that, despite similar experiences in chronic joblessness among African American male and female youths, the developmental implications of such difficulties are quite different for African American males (Bowman, 1984, 1990; Bowman & Saunders, 1988; Harrison, Bowman, & Beale, 1985). Thus, in the face of harsher economic and social realities, African American families now have the added challenge of socializing boys in ways that may protect them from situations that render them vulnerable to drugs, alcohol, gangs, and other aggressive or self-destructive behavior. Bowman and his colleagues found that access to cultural resources, such as those discussed later in this chapter, facilitates adaptive models of coping with such chronic role strain (Bowman & Howard, 1985; Bowman & Saunders, 1990).

Another contemporary explanation for the acting-out behavior of boys is that the absence of African American adult males places the younger African American male, particularly the adolescent, in the position of being a parental child (Boyd-Franklin, 1989; Minuchin, 1974). That is, mothers view their sons as fulfilling the adult roles of the absent fathers or surrogates; yet sons are not socialized into these roles. Moreover, sons who may become overwhelmed by the role may reverse generational boundaries and assume spousal or parental responsibilities for the mother (Boyd-Franklin, 1989). Also, the demands of being a single mother, and in many instances a single working mother, may place task and emotional overloads on women that then transfer to the parental child (McLoyd & Wilson, 1990). It may be easier for girls and their mothers to address the situation (violently or nonviolently) than it is for boys and their mothers. Therefore, boys seek relationships outside the home, usually with peers with whom to express their emotions or have age-appropriate interactions. Acting out, other aggressive behavior, and self-destructive behavior may be manifestations of pent-up hostility or the overwhelming feelings about being unable to adequately fulfill the parental child role (Boyd-Franklin, 1989) or normative adolescent roles (Bowman & Saunders, 1988).

Relatedly, McLoyd and Wilson (1990) empirically tested the association between a mother's communication of problems to her children and the children's sex as predictors of psychological distress in African American mother-only families experiencing economic hardship. Although they found that the frequency with which mothers talked to their children about personal problems and financial matters predicted higher levels of psychological distress in children, there were no differences related to the sex of the children. Thus, while the parental child notion may have important clinical implications for working with male youths in single-mother families, more research is needed to fully understand the intervening processes linking maternal behavior to child outcomes or gender-based differences in parent-child interaction in African American single-mother families.

Moreover, recent research reveals mixed findings on the protective influence of family support for children in single-mother families. As noted above, McLoyd and Wilson found that satisfying contact with family members was associated with lower psychological distress in children; sex-of-child effects were not found. A study by Pearson, Ialongo, Hunter, and Kellam (1994) found, however, that for low-income fourth-grade boys, mother-grandmother extended families are not protective (i.e., boys in these families were not reported as less aggressive as compared with boys in mother-alone families). Pearson et al. speculated that for these older elementary-aged children peers have a greater influence than grandmothers, and therefore the protective effects found for grandmothers with young elementary-aged male children (Kellam, Ensminger, & Turner, 1977) were not found in their sample. It should be noted that study methodologies may have influenced findings: The McLoyd and Wilson (1990) sample was composed solely of African American adolescents, and the Pearson et al. (1994) study sample was fourth graders, 70% of whom were African American (however, race effects were not examined).

Jackson's (1993) study of African American single working mothers in poverty found that parenting (preschool) boys may be especially stressful for mothers balancing work and family roles in poverty, particularly when low education is also a factor. Having no education beyond high school and a male child predicted significantly higher role strain, greater depressive symptomatology, lower ratings of overall life satisfaction, and the least favorable maternal perceptions of children. A mediating factor was willingness/preference for employment; higher levels of strain were associated with reluctant employment. Jackson postulated that higher educational attainment may better prepare mothers with coping abilities to meet the special demands of raising young boys, including knowledge about how to access support networks that moderate their role strain. Also, mothers who preferred to be employed were more energetic in their response to the demanding role of raising sons. However, regardless of the reason for working, mothers with education beyond high school perceived their children (boys and girls) significantly more positively than did mothers with no education beyond high school. Another finding was inconsistent with previous research based on samples of middle-class White wives. That is, regardless of the amount of time mothers spent in paid employment, descriptions of boys were significantly more negative than those of girls. Jackson contends that this supports the notion that the effects of maternal employment may be different for diverse populations.

In general, existing literature paints a mixed picture of children in single-mother families. On one hand, the picture is less than optimistic for children's outcomes and, on the other, many African American children survive and even thrive in these family situations. A number of factors need to be considered as we further examine these families or attempt to intervene to strengthen them, particularly because for African American children this is now the predominant family type, with 51.2% of African American children under 18 years of age living in mother-only families (U.S. Bureau of the Census, 1991). Many of the factors commonly pointed to in the literature are "mother blaming" (Kissman & Allen, 1991) or attribute children's problems to "mother failings" (for a review, see Caplan & Hall-McCorquodale, 1985). These perspectives are akin to the victim-blaming perspectives that view single-mother families and children in them as pathological, deviant, devalued, and disadvantaged.

What has been neglected is the wide range of other factors that contribute to family and child outcomes—family processes, environmental stress, and the cultural and ecological contexts in which these families raise their children. Other systems (political, economic, educational, etc.) are failing single-mother families due largely to sexism and elitism (i.e., the relatively low status of women in society and negative expectations about mothers' abilities to parent alone) (Kissman & Allen, 1991). The situation is amplified for single-mother African American families due to the confounding effects of racism. When viewed within this larger environmental context, the strengths of single-mother families and the positive effects on children can be more fully illuminated. The strategies that African American single mothers use to function effectively within this "double whammy" context (racism and sexism) are discussed after exploring what it means to be raised in a single-mother family and what factors make parenting and growing up easier or more difficult.

Many authors would agree that the type of single-parent family may directly or indirectly affect parent-child interactions or child outcomes. The notion of type encompasses a range of factors: family structure, household composition, family member relationships, and the life events that resulted in the single parenting status. The following discussion examines ways in which these factors may contribute to a better understanding of the realities (strengths and problems) of children in families headed by African American single "mothers."[1]

FAMILY STRUCTURE, HOUSEHOLD COMPOSITION, AND FAMILY RELATIONSHIPS

Family structure and household composition combine to refer to the organization of the family as typically discussed in traditional sociological terms—that is, nuclear, extended, or augmented. Family relationships include the biological, adoptive, or kin and non-kin relationships among members in the family or household. For the purposes of this chapter, the nuclear family is composed primarily of the mother and her children (biological or adopted). In some situations, the mother's partner may reside with the family. An extended family situation comprises the nuclear family and at least one other adult relative who resides with the family. An augmented family is referred to as one in which the nuclear family and one adult nonrelative reside together. The relationships among family members in these types of single-mother families are discussed as they relate to their impact on children's developmental outcomes.

Nuclear Families

In nuclear families, the mothers may lack support from extended networks or fictive kin, may have fewer personal and social resources to offset detrimental outcomes, and are extremely burdened by the same tasks of two-parent families (balancing work and family, finding child care, transportation, health care, parenting, and household maintenance). However, it has also been shown that when mothers in these family types have more income, higher educational levels, are widowed, or have a regular male partner, their children's outcomes are more positive.

Extended Families

In extended family situations, the other adult is likely to be a grandmother. Related to life events, a large proportion of single-mother families results from teenaged pregnancy. Adolescent mothers are more likely to remain in the same household as their mother (children's grandmother). This creates a situation that is more properly referred to as binuclear in that two sets of parents (usually both are single parents) are raising children. Another increasing configuration evident in recent years' national statistics (e.g., in the National Longitudinal Survey of Youth) is the two-single-sisters-with-children household. The potential for children's developmental outcomes in binuclear and extended families is both positive and negative.

On the positive side, an older, usually more experienced mother is available to assist with parenting tasks. An extended family situation may make the parenting role less stressful for the younger mother and thus more facilitative of good parent-child interaction than if she were left alone to raise her child (Furstenberg, Brooks-Gunn, & Morgan, 1987;

Stevens, 1988). By sharing a household the generations also share resources, advice and guidance, and emotional support, in a more direct and focused way than if they were in different households (Pearson, Hunter, Ensminger, & Kellam, 1990). This reciprocal exchange of resources may be a key protective factor in offsetting the impact of poverty on children. Also, the presence of older children from the other family may serve a protective function for the younger child(ren) in terms of socialization as well as cognitive and motor development.

On the negative side, conflicts may arise in parenting when the older generation provides guidance contrary to the younger mother's beliefs and practices. This effect may be related to the age of the mother at first birth (Chase-Lansdale, Brooks-Gunn, & Zamsky, 1994). For example, a recent study found that multigenerational families most likely to provide positive parenting were those where older mothers did not reside with the grandmother, whereas in families with very young mothers, co-residing with grandmothers showed higher quality of parenting than did non-co-residing ones. (Chase-Lansdale et al., 1994). Also, children may be confused as to the roles that their mothers and the other "mothers" (grandmothers or aunts) perform. Distribution or sharing of household resources may also limit the parent's ability to effectively raise her children. For example, mothers with infants and toddlers may qualify for programs like the Women, Infants, and Children (WIC) program that provides vouchers for food. These commodities may have to be shared with the other nuclear family that is not eligible for such assistance; when distribution or sharing is not perceived as equitable by one or the other "mothers," conflicts can result. Because of the potential for such conflicts around child rearing and resource sharing, the most effective extended families are likely to be those in which grandmothers provide support and substitute child care but do not have families of their own to raise.

Among adolescent families, a more prevalent extended family type includes three generations of single parents (mother, grandmother and great-grandmother). Burton (1991) found that in these families the great-grandmother assumes the parenting role for the adolescent mother while the grandmother becomes the chief caregiver for the adolescent's child. This skip in generational parenting may serve a protective function for children in that an older, more experienced caregiver assumes the parenting role and there is less opportunity for conflict between the two closer generations (i.e., mothers and grandmothers or grandmothers and great-grandmothers). This reduction in adult-adult conflict has the potential for lessening stress that could result in difficult parent-child interactions.

Relatedly, in recent attachment research, retrospective accounts of mothers' attachment to their mother have been predictive of mother-infant quality of attachment. Those adults who report difficult attachment relationships with their own mothers have infants who are classified at one year as insecurely attached to their mothers. Secure attachment has been shown to be predictive of more optimal developmental outcomes for preschool- and school-aged children. Insecure attachment has been shown to relate to difficult peer interactions, lower school achievement, and poor relationships in adolescence. The limitation of current attachment research is, however, that it focuses largely on children's attachments to their biological mothers.

In African American single-mother families, an examination of multiple attachments may be necessary to fully explicate how children form socioemotional relationships predictive of optimal performance at later ages. For example, children in extended households or nuclear families with a dysfunctional mother may form attachments to their grandmothers as the principal attachment figure, and even though they show insecure attachment to their mother, they may show secure attachment to their grandmother (Randolph, 1989). An emphasis on multiple attachments may be even more important in cases where children are informally adopted by "other mothers." The extent to which the "other mother" serves a protective role in this regard is tantamount to our developing more culturally appropriate intervention strategies to assist single-mother families. More studies that use an intergenerational framework that respects the cultural integrity of the single-mother African American family are needed to address such issues.

Augmented Families

Little contemporary research has been conducted on augmented family types and the parenting roles played by adult nonrelatives who reside in the same households of single-mother families. However, earlier ethnographic research on the roles of kin and fictive kin in poor African American families (Aschenbrenner, 1973; Martin & Martin, 1978; Stack, 1974) shows that these adult nonrelatives assume significant roles, including parenting, that assist the single parent in managing on limited resources. Such caregivers usually contribute to the family income by paying rent, buying food, or helping with utility payments. This additional resource may buttress the impact of poverty for those who are chronically poor or experience involuntary work interruption, unemployment, or other economic hardship that may result for newly single, formerly married women (i.e., those who are divorced, separated, or widowed). This is important because, as mentioned earlier, the poorer outcomes for single-mother families as compared to two-parent families may be due more to the absence of the father's income than to the absence of the father/male per se (Adams, 1991; Cherlin, 1981). Another factor to consider is the mother's adaptation to the economic hardship, perceived financial strain, and perceived availability of instrumental support (McLoyd et al., 1994). As has been shown by McLoyd et al. (1994), these factors can be indirectly related to children's distress. If the additional "family" member is viewed as offsetting the financial strain, this may result in lower levels of perceived financial strain in mothers and children and thus reduce children's levels of cognitive distress, anxiety, and depressive symptomatology. Thus the augmented family type may provide an alternative to the nuclear type when an extended family arrangement is not available, possible, or desirable.

LIFE EVENTS ASSOCIATED WITH SINGLE-PARENT STATUS: CHOICE OR CIRCUMSTANCE?

> Almost every writer on families headed by single mothers points to the relationship with the larger environment as a determining factor in the well being of those families. (Kissman & Allen, 1991, p. 41)

Throughout the 1980s, teenage pregnancy accounted for the largest proportion of single mothers studied in the literature. Much of the research on single parents has been based on research with adolescents and their children, although more recently multigeneration studies have been conducted (Burton, 1990; Chase-Lansdale et al., 1994). It should be noted that the assumption is that fathers are absent or uninvolved in the lives of children born to adolescents. However, although adolescent fathers and older fathers of children born to adolescents may not function in provider roles, they do value the role of companion to their children (Staples & Johnson, 1993). Other protective factors for children of adolescent single mothers are maternal co-residence with the grandmother for very young mothers (Chase-Lansdale et al., 1994), child intelligence, child self-esteem, quality of the home environment, maternal educational attainment, family support for achievement, and support from caring adults in the community (Nettles & Pleck, 1994).

Although a range of life events contribute to single-parent status (some resulting in more negative or positive outcomes than others), what seems to be important is the interpretation of that event as positive or negative by mothers or surrogate mothers and children. Other factors that influence the well-being of the families are the resources available, the extent to which any issues between the father and mother or children were resolved or remain unresolved, and the mothers' and children's self-perceptions and sense of control (Kissman & Allen, 1991).

Another issue that must be factored in is the meaning of the event to the child. Single-parent status, including divorce, is presumed by some scholars to be a "normative" experience in African American children's worlds (i.e., their neighborhood, church, or school). It is argued that the child is more likely to make a successful transition in this case than if single-parent status is viewed with social disapproval in his or her environment. The presumption of normativeness has not been tested among African American children and their communities. Anecdotal evidence suggests that the phenomenon may not be viewed as normative and that many children face peers who stigmatize them because of their family status; many adults also face such stigma or disapproval from family members, policy makers, educators, and other members of the community (Kissman & Allen, 1991). As with the mother, the child's own sense of control and self-perceptions is an important determinant of his or her adjustment to the situation. Developmental research is needed to examine age-related adjustments to single-parent status among children. Life cycle approaches would help to provide information about how the work history of the parent, presence or absence of varying aged children, and family and household structural changes influence children's interpretation of the meaning of their single-mother family.

Another important issue for children is identity formation, especially for adolescents. For example, at or near age 12, children may become preoccupied with the need to know their father. It should be noted that some parent-child difficulties arise over issues related to the mother either withholding or sharing information that will enable the child to locate his or her father. Again, the precipitating event for the single-parent status may be a major factor influencing the mother's cooperation with or response to her child's request.

Finally, the meaning of the event to the African American community and the larger community may also be factors in successful parenting and child developmental outcomes in single-mother families. Again, although it is presumed by some that single-parent family status is a normative (acceptable) experience among African American families (i.e., that single-parent status is not as stigmatizing as in the majority culture), this is an undocumented presumption. Nonetheless, the community oftentimes assumes responsibility for providing support to assist these families. Whether single-mother status is due to circumstance (adolescent parenting, divorce, death of partner, never-married's unplanned pregnancy) or choice (planned pregnancy, mother-initiated divorce or separation), the extended family or community acknowledges the value of the children in this situation and has typically responded by providing for the basic needs of the mother and child and, in some instances, informally adopting the child. Formal institutions and organizations such as churches and mosques provide educational and recreational activities, male role models and mentors, surrogate fathers, parental support, scholarships, job training, and assistance with daily needs for child care, transportation, and health maintenance (Billingsley, 1993). Also, once a father acknowledges his child, his family becomes an important resource for the single-mother family (Boyd-Franklin, 1989). These and other strengths of African American families and communities protect many children from the harsh reality of problematic single-mother family situations. An elucidation of these strengths follows a discussion about some factors that put some single-mother families at greater risk for poorer maternal and child outcomes.

DYSFUNCTIONAL SINGLE-MOTHER FAMILY TYPES AND IMPLICATIONS FOR CHILDREN'S DEVELOPMENT

Although many children in single-mother families are as successful as those in two-parent families, there are special circumstances that put some African American children at particular risk for poor emotional and academic outcomes. That is, there are some family types that may be dysfunctional. Among the factors which may help to explain these children's problematic behavior is the type of dysfunctional family in which children are being raised. This discussion builds on the earlier discussions on family structure, household composition, and family relationships.

Boyd-Franklin (1989) discusses five types of dysfunctional single-mother African American families and the implications for child development and parent-child interactive outcomes; these types are based on clinical samples:

1. *The underorganized family* has boundaries that are vague, and there is no clarity of rules and responsibilities of the family members. These families are cut off from their extended families or have inconsistent involvement with them. These families often present in mental health settings with one or more children in trouble at home, at school, or in the community.

2. *The overcentralized-mother family* has family power overconcentrated in an overwhelmed, overburdened mother. This may be functional when children are very young but dysfunctional for adolescents when the mother's style may be challenged. These families present with adolescents accused of stealing and lying, who have run away, or displayed oppositional behavior at home and in school.

3. *The dysfunctional-mother family* includes a parental child who may run the family because of the mother's illness, low mental or intellectual ability, mental health problem, or substance abuse problem. The parental child's need for nurturance is neglected, and his or her normative development is negatively affected. Younger children in these families will usually display extreme acting out.

4. *The hidden-family-member family* includes reliance on the mother's boyfriend for financial and emotional support that may result in overload and burnout on his part. His role may also not be clear to all family members, especially the children (e.g., when discipline is concerned). In the case of their mother's transient relationships with men, children may become confused about their relationship with their mother. Young children display acting out and lower school performance, and mother-child relationships are difficult, especially for adolescents.

5. *The multigenerational family* includes types where the extended family network may participate in a reciprocity loop (that is, support is given as well as received by the single-mother family), but there is a perceived imbalance in the reciprocity loop (Boyd-Franklin, 1989) or "kin insurance" (McAdoo, 1981). That is, the single-mother family is providing more support than it is receiving. There may also be confusion about the roles and boundaries of family members. Another critical factor associated with dysfunctional mothers in extended families is loss of an older-generation family member and the unresolved mourning associated with that loss (Lindblad-Goldberg & Dukes, 1985). That is, the single mother is unable to cope with the death of her mother or another adult from an older generation, and this may in turn affect parent-child relations.

McLoyd et al. (1994) also suggest that some families may be dysfunctional when the mother has higher levels of perceived financial strain, which predicts adolescents' perceptions of their family's economic hardship, which in turn is associated with higher anxiety, more cognitive distress, and lower self-esteem in adolescents. Thus in both clinical and empirical samples there is evidence that a complex of variables need to be considered in examining the impact of single-mother family structure on children's developmental outcomes.

STRENGTHS OF AFRICAN AMERICAN SINGLE-MOTHER FAMILIES

Despite the long list of adversities confronting mothers and children in single-mother families, a number of strengths in African American families and communities help to offset detrimental outcomes for many children. These are role flexibility, spirituality, sense of community, and positivity in viewing the situation. These strengths are consistent with an Afrocentric worldview that emphasizes these and other values (Nobles, 1974).

Role Flexibility

African American families have a long history of women working and rearing children. Therefore, there is a long tradition in families of role models for household, family, and resource management. Single mothers faced with emotional and financial overload can consult these role models or rely on their experiences with them to organize and manage their own limited resources in such a way as to be beneficial to family members.

Also, because of this long tradition of working mothers in African American families, expectations for parenting and child rearing have not been as gender based as in White families in the United States. Responsibilities for child care and household maintenance have been shared by men and women, although research suggests that mothers still carry the brunt of the child rearing and housework. In single-mother families where there is a hidden family member, the surrogate father may even function as a househusband and substitute caregiver.

The protective benefits of multigenerational households have been discussed throughout this chapter; the most significant benefit may be role flexibility. In brief, additional role models and substitute caregivers are provided for children, particularly boys when a father surrogate is present; adolescent mothers who have difficult relationships with their own mothers can benefit from having their grandmother as a key attachment figure; respite care provided by older generations is available to mothers who are overloaded; and it has been found that perceived availability of instrumental support, availability of extended families, or satisfying contact with family members may be protective for some children (McLoyd et al., 1994; McLoyd & Wilson, 1990; Taylor et al., 1993). However, it should be noted that under some conditions such familial support may interfere with or impede optimal family functioning, maternal well-being (Frazier, 1989), and child development (Stevens, 1988). For instance, additional adults may model less than optimal child-rearing practices or offer support that is intrusive.

Thus a key ingredient in building on role flexibility as a family strength is clarity in roles and consistency. Without these the potential is high for adult-adult conflict and child-adult interactive difficulty. In the case of families with a parental child, it is important that roles be managed so that the child assumes the adultlike roles while maintaining developmentally appropriate roles and accomplishing normative developmental expectations.

Spirituality

The belief that the nature of all things is spirit is an Africentric principle underlying the development of African and African American religious and social practices (Nobles, Goddard, Cavil, & George, 1987). Thus spirituality refers to a wide range of rituals, rites, and ways of interacting that encompasses more than religiosity. It also assumes that the range of practices is not limited to the Christian experience or only to people affiliated with a religious denomination. Spirituality refers to the reliance on inner strength for self-definition and worth as contrasted with a preoccupation with a material existence.

A mother's sense of spirituality or inner strength enables her to find ways to give positive meaning to potentially stressful life events. This inner strength also communicates to her children the mother's love for them when she cannot directly express it. Social outings and rituals are used as a way to maintain family unity and instill pride and tradition. These outings and rituals may be visits to relatives or fictive kin, family reunions, birthday parties, christenings and baptisms, graduation celebrations, funerals, church picnics and field trips, and other family-focused activities. In these settings, children learn about their connectedness to other family members, both male and female (i.e., their namesakes), become informally adopted by an aunt, uncle, or cousin, and have the opportunity to pursue developmentally appropriate activities with same-age peers even if their mothers have restricted their activity within the neighborhood. Rituals may also include family routines such as eating meals together, saying bedtime prayers, going to worship services together, and having planned outings at regular times.

Although spirituality extends beyond the religious domain, places of worship serve a major role as socializing agents. The educational role is fulfilled through Saturday or Sunday schools, schools run by churches or mosques, and vacation Bible school. Opportunities are provided for mothers and children to engage in diversified roles. For example, mothers serve in leadership roles in auxiliaries, on committees, and on boards of the congregation. This may be the only opportunity that children have to observe her in that leadership capacity. An important socializing function for the mother is that this may be her only time to separate from the children (Boyd-Franklin, 1989). Children have the opportunity to perform as servers and choir members and to participate in plays, speaking events, and other special events that give them a sense of accomplishment and provide for peer interaction in developmentally appropriate activities. Also, role models missing in the family situation may be present in the worship setting. Finally, as has already been mentioned, religious institutions provide family support programs, such as child care, recreation, and nonreligious activities (scouts, girls' clubs, etc.), and may be the only family ritual (Billingsley, 1993).

Sense of Community

The African proverb "It takes a whole village to raise a child" that opened this chapter connotes the sense of community among African Americans. It is best illustrated by the involvement of blood kin as well as fictive kin who rally to support families in times of need as well as prosperity. In single-mother families, the more well known facts about sense of community relate to ways in which the maternal extended family (kin or fictive kin) contributes or in which other women provide support to single-mother families. Discussion rarely focuses on the contribution of the father's family or other men's support. However, there is both anecdotal and empirical evidence to suggest that the roles of the father's family and surrogate fathers are as important and valued.

If a man has acknowledged a child, even if he is physically absent from the home "the community expects the father's kin to help out. . . . By validating his claim as a parent, the father offers the child his blood relatives and their husbands and wives as the child's kin—an inheritance so to speak" (Stack, 1974, pp. 51-52). In the past two decades, however, the sense of community may be changing as African Americans have expanded the range and composition of the neighborhoods in which they reside. Also, as suggested earlier, the extent to which in-law families assist and the types of assistance rendered depends to a large extent on the nature of the relationship between the father and mother. In never-married mother families, assistance may be more likely to be forthcoming than in divorced or separated families, for example.

"Play daddies" for children in single-mother families are often uncles, older brothers of their mother or father, grandfathers, godfathers, and the partners of their mothers (Boyd-Franklin, 1989). Indeed, as Boyd-Franklin and others have noted, often the men who are involved with single mothers as boyfriends are involved with their children as well. A passage from Stack (1974) illustrates that these "play daddies" include those from the father's family: "My kid's daddy's people really take to them—they always doing things and making a fuss about them. We help each other out and that's what kinfolks are all about" (p. 45).

Another source of support for single mothers that is often overlooked in the literature is that of other parents in the neighborhood. A tradition in African American communities that is eroding somewhat due to changing social conditions is that of a neighbor parenting a child in a mother's absence. That is, while a mother is at work or away from home any other parent in the neighborhood would "keep an eye" on her children. There was also implied permission for the neighbor parent to discipline children in the mother's absence. Also, what a mother did or did not do was under the watchful eye of these surrogate mothers. A positive aspect to this sort of public parenting was that mothers shared in child care and child rearing.

An important element in effectively using kin and fictive kin networks, play daddies, and neighbor parents is consistency. If available, maternal and paternal extended families can be used unless such use would be dysfunctional for the target family. However, as with role flexibility, the nature of their involvement should be made clear. Mothers should not abdicate their parenting roles, nor should the role of the mother be undermined or compromised, even if she is overburdened and overwhelmed. A more effective way to build on this strength of African American families is to ensure that decision making for the family resides with the mother but is supported by these significant others and this sense of community.

Positivity: "Making a Way Out of No Way"

African American families have a legacy of making the best out of a bad situation or being able to see the good in what to others might appear to be an adverse situation. Even though they may be in the dire straits of poverty, African American mothers make sacrifices to provide for their children because they want them to have a better life than they did. Therefore, many will purchase expensive or fad clothing for infants and toddlers, enroll their children in parochial or private schools, or go to great expense to present a middle-class image. To service providers, educators, and agency officials this may seem frivolous given the family's economic status, but it is mothers' attempts to provide wider opportunities for their children, instill pride in their children, and enhance their own self-worth. It is also reflective of the peer group pressure that influences many mothers.

Many of the child-rearing practices of African American single mothers have been viewed as less than optimal, particularly those in the area of discipline. However, several authors note that these are adaptive strengths. Looney and Lewis (1983) point out that when a mother is strict in her punishment, adolescents see this as a source of family strength and regard their mother as the center of the family. Strictness is seen by African American mothers as protection from the streets (Boyd-Franklin, 1989; McGoldrick, 1982). Parents emphasize obedience, but this is not seen by them as negative; instead, it is viewed as necessary because it "would make life easier for my child," "means respect," "is equated with my love," or "is necessary if my child is to achieve in school" (Peters, 1981, pp. 216-217).

These ways of "making a way out of no way" may be the key element to ensure that children in single-mother families thrive, particularly those living at or below the poverty level. Further examination of the strategies these mothers pursue to protect their children from the risks so often identified in the literature would greatly enhance the quality of life for all children in single-mother families.

CONCLUSION

The existing literature on African American children in single-mother families presents a varied picture with respect to their outcomes. The effects of father absence per se has received less attention recently than the mother-child relations and the impact of economic hardship on child outcomes. As a consequence of the absence of a male income and the "double whammy" of racism and sexism for African American women, many children live in families at or below the poverty level. The economic, social, and political realities for African Americans make it doubtful that these children and their families will see relief from poverty in the near future. Mounting social problems are likely to increase the numbers of children in single-mother families as well as put the children in these families at even greater risk for poor developmental outcomes. Moreover, the limited opportunity structure for African American adolescents and adults, particularly males, suggests that there are substantial societal barriers to an improved quality of life, even if one has superb individual and familial resources. Even so, some single mothers show amazing resilience that translates into resilience for their children (Nettles & Pleck, 1994).

Scholars need a better understanding of the factors that put some families and not others at risk, or how in the face of adversity some families survive better than others. Qualitative research examining families' daily living and adjustments to the single-mother family structure is needed. Using the data from such research, the adaptive strengths of individuals, families, and communities need to be articulated in such a way that program planners, service providers, and policy makers can develop strategies that respect the cultural integrity of the African American single-mother family.

The presumptions about the lack of male presence or father involvement in African American children's lives have been overstated and thus perpetuate the Moynihan-like, mother-blaming answers to why children in these families fare less well when the evidence points that way. Thus mothers in these families are devalued by society and a self-fulfilling prophecy is created—mothers blame themselves also and give up on self-help, and this translates into poor outcomes for children.

More responsive approaches should be sought in understanding the realities of motherhood and singlehood for African American women, the ways they respond to the stress associated with racism and sexism, how they buffer these stressors, and the impact of their individual development on the development of their children. This will require no less than going straight to the source—single mothers who are single for varied reasons noted in this chapter and others in this volume. These mothers have children of different ages (infancy, preschool, adolescence, adults); come from varied geographic locations and types of communities (urban, rural, suburban); and have varied other demographic factors (age, age at first child's birth, family history, etc.). The immediate purposes of this research strategy would be to (a) dispel the myths about single-mother families that currently limit our ability to respond to their needs and (b) provide needed data for a more responsive approach to meet their needs and the developmental needs of their children.

A transactional approach to the study of child outcomes in single-mother families is needed. That is, if we are to fully understand the risk and protective factors associated with being a child in a single-mother family, we must examine individual characteristics of the child (e.g., age, health status, perception of family status, cognitive processes, socioemotional status, and perception of parent-child relationship); personal characteristics of the mother (perceived life strain, perceptions of maternal role, perceptions of parent-child relationship, reason for singlehood, age at first child's birth, cognitive status, and socioemotional functioning); characteristics of the caregiving environment (availability of instrumental and emotional support, support network characteristics, household composition, and opportunity structure); and the interrelationships among these variables. Models are needed that predict whether the single-mother family structure has a direct or indirect effect on children's developmental outcomes and which family processes, caregiving environment characteristics, and child-rearing practices function as mediating variables.

Inherent in this transactional approach is an individual difference approach that uses a risk and resilience model to examine the family processes and socialization practices underlying the diversity in single-mother African American families. Previous work in this area provides theoretical and empirical arguments for viewing the varied adjustments of family members, especially children, in African American single-mother families (Chase-Lansdale et al., 1994; McLoyd & Wilson, 1990; Nettles & Pleck, 1994; Slaughter, 1988; Spencer, Brookins, & Allen, 1985). Sorely needed are studies that include an expanded range of child outcome variables (e.g., physical and mental health) that are investigated in developmentally appropriate ways.

Finally, grounded theory, ethnography, and other qualitative approaches are needed to fully explicate factors that may provide better insight into the intervening processes linked to developmental outcomes for children in these families. This is especially crucial if we are to intervene on behalf of African American male youths. As suggested by Myers (1989),

> Since theoretical or empirical literature in the past has failed to provide an account of how early gender role socialization may or may not affect role performance among Black women or Blacks in general, there is a need for Black social and behavioral scientists to pursue this kind of research in an attempt to develop as complete a descriptive account of this process as possible. (p. 177)

Regarding practical implications, support groups or community-level supports are needed for mothers and children cut off from family or friendship networks. Support groups can assist mothers in reframing their parenting situation and identifying family strengths (Richards & Schmiege, 1994). To assist mothers in successfully performing their varied roles without taxing their children to assume adultlike roles, these support networks could also include respite care to provide child care for mothers with very young children, trade services for household management, and assistance for mothers and their adolescent children in job search. These groups could also assist mothers with parent-child communication and alert them to the possible deleterious effect of sharing worries and problems with younger children, as noted by McLoyd and Wilson (1990) in their sample of African Americans. That is, the support group could provide an outlet for mothers to discuss their problems and worries and to generate solutions or strategies for coping.

In developing this support network, it is critical to understand that the role of the mother should not be undermined or supplanted by the help network; mothers should be involved in all decisions related to their families. When mothers have naturally occurring networks, support programs should be family focused to ensure that kin networks do not interfere with the possible enhancements of the support group. Frazier (1989) found, for example, that the receipt of kin child care support and African American mothers' life satisfaction scores suggested a detriment to their well-being and that mothers' receipt of financial/material support was related to lower levels of self-esteem and mastery.

Single mothers need assistance to negotiate the complexities of role flexibility, capitalize on spirituality and inner strengths, take advantage of community supports, and continue to see a way out when the walls appear to be closing in. Single mothers are our best resource to ensure that children have the best chance. Foster care and other out-of-home placements should not be presumed to be more viable alternatives for children in dysfunctional single-mother families; these problems are increasing and the system is already overloaded. Therefore, support will also be needed for the nonbiological mothers of these children. Moreover, for some African American women (e.g., divorced women) the single-mother status may result in coping with increased or newly experienced economic hardship. As a result, they may not have a long history of adjustment to the single mother role, managing role flexibility in a binuclear household, or use of extended family supports for assistance. Governmental policies and programs must be reformulated to accommodate the varied needs of children in African American single-mother families. Relief of maternal financial strain and access to instrumental support will require widening the opportunity structure for mothers, including education beyond high school, job search assistance, job placement, child care assistance, financial subsidies or noncash provisions, housing, and family-centered programs for treatment of mental health problems. That education beyond high school has a favorable consequence for maternal perceptions of children, especially preschool boys, provides support for developing intervention programs that go beyond GED (general equivalency diploma) training. Financial support for college education would be a start. Single mothers could mentor each other, with those with experience of college education providing support for those just beginning. Such a program could also be viewed as a preventive approach to the problems experienced by children at later ages, particularly boys (Jackson, 1993).

Thus the larger cultural context in which single-mother families are existing has to be considered as we move toward a better understanding of the outcomes for African American children in these families and as we mobilize resources to ensure these children's optimal development. Undoubtedly, as the numbers of African American children in single-mother families increase, we will find "It *still* takes a whole village to raise a child."

NOTE

1. "Mothers" in this context refers to biological and formal or informal adoptive mothers who serve as head of households or live in family situations where they have major responsibility for parenting an African American child.

REFERENCES

Adams, P. L. (1991). Effects of poverty and affluence. In W. R. Hendee (Ed.), *The health of adolescents: Understanding and facilitating biological, behavioral, and social development* (pp. 118-138). San Francisco: Jossey-Bass.

Aschenbrenner, J. (1973). *Lifelines: Black families in Chicago.* New York: Holt, Rinehart & Winston.

Billingsley, A. (1993). *Climbing Jacob's ladder: The enduring legacy of African American families.* New York: Simon & Schuster.

Bowman, P. J. (1984). A discouragement-centered approach to studying unemployment among Black youth: Hopelessness, attributions, and psychological distress. *International Journal of Mental Health, 13,* 68-91.

Bowman, P. J. (1988). Post-industrial displacement and family roles strains: Challenges to the Black family. In P. Voydanoff & L. C. Majka (Eds.), *Families and economic distress* (pp. 75-96). Newbury Park, CA: Sage.

Bowman, P. J. (1990). The adolescent-to-adult transition: Discouragement among jobless Black youth. *New Directions for Child Development, 46,* 49-69.

Bowman, P. J., & Howard, D. S. (1985). Race-related socialization, motivation, and academic achievement: A study of Black youth in three-generation families. *Journal of the Academy of Child Psychiatry, 24,* 134-141.

Bowman, P. J., & Saunders, R. (1988). Black unmarried fathers across the life cycle: Provider role strain and psychological well-being. In J. L. McAdoo (Ed.), *The twelfth conference on empirical research in Black psychology* (pp. 9-15). Washington, DC: National Institutes of Mental Health.

Boyd-Franklin, N. (1989). *Black families in therapy: A multisystems approach.* New York: Guilford.

Burton, L. (1990). Teenage childbearing as an alternative life-course strategy in multigeneration Black families. *Human Nature, 12,* 123-143.

Burton, L. (1991, April). *When parents can't: The cost of rearing grandchildren to Black grandparents and great-grandparents.* Paper presented at the biennial meeting of the Society for Research in Child Development, Seattle.

Caplan, J. J., & Hall-McCorquodale, I. (1985). Mother-blaming in major clinical journals. *American Journal of Orthopsychiatry, 55,* 345-353.

Cashion, B. G. (1982). Female-headed families: Effects on children and clinical implications. *Journal of Marital and Family Therapy, 8*(2), 77-86.

Chase-Lansdale, P. L., Brooks-Gunn, J., & Zamsky, E. S. (1994). Young African-American multigenerational families in poverty: Quality of mothering and grandmothering. *Child Development, 65,* 373-393.

Cherlin, A. (1981). *Marriage, divorce, remarriage: Changing patterns in the postwar United States.* Cambridge, MA: Harvard University Press.

Davidson, N. (1990). Life without father: America's greatest social catastrophe. *Policy Review,* No. 5, 40-44.

Frazier, S. C. (1989). Psychological well-being of Black single-parent women: Child care, social support, and sex-role attitudes. *Dissertation Abstracts International, 50,* 1153B.

Furstenberg, F. F., Jr., Brooks-Gunn, J., & Morgan, S. P. (1987). *Adolescent mothers in later life.* Cambridge, UK: Cambridge University Press.

Grossman, A. S., & Hayghe, H. (1982). Labor force activity of women receiving child support or alimony. *Monthly Labor Review, 105,* 39-41.

Harrison, A. O., Bowman, P. J., & Beale, R. L. (1985). Role strain, coping resources, and psychological well-being among Black working mothers. In A. W. Boykin (Ed.), *Empirical research in Black psychology* (pp. 21-28). Washington, DC: National Institutes of Mental Health.

Hill, J. P., & Lynch, M. E. (1983). The intensification of gender-related role expectations during early adolescence. In J. Brooks-Gunn & A. C. Petersen (Eds.), *Girls at puberty: Biological and psychological perspectives* (pp. 201-228). New York: Plenum.

Jackson, A. (1993). Black, single, working mothers in poverty: Preferences for employment, well-being, and perceptions of preschool-age children. *Social Work, 38,* 26-34.

Johnson, B. L., & Waldman, E. (1983). Most women who maintain families receive poor labor market returns. *Monthly Labor Review, 106,* 30-34.

Kellam, S. G., Ensminger, M. E., & Turner, R. J. (1977). Family structure and the mental health of children. *Archives of General Psychiatry, 34,* 1012-1022.

Kissman, K., & Allen, J. A. (1993). *Single-parent families.* Newbury Park, CA: Sage.

Lindblad-Goldberg, M., & Dukes, J. (1985). Social support in Black, low-income, single-parent families: Normative and dysfunctional patterns. *American Journal of Orthopsychiatry, 55,* 42-58.

Lloyd, M. A. (1985). *Adolescence.* New York: HarperCollins.

Looney, J. G., & Lewis, J. M. (1983). Competent adolescents from different socioeconomic and ethnic contexts. *Adolescent psychology, 11,* 64-74.

Martin, E., & Martin, J. M. (1978). *The African American extended family.* Chicago: University of Chicago Press.

McAdoo, H. (Ed.). (1981). *Black families.* Beverly Hills, CA: Sage.

McGoldrick, M. (1982). Normal families: An ethnic perspective. In F. Walsh (Ed.), *Normal family processes* (pp. 379-424). New York: Guilford.

McLanahan, S, & Booth, K. (1991). Mother-only families. In A. Booth (Ed.), *Contemporary families: Looking forward, looking back.* Minneapolis: National Council on Family Relations.

McLoyd, V. C., Jayaratne, T. E., Ceballo, R., & Borquez, J. (1994). Unemployment and work interruption among African American single mothers: Effects on parenting and adolescent socioemotional functioning. *Child Development, 65,* 562-589.

McLoyd, V. C., & Wilson, L. (1990). Maternal behavior, social support, and economic conditions as predictors of distress in children. *New Directions for Child Development, 46,* 49-69.

Minuchin, S. (1974). *Families and family therapy.* Cambridge, MA: Harvard University Press.

Myers, L. W. (1989). Early gender role socialization among Black women: Affective or consequential? *Western Journal of Black Studies, 13,* 173-178.

Nettles, S., & Pleck, J. H. (1994). Risk, resilience, and development: The multiple ecologies of Black adolescents in the United States. In R. J. Haggerty, N. Garmezy, M. Rutter, & L. Sherrod (Eds.), *Stress, risk, and resilience in children and adolescents: Processes, mechanisms and intervention* (pp. 147-181). New York: Cambridge University Press.

Nobles, W. W. (1974). Africanity: Its role in Black families. *The Black Scholar, 5,* 10-17.

Nobles, W. W., Goddard, L. L., Cavil, W. E., & George, P. Y. (1987). *African-American families: Issues, insights, and directions.* Oakland, CA: Black Family Institute.

Pearson, J. L., Hunter, A. G., Ensminger, M. E., & Kellam, S. G. (1990). Black grandmothers in multigenerational households: Diversity in family structure and parenting involvement in the Woodlawn Community. *Child Development, 61,* 434-442.

Pearson, J. L., Ialongo, N. S., Hunter, A. G., & Kellam, S. G. (1994). *Family structure and aggressive behavior in a population of urban elementary school children.* Unpublished manuscript via personal correspondence.

Peters, M. F. (1981). Parenting in Black families with young children: A historical perspective. In H. McAdoo (Ed.), *Black families* (pp. 211-224). Beverly Hills, CA: Sage.

Randolph, S. M. (1989). Infant attachment in Black American families: An interim report. In A. G. Harrison (Ed.), *Proceedings of Conference XII, Empirical Research on Black Psychology* (pp. 133-165). Washington, DC: National Institutes of Mental Health.

Richards, L. N., & Schmiege, C. J. (1994). Problems and strengths of single-parent families: Implications for practice and policy. *Family Relations, 42,* 277-285.

Rosser, P. L., & Randolph, S. M. (1991). Black American infants: The Howard University Normative Study. In K. Nugent, B. Lester, & T. B. Brazelton (Eds.), *The cultural context of infancy* (pp. 133-165). Norwood, NJ: Ablex.

Slaughter, D. T. (Ed.). (1988). *Black children and poverty: A developmental perspective* (New Directions in Child Development, No. 42). San Francisco: Jossey-Bass.

Spencer, M. B., Brookins, G. K., & Allen, W. R. (Eds.). (1985). *Beginnings: The social and affective development of Black children.* Hillsdale, NJ: Lawrence Erlbaum.

Stack, C. (1974). *All our kin: Strategies for survival in a Black community.* New York: Harper & Row.

Staples, R., & Boulin Johnson, L. (1993). *Black families at the crossroads: Challenges and prospects.* San Francisco: Jossey-Bass.

Stevens, J. H., Jr. (1988). Social support, locus of control, and parenting in three low-income groups of mothers: Black teenagers, Black adults, and White adults. *Child Development, 59,* 635-642.

Taylor, R. J., Chatters, L. M., Tucker, M. B., & Lewis, E. (1990). Developments in research on Black families: A decade review. *Journal of Marriage and the Family, 52,* 993-1014.

U.S. Bureau of the Census. (1991). *Marital status and living arrangements: March 1990* (Current Population Reports, Series P-20, No. 450). Washington, DC: U.S. Government Printing Office.

Weiss, R. S. (1979). Growing up a little faster: The experience of growing up in a single-parent household. *Journal of Social Issues, 4,* 97-111.

SUGGESTED READINGS

Adams, P. L., Milner, J. R., & Schrepf, N. (1984). *Fatherless children.* New York: Wiley Interscience.

Billingsley, A. (1968). *Black families in White America.* Englewood Cliffs, NJ: Prentice Hall.

Brisbane, F. L., & Womble, M. (1985-1986). Treatment of Black alcoholics. *Alcoholism Treatment Quarterly, 2*(3-4), 1-16.

Demo, D. H., & Acock, A. C. (1991). The impact of divorce on children. In A. Booth (Ed.), *Contemporary families: Looking forward, looking back* (pp. 162-191). Minneapolis: National Council on Family Relations.

Downey, D. B., & Powell, B. (1993). Do children in single-parent households fare better living with same-sex parents? *Journal of Marriage and the Family, 55*, 55-71.

Hunt, J. G., & Hunt, L. L. (1975). Race and father-son connection: The conditional relevance of father absence in the orientation and identities of adolescent boys. *Social Problems, 23*, 35-52.

Hunt, J. G., & Hunt, L. L. (1977). Race, daughters, and father loss: Does absence make the girl grow stronger? *Social Problems, 25*, 90-102.

Jayakody, R., Chatters, L. M., & Taylor, R. J. (1993). Family support to single and married African American mothers: The provision of financial, emotional and child care assistance. *Journal of Marriage and the Family, 55*, 261-276.

Kinard, E. M., & Reinherz, H. (1984). Marital disruption: Effects on behavioral and emotional functioning in children. *Journal of Family Issues, 5*, 90-115.

Slaughter, D. T. (Ed.). (1988). Black children and poverty: A developmental perspective. *New Directions in Child Development*. Special Issue No. 42. San Fransisco: Jossey-Bass.

8

The Role of the Grandmother in Poor Single-Mother Families and Households

Susan M. George
Bette J. Dickerson

There is an assumption in America about African American grandmothers. According to that assumption, they are the indomitable sources of material and spiritual strength. African American grandmothers are perceived as the central figures in large interconnected extended families, watching over their children and grandchildren as they face a world of prejudice and adversity. It is taken for granted that no matter what circumstances they face African American grandmothers can take care of their families. Juxtaposed with this assumption is the reality that their grandchildren have a 50% chance of having single mothers, nearly half of whom live below the poverty line, and that more than one in five of their grandchildren have single mothers under the age of 20, 77% of whom live below the poverty line (Garwood, 1992; Jacob, 1992; National Urban League Research Staff, 1992; U.S. Bureau of the Census, 1991).

When the assumption about African American grandmothers is contrasted with the reality of continuing deprivation and poverty for many African

AUTHORS' NOTE: Susan M. George developed the first draft of this chapter, which consisted of the initial literature review and preliminary data analysis. Bette J. Dickerson made all the revisions necessary for the final draft.

American single mothers and their children, a fundamental question arises: Can African American grandmothers continue to perform their traditional roles in the face of these conditions, and if not, what does this mean for the quality of life for African American single mothers and their families?

Three topics are addressed in this chapter:

- The roles that have been traditionally assumed by African American grandmothers
- The challenges that grandmothers today are facing in trying to fulfill their traditional roles
- The social policy implications with respect to supporting the role of grandmothers in poor and single parent families

These topics are addressed largely through the examination of findings from select small-sample studies. Large-sample quantitative data, such as that collected by the U.S. Bureau of the Census, provide information about the changes in household composition but do not, however, provide reasons for the changes. By interviewing participants in small-sample studies, insights are provided into the reasons why changes have taken place. The research reviewed in this section discusses small-sample studies of African American grandmothers and mothers with respect to their day-to-day "ordinary" lives. The data come primarily from firsthand accounts collected through interviews and questionnaires. The strength of such "firsthand account" research is its ability to provide a frame of reference and a rationale for the findings from census and other large-sample studies. In this type of research, participants examine their own realities and share in identifying the underlying reasons for the findings. This results in information shared in the participants' own voices that is situated in their standpoint (Dickerson, 1994).

THE RISING NUMBER OF POOR, FEMALE-HEADED, EXTENDED AFRICAN AMERICAN HOUSEHOLDS

Between 1960 to 1985 there was a dramatic increase in the number of families headed by single African American females. The proportion of families with children under 18 years of age headed by married couples fell from 78% to 40% while the proportion of those headed by single women rose from 22% to 57%. In 1980, the proportion of African

American families headed by single females (49%) exceeded the proportion headed by married couples (48%) for the first time. The percentage of families headed by single females has continued to rise ever since (Billingsley, 1990).

The relationship between family, household composition, and socioeconomic status is profound. In 1986, in the African American community, married couples made up the majority of the nonpoor working, middle, and upper classes while single parents constituted the majority among the working poor and the underclass (Billingsley, 1990). Not only are single-parent-headed households the fastest growing type of household among African Americans, they are some of the poorest households in America (Jones, 1983).

Many poor African American single mothers rely on the support and assistance provided by extended families and many reside in extended households. In fact, the most common type of extended household consists of three generations: a single mother and her child(ren) living in the home of the maternal grandmother. Grandparents play a central role in extended families, as demonstrated by the 1.2 million children who were living with their grandparents in 1989. Of these children, 38% were being reared by the grandparents alone, with neither parent present. In instances where the grandparents were the household heads but the parents were present, both parents were present for 4%, only the father was present for 2%, and for over half (56%) only the mother was present (Billingsley, 1992).

In summary, single female heads of households are the fastest growing segment of the African American population. Three of every four African American children living in a female-headed household are poor. Along with the increase in the number of female-headed families has come an increase in three-generation households, the majority of which are composed of a single female head of household, her daughter, and her daughter's children. These trends suggest that an increasing number of grandmothers are involved in the day-to-day caregiving of their grandchildren.

THE ROLE OF GRANDMOTHERS
IN AFRICAN AMERICAN FAMILIES:
AN OVERVIEW

In a recent study by the American Association of Retired Persons (1993), the issue of "grandparents raising their grandchildren" was found to be "a concern for you or people you know in your age group" for 61% of the Black respondents compared to only 29% of the White respondents. The issue was also found to be of greater concern for older women, many of whom were probably grandmothers, than for older men. Findings such as these are related to the fact that African American grandparents in general, and maternal grandmothers in particular, have traditionally served as a significant resource for African American families (Gutman, 1976; Hill, 1980). Grandmothers are actively involved with their grandchildren, and child care is the form of family assistance they most frequently provide (Billingsley, 1992; Jackson, 1970, 1971; Minkler & Roe, 1993). Grandmothers who live with their grandchildren or in a household where the parent is a single parent are more actively involved with their grandchildren than are grandmothers who live in a two-parent household or do not live with their grandchildren (Wilson, 1982, 1984, 1986a, 1986b).

More recently, grandmothers have been increasingly recognized as an important source of support for adolescent mothers (Apfel & Seitz, 1991; Smith, 1975). However, at the same time, research is beginning to suggest that multiple generations of adolescent and single mothers as well as high rates of poverty among single mothers may be depleting the resources that grandmothers have traditionally provided to their extended families (Burton, 1987; Burton & Bengston, 1987). This is leading to a weakening of the extended family and a breakdown of intergenerational supports in some contemporary African American extended families (Burton, 1987; Burton & Bengston, 1987; Furstenburg, 1976; Ladner & Gourdine, 1984).

THE ORIGINS OF THE CENTRALITY
OF EXTENDED KIN IN
AFRICAN AMERICAN FAMILIES

The participation of African Americans in extended family networks, and particularly the sharing of child care responsibilities by adult kin other than the biological parents, has its origins in the values and practices of traditional African communities (Abu, 1983; Kayongo-Male & Onyango, 1984; Wei, 1982). Chief among the qualities that characterize traditional African family life is the central importance of the extended family (Billingsley, 1968). Kayongo-Male and Onyango (1984) state, "The most significant feature of African family life is probably the *importance of the larger kin group* beyond the nuclear family" (p. 6, emphasis added). The conjugal nuclear family is often weaker than the larger kin group in residential, economic, and emotional support. In the Ashanti extended family system, for example, spouses frequently do not live together, particularly if the husbands are not able to provide the accommodations necessary for a shared residence (Abu, 1983).

The extended family often has a great deal of influence with regard to marital issues and family members are linked in a complex network of mutual exchanges, obligations, affection, and economic/material and religious/spiritual support (Billingsley, 1968). Among the Avatime of the Volta region of Ghana, a residential group headed by a woman usually contains her children and/or grandchildren and is considered a practical solution to the child-care problems faced by women who work outside the home (Brydon, 1983). Young Ashanti mothers are considered not yet competent enough to manage alone and are often found residing in their matrilineal compound where they receive assistance from older women and other young mothers in looking after their babies (Abu, 1983).

Children belong not just to their respective father and mother but also to the wider kinship network. Within this extended network of family life, therefore, the importance of children extends well beyond their value to their biological parents. Children are considered a symbol of God's blessings, a vital link between the living and the dead, the eventual keepers of family shrines, and representations of kinship solidarity as well as viable contributors to the family economy (Kayongo-Male & Onyango, 1984). Unlike children raised in nuclear families in Western societies, African children are not considered the sole possessions of their biological parents but, rather, belong to and are the responsibility of both the parents and the larger kin group. For the matrilineal Ashanti, children may be found living with either or neither parent or with the maternal grandmother or aunt. As a result, they receive a high quality of care and protection (Abu, 1983; Billingsley, 1968).

In West African societies, the elders, including grandparents, are honored and command immense respect (Etienne, 1983). The elders' highly respected status is derived partly from the community's view that they hold a mediating position between living people and the deceased ancestors (Bascom & Herskovits, 1959; Billingsley, 1968). On the individual level, the relationship between mother and child is the closest but that between the child and the grandparents is the most revered. Among the Ashanti, for example, "The grandparents are felt to be the living links with the past" (Fortes, cited in Billingsley, 1968, p. 47).

African grandmothers—both maternal and paternal—exercise great influence and responsibility in the care and protection of children (Billingsley,

1968). Older women are socialized to the roles of caregiving grandmother and maternal aunt. In fact, the Baule women of Ivory Coast actually increase in status as they progress from "sister" to "mother" to "grandmother" (Etienne, 1983).

THE EXTENDED FAMILY AS ECONOMIC UNIT

Multigenerational households and extended family structure among African American families have traditionally served as a safety net for poor families. Living in extended families allows the family members to pool resources and share family obligations and responsibilities. African Americans, especially those who are poor, are more likely to live in three-generation-households and to participate in a mutual exchange of goods and services with members of their extended family than are their White counterparts (Allen, 1979; Mitchell & Register, 1984).

Studies that have looked closely at the factors influencing the quality of life among poor African American families indicate that participation in extended family networks serves to increase the economic viability of poor families. Stack (1974) drew the following conclusions about the high level of participation in extended family structures among poor African American families:

> Those living in poverty have little or no chance to escape from the economic situation into which they were born. Nor do they have the power to control the expansion or contraction of welfare benefits or of employment opportunities, both of which have momentous effects on their daily lives. In times of need, the only predictable resources that can be drawn upon are their own children and parents, the fund of kin and friends obligated to them. (p. 107)

THE ROLE OF GRANDMOTHERS IN EXTENDED FAMILIES AND HOUSEHOLDS

Although the research literature about the functioning of grandmothers in multigenerational African American families is relatively small, several trends seem clear. Research findings support the assumption that many African American grandmothers do play an important role in the day-to-day lives of their children and grandchildren. The aid of the grandmother is more significant and more likely to be used when families are poor, female headed, and the grandmother resides with her children and grandchildren.

Grandmothers have been found to assume a variety of roles, ranging from becoming the primary parent to their grandchildren to sharing the burden of childcare so that a young mother can finish her education to becoming the household "manager," overseeing and directing the activities of their daughters and grandchildren.

Jackson (1970, 1971) looked at the relationship between role interactions and subjective characteristics of the relationship between Black grandparents and grandchildren living in a southern, urban, low-income area. The majority of the subjects verbalized strong affectional closeness between themselves and their grandchildren. The most common form of grandparent-grandchild assistance was found to be child care, and the grandmothers carry out important tasks in the rearing of grandchildren. Almost 44% of the grandmothers actually had grandchildren residing with them. A smaller proportion of the subjects "baby-sat" with school-aged children. Jackson (1971) concluded that "many Black grandparents serve a point of anchorage for grandchildren and provide kinds of support for them unavailable from their own parents" (p. 271).

Wilson (1982, 1984, 1986b) studied the effect of family structure (single-headed or dual-headed nuclear families) and the grandmaternal domicile (grandmother living with the nuclear family or in the local community) on the perception of grandmother-grandchild and parent-child interactions. The primary purpose was to delineate the perceived role of the grandmother within the Black family with regard to child rearing and to analyze the perceived involvement of the grandmother as a possible surrogate parent in single-headed families. His sample consisted of 60 families made up of grandmothers, parents, and children. Results indicated that grandmothers perceived (and were perceived as) having greater numbers of interactions with their grandchildren when they lived in the home and when it was a single-parent family structure. Wilson's findings support the proposition that grandmothers tend to serve as surrogate parents in single-parent households and are more actively involved with their grandchildren than are grandmothers who live in dual-parent households. His findings suggest that the increased involvement of grandmothers in single-parent households is an adaptive support mechanism for single parenthood.

THE BREAKDOWN OF
INTERGENERATIONAL SUPPORT

Among the Western industrialized nations, the United States has the highest rate of adolescent pregnancy and childbirth, with one in five female adolescents bearing children. More than one in four African American women have had at least one child by the age of 18, and the rate of African American adolescent childbirths is more than 2½ times greater than that of European Americans ("Hell in a Handbasket," 1994).

Most African American adolescent mothers bring their babies home and the maternal grandmother plays a critical role in the rearing of these babies (Flaherty, Facteau, & Garver, 1987). Research indicates that extended kin, especially grandparents, offer close physical and psychological connections of instrumental and psychological value (Jackson, 1970, 1971; Wilson, 1982, 1984, 1986b). The involvement of grandmothers in adolescent mothering is particularly significant because the family of the adolescent mother is usually the most consistent source of emotional and economic support (Furstenburg, 1976). Smith (1975) explains that a teenager who plans to keep her child often stays at home during her pregnancy and her mother provides some degree of care for the newborn. As such, he advised health care professionals who work with adolescent mothers to consider the centrality of the adolescents' mothers and families in providing the essential supports the adolescent mothers need to sufficiently parent their children.

In the case of adolescent mothers, the availability of an alternative caregiver is often critical to the adolescent's achievement of her dual roles as teenager and mother (Flaherty et al., 1987). Smith (1975) emphasizes the importance of the adolescent mother's family, particularly her mother, in determining the quality of life for the mother (e.g., her ability to finish her education) and the quality of life of the child (e.g., as additional caregiving resources for the child). Coletta and Lee (1983) examined the relationship between social support and adolescents' responses to early motherhood. The sample was composed of 64 African American adolescent mothers who averaged 16.3 years of age when their children were born. Structured interviews were used to assess the young mothers' emotional stress as well as the amounts, sources, and kinds of support available. Self-esteem and sense of control were assessed via standardized instruments. A major finding was that support from individuals is related to a decrease in stress and an increase in self-esteem. For 66% of the sample the main source of assistance from individuals was the adolescent's own mother who was also found to be the most effective source of support. Assistance also came from other relatives, typically the adolescent's grandmother, older sister, or aunt.

There is growing concern that the support structure provided by grandmothers in past generations is beginning to weaken. The increase in the proportion of single female heads of household over the past 30 years, the high rate of poverty among these households, and the likelihood that a majority of young and adolescent mothers bring their babies home to their mother's home means that more and more women are becoming the head of poor three-generation households (Billingsley, 1990; Flaherty et al., 1987). Multiple generations of poor single female heads of households leave the extended family depleted and no longer able to serve the traditional role of "safety net." This seems to be particularly true of young grandmothers (35 years of age and younger), many of whom were adolescent mothers themselves. Most single mothers and grandmothers have fewer economic resources than their married counterparts and therefore have less to pass down to succeeding generations. Increasingly, there is a concern that multiple generations of poor single mothers who never married are depleting the resources that the extended family has traditionally provided (Billingsley, 1990; Burton & Bengston,1987; Ladner & Gourdine, 1984).

Multiple generations of adolescent mothers also mean that women are becoming grandmothers in their late 20s and early 30s. Those who feel they are too young to be grandmothers are often less ready for and less accepting of that status. These young grandmothers are generally less willing and able to provide the same supports as their older counterparts. Many of these young grandmothers moved themselves toward adulthood with limited resources, simultaneously raising their own children in an atmosphere of economic scarcity. Their daughters are at greater risk of duplicating the familial patterns of their mothers' adolescence, resulting in a rise in the incidence of poverty for both generations of women (Ladner, 1986).

African American families do not always unqualifiedly accept the pregnancy of an unmarried adolescent girl. The family of a pregnant unmarried adolescent may be angry and unaccepting initially and concerned with the added financial burden and all the responsibilities an additional child will bring. Concern may also be expressed for the adolescent's chances of finishing her education. The mother of the pregnant adolescent may also express concern for herself. She may be a working mother without the time to give to quality child caring characteristic of the traditional grandmother role. If she is still relatively young, she may be just beginning to see some freedom from responsibilities toward her own children. Becoming a grandmother—especially when this may mean having to assume at least part of the responsibility for a daughter and her child—may be an initially unwelcome life event (Burton, 1987; Burton & Bengston, 1987; Furstenburg, 1976; Ladner, 1986; Ladner & Gourdine, 1984; Smith, 1975).

Burton and Bengston (1987) studied the effect of age on role satisfaction among 41 African American grandmothers. The grandmothers were divided in two categories: early grandmothers between the ages of 25 and 38 and on-time grandmothers between the ages of 42 and 57. They found that the timing of entry into the grandmother role affects role behavior and satisfaction. The young grandmothers often experienced "crisis accumulation" when their own adolescent daughters brought infants into a household where the grandmothers were still raising young children of their own. Young grandmothers often expressed resentment of being put in the role of an "elder" while they still perceived themselves as young. On-time grandmothers were more likely to express satisfaction in their role and more likely to perceive themselves as "ready" to assume the job of helping their daughters raise their own children.

Ladner and Gourdine (1984) interviewed 30 adolescent mothers, all of whom had been born to poor adolescent mothers. The grandmothers were also interviewed and it was found that they, as a group, did not unqualifiedly welcome their daughters' pregnancies. They were opposed to their daughters repeating their own "mistakes" and viewed having another child to take care of as an additional burden. Among the young grandmothers,

> the perception of roles seems to be a departure from traditional low income, African American families in which grandparents assumed a far greater responsibility. What appears to be the case now is that due to the younger ages of these grandparents, they are no longer taking on the traditional roles of grandmothers. Often they are still in their childbearing years and devote their primary time to their own children. (p. 24)

In a study of the functions of 19 African American grandmothers, aged 29-59, who were engaged in the care of their adolescent daughters' infants, adolescent mothers were found to be the primary caretakers. In these three-generation households, the grandmothers, acting in the role of advisor, were outspoken in their approaches to their daughters and grandchildren. They expected their daughters to care for their infants. The grandmothers provided child care but did not assume primary responsibilities. Instead, they saw themselves as "back up" persons (Flaherty et al., 1987). They often assumed an instrumental role, that of managers of family life and resources. Managing activities included controlling family members' behavior, overseeing the recovery of new mothers, fitting work, school, and infant care needs into schedules, and providing safety for "their grandbabies." Although most grandmothers were involved in direct caretaking of infants, the significance of this function was mediated by the constraints that grandmothers placed on these child-care activities. For example, the study subjects said, "I'll help her for now" and "until she gets back on her feet." The grandmothers saw their responsibilities as temporary and hoped this would be the case.

In a study of the role of grandmothers and other family members in the continuing development of adolescent mothers, Apfel and Seitz (1991) conducted interviews at 18 months postpartum with 119 African American inner-city adolescents who were less than 19 years old when they gave birth to their first child. During the same time period, interviews were also conducted with the adolescent's mother or mother surrogate (103 of the available 113 grandmothers agreed to be interviewed). The interviews covered a broad range of issues related to the family's adjustment to the birth of a new grandchild, and four models of familial adaptation emerged: Parental Replacement, Parental Supplement, Supported Primary Parent, and Parental Apprentice.

In the *Parental Replacement Model* (adopted by approximately 10% of the sample), the mother of the adolescent mother assumes total responsibility for rearing the baby. Child-care responsibilities are not generally shared with the biological mother, and the grandmother becomes, in effect, the functional and psychological parent to the child.

The potential benefits of this model are the following:

1. It allows the daughter to continue her education and development without the burdens of early parenthood.
2. The child is able to more clearly identify the maternal figure in his/her life than are children in a home where responsibility for child care shifts back and forth between grandmother and mother.

3. Grandmothers may be better able to be a more skilled parent than their adolescent daughters.

The potential drawbacks to this model of familial adaptation are the tension that may arise when the decision for the grandmother to raise the child did not come from an agreement between the child's mother and grandmother. For example, tension could arise when a mother is forced to give up her child to be raised by the grandmother or when the mother abandons her child, leaving the baby to be raised by a grandmother who does not welcome the responsibility. A variety of psychological and practical problems may arise for the child if the mother attempts to reestablish her role as primary maternal figure. Assuming the burden of child care may have a negative and possibly unwelcome impact on the grandmother's life course, or her age and health may interfere with her ability to parent.

In the *Parental Supplement Model* (adopted by slightly more than 50% of the sample),

> the care of the child is shared between the grandmother and her daughter. Often the teen's siblings or other relatives also help. There may be one steady childcare provider or many providers: In some households childcare depends on who is present, whereas in others it is divided by tasks. . . . The young mother may live with her family or apart—the distinguishing feature of the Parental Supplement Model is the child's care is regularly shared. (Apfel & Seitz, 1991, p. 424)

There are two potential benefits of this model:

1. Sharing the burden of child care with other family members may allow the young mother to finish school and consequently decrease the likelihood that she will become permanently dependent on welfare.
2. The young child will be cared for, at least in part, by older, more experienced, and potentially more capable caregivers than the child's own adolescent mother.

The success of this model of caregiving is highly dependent on the various caregivers' ability to communicate and cooperate with each other as the responsibility for child care shifts from caregiver to caregiver throughout the day, week, or month. Chief among the potential drawbacks of this system are the following:

1. No one person may assume responsibility for overseeing all aspects of the child's care, and inadequate care by some caregivers may be allowed to go on undetected.

2. With so many caregivers the child may not be able to identify and form a secure attachment to a "primary psychological parent."

In the *Supported Primary Parent Model* (adopted by approximately 20% of the sample),

> the young mother is primarily responsible for the full-time care of her child. She may receive family support in the form of regular communication, visiting, financial contributions, occasional baby-sitting and help with household tasks.... The assumption made by families in the Supported Primary Parent model is that the adolescent is able to make a rapid transition to full-time parenthood with minimal guidance and supervision. (Apfel & Seitz, 1991, pp. 424-425)

Among the chief benefits of this system of child care are that the lines of responsibility for childcare are clear, which may facilitate the young mother's ability to identify with the roles and responsibilities of motherhood and also help her child identify a "primary psychological parent." However, assuming the responsibilities of full-time child care may prevent a young mother from completing her education and becoming employed. In addition, the children of young mothers who are unable to successfully assume the role of primary caregiver may be at risk for receiving inadequate care.

The last model identified, the *Parental Apprentice Model* (adopted by approximately 10% of the sample), "could be viewed as a developmentally higher level of adjustment made by grandmothers to their 'premature grandparenthood' " (Apfel & Seitz, 1991, p. 426). The grandmothers tended to assume the role of mentor to their adolescent daughters—providing support and assistance to the young mother while attempting to teach her how to function independently as a competent parent. They acknowledged their daughters' youthful inexperience yet maintained the belief that their daughters would become competent parents.

The primary benefits of this approach are that it does not diminish the role of the young mother as primary caregiver or interfere with the primary attachment between a young mother and her child. At the same time, this approach is less likely to force a young mother prematurely into a role or function she is not able to fulfill, a situation that may result in poor or inadequate child care.

The risks of this approach are that the focus on becoming a capable and responsible caregiver may interfere with a young mother completing her education and that not all young mothers may be able to become capable primary caregivers regardless of the grandmother's efforts to educate her into that role.

Apfel and Seitz (1991) concluded:

> Each of these models, except the Parental Replacement Model, has the potential for a successful transition to parenting for the young mother. The Parental Supplement and the Supported Primary Parent Models seem to have more inherent risks that the transition might go awry. The model with the highest potential for creating a well-functioning mother out of an adolescent would appear to be the Parental Apprentice Model. (p. 428)

They suggest that practitioners involved in the delivery of services to families with adolescent mothers first determine which of the four models (or aspects thereof) a family has adopted as their response to the adolescent becoming a mother. With this information in hand, practitioners can then target their services and interventions to support the well-functioning aspects of a family's response and guard against the potential risks inherent in each model.

CONCLUSION

African American grandparents, particularly in poor families, are more likely to be actively involved in the rearing of their grandchildren than are their European American counterparts. Maternal grandmothers, in particular, frequently share households with their children and grandchildren and provide child care and economic assistance. The grandmothers who live with grandchildren or in a household where the parent is a single parent are more actively involved with parenting activities than are grandmothers who do not live with their grandchildren or live in a dual-parent household. The grandmother role is especially important when the mother is a single adolescent. It is the level of involvement of the grandmother that often determines the mother's chances of finishing her education. Grandmothers may provide, or help to provide, a better home environment than the mother and grandchild may otherwise experience.

The cultural origins of this practice of participation in extended family networks characterized by mutual exchange of services and shared responsibility for child care are in the values and practices of traditional African communities. Within these kinship networks, the caregiving role of grandmothers is not new, but it is little understood and faces new challenges. There is growing concern that the support structure provided by grandmothers in past generations is beginning to weaken (Minkler & Roe, 1993). Multiple generations of adolescent and single mothers, as well as high rates of poverty among single mothers, are depleting the resources of the extended family and creating a breakdown in the intergenerational support that has traditionally existed. Single mothers and single grandmothers tend to have fewer economic resources and less education than their married counterparts; consequently, they often have less to share with succeeding generations. Furthermore, multiple generations of adolescent mothers mean that women are becoming grandmothers at an earlier age, some of whom are less ready for and less accepting of their status as grandmother. Finally, for working mothers, the availability of adult supervision for their children is a major problem resulting in the increasing number of "latchkey" children. Grandmothers once provided much of the support needed, but now many of these grandmothers are themselves working (Billingsley, 1992).

Social programs are usually most effective when they support the traditional support systems already at work in communities. More exploratory "firsthand account" research that gathers data from small samples is needed so that program frameworks can be relocated in the standpoint of African American women who are grandmothers. Centered models could then be developed that would assist social service and health care professionals in more fully understanding how the families of adolescent single mothers adapt and can help shore up those areas where such families are having the greatest difficulties—whether that is teaching a young mother how to recognize and respond to her child's day-to-day needs in a mature and competent manner or providing sufficient child care so that a young mother can return to school. Giddings argues that "less attention should be paid to the configuration of the family and more to empowering the mother with adequate child care so that she might remain in school" (cited in Billingsley, 1992, p. 15), but in the case of grandmothers in African American extended households, attention to family configuration is a vital part of the process leading to the empowerment of adolescent mothers.

Social programs designed to support and reinforce the role of grandmothers and that attend to the process of socialization to the role of grandmother are needed to prevent the extended family system from being overwhelmed and thereby taking away one of the few resources that African American single mothers and their children can turn to in times of adversity.

REFERENCES

Abu, K. (1983). The separateness of spouses: Conjugal resources in an Ashanti town. In C. Oppong (Ed.), *Female and male in West Africa* (pp. 156-168). Boston: Allen & Unwin.

Allen, W. (1979). Class, culture, and family organization: The effects of class and race on family structure in urban America. *Journal of Comparative Family Studies, 10,* 301-303.

American Association of Retired Persons. (1993). *Issues of concern among adults aged 45 years and older.* Washington, DC: Chilton Research Services.

Apfel, N. H., & Seitz, V. (1991). Four models of adolescent mother-grandmother relationships in Black inner-city families. *Family Relations, 40,* 421-429.

Bascom, W. R., & Herskovits, M. J. (Eds.). (1959). *Continuity and change in African cultures.* Chicago: University of Chicago Press.

Billingsley, A. (1968). *Black families in White America.* Englewood Cliffs, NJ: Prentice Hall.

Billingsley, A. (1990). Understanding African American family diversity. In J. Dewart (Ed.), *The state of Black America 1990* (pp. 85-108). New York: National Urban League.

Billingsley, A. (1992). *Climbing Jacob's ladder: The enduring legacy of African American families.* New York: Simon & Schuster.

Brydon, L. (1983). Avatime women and men, 1900-80. In C. Oppong (Ed.), *Female and male in West Africa* (pp. 320-329). Boston: Allen & Unwin.

Burton, L. M. (1987). Young grandmothers: Are they ready? *Social Sciences, 72,* 191-194.

Burton, L., & Bengston. V. (1987). Black grandmothers: Issues of timing and continuity of roles. In L. Burton (Ed.), *Grandparenthood: Research and policy perspective* (pp. 61-77). Newbury Park, CA: Sage.

Coletta. N. D., & Lee. D. (1983). The impact of support on Black adolescent mothers. *Journal of Family Issues, 4,* 127-143.

Dickerson, B. J. (1994). Ethnic identity and feminism: Views from leaders of African American women's associations. In G. Young & B. J. Dickerson (Eds.), *Color, class and country: Experiences of gender* (pp. 97-114). London: ZED Books.

Etienne, M. (1983). Gender relations and conjugality among the Baule. In C. Oppong (Ed.), *Female and male in West Africa* (pp. 303-319). Boston: Allen & Unwin.

Flaherty, M. J., Facteau, L., & Garver. P. (1987). Grandmother functions in multigenerational families: An exploratory study of Black adolescent mothers and their infants. *Maternal-Child Nursing Journal, 16,* 61-73.

Furstenburg, F. F. (1976). The social consequences of teenage parenthood. *Family Planning Perspective, 8,* 148-164.

Garwood, A. N. (1992). *Black Americans: A statistical handbook.* Boulder, CO: Numbers and Concepts.

Gutman, H. G. (1976). *The Black family in slavery and freedom: 1750-1925.* New York: Vintage.

Hell in a handbasket. (1994, February 6). *Washington Post,* p. C5.

Hill, R. (1980). Black families in the 1970s. In J. Williams (Ed.), *The state of Black America 1980* (pp. 29-58). New York: National Urban League.

Jackson, J. J. (1970). *Negro grandparent: Interactional and subjective role aspects.* Paper presented at the annual meeting of the Southern Sociological Society, Atlanta.

Jackson, J. J. (1971). Aged Blacks: A potpourri in the direction of the reduction of inequities. *Phylon, 32,* 260-280.

Jacob, J. E. (1992). Black America, 1991: An overview. In B. J. Tidwell (Ed.), *The state of Black America 1992* (pp. 1-9). New York: National Urban League.

Jones, B. (1983). The economic status of Black women. In J. Williams (Ed.), *The state of Black America 1983* (pp. 115-154). New York: National Urban League.

Kayongo-Male, D., & Onyango, P. (1984). *The sociology of the African family.* London: Longman.

Ladner J. (1986). Teenage pregnancy: The implications for Black Americans. In J. D. Williams (Ed.), *The state of Black America 1986* (pp. 65-84). New York: National Urban League.

Ladner, J. A., & Gourdine, R. M. (1984). Intergenerational teenage motherhood: Some preliminary findings. *SAGE, 1,* 22-24.

Minkler, M., & Roe, K. M. (1993). *Grandmothers as caregivers: Raising children of the crack cocaine epidemic.* Newbury Park, CA: Sage.

Mitchell, J., & Register, J. (1984). An exploration of family interaction with the elderly by race and socioeconomic status and residence. *The Gerontologist, 24,* 48-54.

National Urban League Research Staff. (1992). African Americans in profile: Selected demographic, social, and economic data. In B. J. Tidwell (Ed.), *The state of Black America 1992* (pp. 309-325). New York: National Urban League.

Smith, E. (1975). The role of the grandmother in adolescent pregnancy and parenting. *Journal of School Health, 45,* 278-283.

Stack, C. (1974). *All our kin.* New York: Harper & Row.

U.S. Bureau of the Census. (1991). *Poverty in the United States: 1991* (Series P-6, No. 181). Washington, DC: U.S. Government Printing Office.

Wei, J. L. (1982, April-May). Historical continuities in the Afro-American family. *Research News,* pp. 18-23.

Wilson, M. (1982, August). *Perception of parent-child interaction in three generational Black family.* Paper presented at the annual meeting of the American Psychological Association, Washington, DC.

Wilson M. (1984). Mothers and grandmothers' perceptions of parental behavior in three generation Black families. *Child Development, 5,* 1333-1339.

Wilson, M. (1986a). The Black extended family: An analytical consideration. *Developmental Psychology, 22,* 246-258.

Wilson. M. (1986b). Perceived parental activity of mothers, fathers, and grandmothers in a three generational Black family. *Journal of Black Psychology, 12,* 43-56.

SUGGESTED READINGS

Bernard, J. (1965). *Marriage and family among Negroes.* Englewood Cliffs, NJ: Prentice Hall.

Edelman, M. W. (1987). *Families in peril: An agenda for social change.* Cambridge, MA: Harvard University Press.

Glick, P. (1988). A demographic picture of Black families. In H. P. McAdoo (Ed.), *Black families* (2nd ed., pp. 106-126). Newbury Park, CA: Sage.

Kotlowitz, A. (1992). *There are no children here.* New York: Doubleday.

Lewis, H., & Herzog, E. (1971). The family: Resources for change. In J. Bracey, A. Meier, & E. Rudwick (Eds.), *The Black matriarchy: Myth or reality* (pp. 160-184). Belmont, CA: Wadsworth.

9

Gender, Poverty, Culture, and Economy: Theorizing Female-Led Families

Rose M. Brewer

The heated debate on African American families reaches a fevered pitch on the issue of single parenthood and poor African American women. However, families of whatever ethnicity, if led by women, are at the center of this discussion (Jencks, 1992; Moynihan, 1965; Wilson, 1987). The idea that something is wrong with the American family via the "absent father syndrome" galvanizes liberal and conservative policymakers alike in an attempt to restore the "two-parent family." My aim is to shift the conceptual terrain. My argument in this chapter is that poor African American female-led families must be understood historically, comparatively, and on their own terms. Conceptually, this means examining capitalist labor markets, racial stratification, gender inequality, and Black culture remade as an interrelated dynamic in which family formation occurs.

I believe that changes in cultural meanings and practices are constructed in the urban and rural capitalist context where African American female and male domestic networks appear to be the "spokes" around which many "poor" Black families revolve. Yet the idea of family is powerful for African Americans, and this must be understood in its current expression. In short, the current policy debate on families is too narrow. Explaining the complexities of poor African American female-led households is far from realized. Accordingly, I argue for a complex analytical framework grounded in social-historical context to begin constructing the complicated explanation of the growth of poor African American female-led families.

I attempt to move the discussion from current popular discourse about Black family pathology to a theoretical and empirical analysis. Given this, three conceptual principles are at the organizational core of this chapter:

1. The complex interplay of gender, race, poverty, culture, state, and economy is at the center of the growth of poor female-led families among African Americans.

2. Micro and macro realities intersect. Here, I mean that agency and social structure interplay in the formation of female-led households. Everyday actions are embedded in social structure, and social structural restraint is the context in which these families are formed.

3. Because of the complex interrelationship of race, class, and gender, theorizing racial and gender inequality autonomously as separate social forces must give way to interactive conceptual frameworks. Interactive frameworks focus on the embeddedness and relationality of these inequalities. They operate simultaneously in the lives of African Americans and are crucial in the growth of poor Black female-led families.

The complex interplay of gender, race, poverty, culture, and economy refers to broadscale macrohistorical processes that are deeply embedded with the other. Thus gender is centered in the social construction of maleness and femaleness in institutional arrangements and identity formation. Race is also a social construction predicated on so-called physical differences—skin color, hair, features—which have taken on social meanings and practices that are deeply embedded in everyday life and institutional arrangements. Indeed, a whole culture and social system of racism characterizes life in the United States centered in an ideology of White supremacy. Relatedly, economy and poverty are class and racial demarcations. The economic arrangement (structural underpinning) of the United States today is capitalist: state, corporate, and multinational. The private ownership of social wealth is the key indicator of this economic arrangement. Poverty in this context refers to the economic positioning that places families or individuals at or below subsistence levels. There is not enough income to provide adequate housing, clothing, food, and resources. For a family of four today this means being wealth poor with an income of about $13,950, according to formal government measures of poverty. This indicator does not measure the substantial class cleavages undergirding this income figure. Relatedly, culture embodies meaning and social practices through which individual and group life is expressed.

The state in this analysis is conceived of as not simply a structure of material domination manipulated by leaders and interest groups in the interest of capital (see Skocpol, 1979) but embodies in its structure the interplay of racial/class/gender relations. Thus the state is made in the context of racial/class resistance as well as domination. It also embodies race as a central organizing principle of American society (Omi & Winant, 1987). This conceptualization differs from some neo-Marxist analyses (Offe, 1974; Poulantzas, 1973) in that it places racial and gender cleavages at the center of state formation and change in the United States.

I propose that gender, race, ideology, culture, state, and economy operate simultaneously and interactively in the family formation and change process. Capitalist racial patriarchy profoundly shapes male and female relations generally but is also conflated with cultural and ideological realities. I mean by capitalist racial patriarchy a structure of White-male-dominated social arrangements. These institutional arrangements severely disadvantage Black women, men, and children. The system is material and ideological in form, operating at personal, organizational, and societal levels.

This is important to understand because gender/racial inequality and the complicated positioning of African American women often are not systematically theorized in discussions of family formation. Frequently, researchers cast Black women's involvement in family formation and change in the pathology model (Frazier, 1939; Klaus, 1986; Mead, 1986; Moynihan, 1965; Wilson, 1987). They say the problem lies within the cultural practices of the poor in the form of destructive values—a culture of pathology. I say that this perspective is a profound misspecification. Alternatively, I attempt to theorize in a way illuminative of the interaction of race, class, and gender, social relations in which poor families are formed. In the next sections, these processes are detailed further.

STATE, ECONOMY, GENDER, RACE, AND CULTURE IN COMPLEX INTERPLAY

Black families are more than personal spheres in which internal/interpersonal dynamics alone determine form, content, and structure. As an extension of this observation, family culture is more than "pathology." A structural and cultural analysis is key here. Familial decisions and responses are made in the context of shifting economic, cultural, and social possibilities. Thus it is arguable that the key issues for Black family formation and change are rooted in advanced capitalist political, economic, and cultural realities. Indeed, I say that deindustrialization and the "servicizing" of the economy are at the center of this process (Bluestone & Harrison, 1982).

By the 1990s many more African Americans had fallen into poverty during a period of so-called expansion and recovery (Urban League, 1993). Strikingly, the historical process of uneven capitalist growth has been devastating to inner-city communities and Black families. This means there is not enough money in central cities to sustain either growth or two-parent family formation. With the transfer of capital or the shutdown of plants there has been massive marginalization of African American workers from the economy (Brewer, 1993).

Black workers and families are at the center of this economic restructuring process. This is true because the processes of deindustrialization and economic restructuring to cheaper labor enclaves have been exceedingly hard on the Black poor, and it is true because many of these multinational decisions are, in fact, explicitly racial. Corporate actors who are the CEOs and decision makers choose to move out of Black communities on racial and economic grounds. Manning (1992) points out that "the disadvantaged class position of most African Americans entails that the rewards of U.S. industrial restructuring accrue disproportionately to higher status white and other non-black ethnic groups" (p. 20). I would argue further that restructuring expresses the deep embeddedness of race and class in Black disadvantage.

Nonetheless, Black resistance to this structural disadvantage occurs. Recent efforts by African Americans to obtain social and economic parity reached an intense scale in the 1960s and peaked again with South Central in 1992. By the late 1960s and early 1970s a larger proportion of the social wages went to Blacks and working people (Bluestone & Harrison, 1982). Today, though, economic shifts have largely undercut these gains. Capital is now being restructured globally (Williams, 1985). An international division of labor enables the pursuit of new profits (Gordon, Edwards, & Reich, 1982).

Of considerable structural importance also are the changes in social welfare as a form of redistribution to the poorest sectors of American society. The U.S. *social* welfare state has been severely cut (O'Connor, 1973). The negative impact of these cuts affects large numbers of African Americans and other working people in the United States. The minimalist welfare state is targeted at the Black poor. Recent welfare reform (i.e., Welfare Reform Act of 1988) served the twofold purpose of retracting the social welfare state and creating a potentially exploitable class of female labor. Even more recently, President Clinton has proposed welfare reforms that allow AFDC participants a maximum of two years' benefits and provide job training. However, Clinton's proposal does not raise the issue of the availability of jobs once training is over. There is a high likelihood that jobs, health care, and child care will not be there (Law, 1983). Legislators are pushing for cutbacks in the AFDC rolls. A form of "stringent welfare" is now being tried in states such as Wisconsin. In that state, the birth of a second child does not increase AFDC benefits.

Accordingly, Black women have been affected twofold by state policy and advanced capitalism:

1. They are disproportionately represented as AFDC recipients and have received the brunt of recent state AFDC cutbacks. These actions have occurred under the rubric of so-called welfare reform.
2. Black women suffer high levels of economic marginalization in the labor force in the form of underemployment and unemployment.

Simultaneously, many Black men are jobless (Staples, 1992, 1993). While African American women are disproportionately employed in low-wage service work, Black men are more likely to be without work, marginalized from the formal economy altogether (Beverly & Stanback, 1986; Simms & Malveaux, 1986).

More concretely, closure of industrial jobs continues. By the end of the 1980s, only 18.8 million Americans, or 21.7% of the nonagricultural workforce, held manufacturing jobs. Beverly and Stanback (1986) capture this process for the Black poor:

Today's underclass has emerged from what would have been that marginally employed sector. Moreover, that group which would have had more stable manufacturing jobs is now in the marginal service sector employment. The changes that have occurred in the economy over the past 15 to 20 years have simply pushed black people who would have been in two employment sectors down. (p. 26)

The two manufacturing sectors they are referring to are small manufacturing firms or large heavy manufacturing firms and public service employment. A substantial number of these jobs are gone. A disproportionate number of the new jobs in the service sector are sex typed as women's work. Women generally are in sex-segregated jobs. Black women are likely to be employed in race- and sex-typed jobs (Simms & Malveaux, 1986). These jobs range from nurses' aides to data entry operators. The structural shift in employment means that many African Americans have been pushed down and out. Indeed, Black male joblessness has been matched by the marginalization of Black women into low-wage, low-status, no-fringe-benefits service work. Neither sector of the economy provides enough money to support families adequately. It appears that the poorest African Americans are heavily economically exploitable or expendable under current political economic realities.

RACE AND STATE HISTORICALLY

The interplay of race, class, and gender in the current expression of the welfare state has deeper roots in the formation of the racial state. This began at the very inception of the United States. So, the unwillingness of the state to embody the needs of African Americans is not new (Thomas, 1991). It would not be until the inception of the general welfare state initiatives of the New Deal, under the pressures imposed by the Great Depression of the 1930s, that some support was extended. Unfortunately, racism marked the programs of the New Deal (Quarles, 1964). Many African Americans were not served by the programs and were treated highly unequally. Newman et al. (1978) point out the asymmetry in the social welfare system, with more poor Whites than Blacks receiving benefits.

The more recent formal withdrawal of state-supported social welfare intensified with the passage of the 1983 Omnibus Act, which severely cut the AFDC rolls of poor women and children—the act reduced the national AFDC caseload by 8% in one year. By 1986 AFDC had not returned to the pre-Omnibus levels. Whereas during the 1970s about 83% of all poor families with children under 18 years of age received AFDC benefits, by 1983 it had dropped to 63%. In 1988, the Welfare Reform Act served the twofold purpose of retracting the social welfare state and creating a group of highly economically vulnerable labor. Under conditions of the Act, young mothers were to be drawn into a workfare structure. Work is supposed to occur even if jobs are not available.

In 1994, President Clinton proposed welfare reform that allows AFDC recipients a maximum of two years' benefits. Indeed, the political economy of Black female-led households is an expression of advanced capitalist economic and state restructuring, institutionalized racism, and gender inequality. Even today, labor market segmentation in the United States means that a disproportionate number of Black workers are in a racially splintered labor market (Tomaskovic-Devey, 1993). This secondary work is the life blood of the working poor, and many families that are poor work all year long. Without raising the income of this working poor population, these Black families are in real economic trouble.

The broader parameters of the welfare state have been reconstructed over time with profound implications for African American families. This restructuring more deeply involves the state in private capital accumulation. The welfare state in the United States meshes with private corporate practices (Devine & Canak, 1986). These private corporate economic decisions include plant closures, discriminatory hiring practices, and labor market segmentation along racial/gender lines. These corporate practices intersect with the racial contours of the welfare state, including the fact that Blacks are disproportionately underrepresented as social security recipients and as beneficiaries of FHA housing loans and government loans to small businesses (Newman et al., 1978).

In summary, most significantly for African American families is the fact that economic and state restructuring in the United States means severe cuts in the social wage and redistribution of income upward (Devine & Canak, 1986). This process also undergirds the minimalist social welfare state impulse of policy makers, represented by deep cuts in food stamps, low-income housing, and WIC and school lunch subsidies (Leashore, 1993). Under these economic and political realities, African Americans who live in declining cities or in deindustrialized areas and confront massive unemployment are often economically expendable. Indeed, labor force participation is down for African American men and women, which has created a profound economic crisis among the masses of African American people. *The State of Black America* (Urban League, 1993) characterizes the situation as an economic depression. For African Americans, this is a *racial, class,* and *gender* reality.

Because of these processes, the poor female-led family is one of several institutions through which these inequalities are expressed. This point is brought home by Cassety and McRoy (1983), who aptly note that "in 1978, the percentages of children living in white, black, and Hispanic headed households were 12, 43, and 20 percent respectively, while the proportions of those who were poor were an alarming 31, 58 and 61 percent" (pp. 37-38).

Nevertheless, the contemporary impact of welfare on Black family life cannot merely be conceptualized in its AFDC and general welfare assistance forms. A disproportionate number of Black households depend on AFDC and general assistance as well as supplementary services such as food stamps, energy and housing allowances, and public service work (see Children's Defense Fund, 1983). These supports have all been cut. Life is severe for poor female-led families.

And the situation of economic marginalization continues. More than 60% of all Black children are now living in poor Black female-led households (Staples, 1993). This is one significant indicator of economic crisis in the African American community. Indeed, poor Black female-led households are the end products of a more insidious process of educational exclusion, poor job opportunities, gender inequality, and the general economic crisis affecting all Black inner-city communities in this country. The confluence of these social forces is crucial to the growth and development of poor Black female-led households. These structural realities are macrolevel processes that interplay with the everyday life experiences of African Americans. The microlevel realities are also important in the explication of family formation and change among the Black poor. These issues are discussed further in the following section.

FAMILY FORMATION, CULTURE, ECONOMY, AND STATE

The welfare state practices associated with AFDC and public assistance may be particularly undermining of the family given the state and economic realities and historical strategies of family making (Jewell, 1992). Under these circumstances, African American families have to spread out the risks of daily life, largely through survival networks, to reproduce themselves (Rapp, 1982). In this sense, family becomes a social and cultural construction of its participants. Thus collective living and kinship are at the center of Black urban life. However, Blaydon and Stack (1977) point out in their research that welfare undermines cooperative familial extension.

Welfare, as presently constituted in the United States, is viewed as the social support strategy for the undeserving poor. This means that the recipients are viewed as unworthy of any support, and the policies have been for the minimal survival of this group—consequently, debilitating for many poor families. Blaydon and Stack (1977) provide further insight on the relationship between kinship and welfare:

While it is a fact that the welfare system has not been able to disrupt the cooperative strength and collective survival of poor urban blacks, that is not the crucial issue. The important point is that we have developed a welfare system that treats many low-income families and individuals unfairly. (1977, p. 148)

Thus micro and macro realities must be viewed as intersecting in explicating the growth of female-led families. Agency and social structure interplay in the formation of female-led households and can be understood as a dialectic. That is, social constraints, exploitation, and oppression represent one side of the equation of poor female-led families; the other side is how women resist and act in the world. Poor Black women have a history of acting in the world. This resistance is often overlooked or misnamed. For example, the welfare rights movement of the 1960s represents the most notable social movement of poor Black women. On an everyday level, sharing and acting in the interests of family and community, "making a way out of no way," are microlevel actions on the part of poor women leading families.

Theorizing poor female-led Black families is thus a twofold reality: macro and micro. Female-led families represent a site of control and inequality as well as one of opposition. Among young women who may be deprived of mobility, husbands, and the right to have children, in fact, to have a child entails a degree of agency under profoundly problematic conditions. This is often accomplished in the context of extended kin and domestic networks. Yet more and more these young women appear to be alone (Jewell, 1992).

If there are kin, the cultural continuity, depending on extended kin, is illustrative of how culture interplays with class, gender, and race. From our Minneapolis Study of Family Formation Among Young Unmarrieds, conducted in 1989-1990, we found support for this interplay of culture, kin, and economy. We sampled mothers, aged 21 and younger, who had a child 12 months of age or younger and were listed in the AFDC data file. Fathers' names, linked to mothers' names, were obtained from the maternity unit of the IV-D office.[1] Ultimately some 126 dyads of Whites, Blacks, interracial, and Native American unmarried parents were interviewed. The experience of one of the interviewees is indicative of social relations found in our African American sample.

A young Black woman I call Kim has a family life illustrative of the dialectic among kin, culture, and economy. She firmly stated in her interview that without the support of her baby's paternal grandmother she could not make it. She and the baby lived with this "other mother." Kim had been unemployed for over a year at the time of the interview. Although she had been a fairly good student and a high school graduate, she found work only in the low-wage service sector. When she discovered she was pregnant, she was working at Wendy's, a fast-food chain. That job lasted for a year. She worked at blue-collar temporary services packing goods for about a year and at Target (a discount department store chain) for about 6 months as a cashier. None of these jobs paid enough to support a family. Without welfare and kin support, it would have been impossible for her to survive. The father of her child was connected to the baby but also had few financial resources.

So, for Kim, as for all women, social reproduction is not simply the biological reproduction of human life but the whole set of social relationships that go into the maintenance and persistence of that life, including food, care, nurturance, and socialization. In this poor female-led African American family, a heavy tie to the baby's paternal kin was constitutive of family. Given this reality, a crucial question is "Who bears the brunt of the social reproduction of African Americans and under what conditions?" The answer is chilling: The most vulnerable women in this society—young, Black, and poor—with all the implications thereof.

The partners of the young women in our study were also severely constrained. A young man I call Don was involved in a different dyad but also faced family formation under severe economic conditions. He had worked on a series of low-paying unskilled jobs: dishwasher, busboy, and temporary worker. He was unemployed at the time of the interview, yet very much wanted additional training. However, the Minneapolis labor market is not good for unskilled Black males. Indeed, the secondary labor market—low-waged and temporary—provides too small an income for many of these young men.

Under these conditions, traditional family formation (married with children) often does not occur for the African American poor.

The Ideology of Black Female-Led Families

This discussion would be incomplete without raising the issue of how ideology figures into an analysis of poor, female-led African American families. I use the notion that ideology mediates social structural realities. Everyday worlds are built in the context of ideological mystifications, structural realities, and cultural creation.

Importantly, the broader societal construction of poor African American families is often heavily ideological. The reappearing icon, highly discursive in its academic and popular constructions today, is the young, fecund Black woman having babies that a racist society cannot afford. Although this racial/gender imagery around the African American family is tied to material realities, such ideology is firmly rooted in racism. Accordingly, the ideological construction of "pathological Black family formation" becomes the linchpin refrain of a discernible number of policy analysts. This ideology can be traced over time. In fact, Carby (1987) places the ideology of Black womanhood in the context of slavery. Her analysis is deeply revealing. This ideology, she says, is a process constituting Black women racially and sexually. Collins (1990) also delineates the racial/gender ideology that frames discourse on Black women who are on welfare. She notes the reconstitution of older negative images of Black women into the more recent one of "welfare queen."

Material arrangements are important in the determination and confirmation practices within societies (Sayer, 1984). In ideology inheres the rationalizations regarding the inferiority of groups or individuals who are considered social failures. Indeed, part and parcel of late capitalist economic restructuring is the stepping up of the rhetoric on the so-called undeserving poor—unmarried poor Black women with children. This polemic is racialized and gender coded. It represents an ideological conduit to the material shifts of U.S. society: the growth of poverty across race and gender lines. Thus the ideology of Black female unworthiness is key here. Such a conceptualization is at the center of the racial/gender hierarchy, the justification for economic exclusion, and the current push toward punitive welfare today.

Especially for young Black women who do not work, it can mean literally coercion into forced labor. Many of these women will end up with the least desirable, least well paid jobs of the service economy or the meanest form of "welfare." In this outcome, ideology, state, and economy have converged in the creation of the vulnerable female-led poor Black family. As "Melba," an African American woman in her early 30s (but a teenager when she had her first child), incisively explains,

> I despise AFDC and everything that it represents. I look forward to its reconstruction and expect that several thousands of people would be just as anxious as I am. If an alternate program was implemented that was sensitive to the status of the poor, AFDC could be the program it should be. It would not be used as a tool to isolate and segregate the poor from the general population.

CONCLUSION

At the center of this analysis is the assumption that racism has been as powerful a determinant of oppression as class exploitation and gender oppression in family formation for poor African American women. It is the deep interrelationship and embeddedness of these social forces that is constitutive of poor Black women's positioning in American society. Simultaneously, gender is highly conflated with race and class. This is an interactive, multiplicative relationship rather than an additive reality. Indeed, King (1988) made a significant distinction between additive models that conceive of Black women's position as *race + class + gender* and multiplicative conceptualizations built on the idea of *race × class × gender.* Additive models cannot capture the complexity and the intensifying effect of race, class, and gender in African American women's experiences, argued King. As discussed, there are material, cultural, and ideological dimensions to poor Black female-led families.

Finally, young Black men and women face a treacherous rite of passage into adulthood. The normative markers of an earlier generation are now shifting in the context of a late capitalist culture and economy. This is especially true regarding family formation. Taken-for-granted notions about marriage, family, and kin must be retheorized. Centrally, poor Black female-led families are structurally shaped and culturally expressed. Yet they are also ideologically defined and heavily stigmatized as undeserving. In this sense, the family becomes a social construction of a racist/ sexist social order. In a more culturally resistive way, family is a crucial cultural construction of African Americans living on the edge. As such, the economic realities are mediated by cultural practices and assumptions that place collective living and kinship at the center of family life. Thus the family remains culturally and ideologically meaningful to African Americans, essential to survival, sustenance, and emotional support.

What seems clear to me is that for poor Black women motherhood and family formation are embedded in harsh racial, gender, and economic realities. Nonetheless, as noted, family life is often expressed in the context of female-centered, female-anchored, and female-dominated kin networks that function in interaction with male-centered, male-anchored, and male-dominated kin networks (Scott & Black, 1992). The cultural expression of family continues.

In closing, I believe that thinking about African American family formation must be firmly embedded in a paradigm expressing the interaction of culture, economy, race, and gender. The complex interplay between micro and macro social realities is not easily sorted out but is essential to an explanation of the expansion and creation of female-led families among African Americans. I am sure that singular explanations focusing on one or another of these social forces are simply insufficient for analyzing what is happening with poor Black women and their families.

NOTE

1. *IV-D* is the term applied by the Hennepin County Department of Social Welfare, Minneapolis, MN, to fathers who have children who do not pay child support and for whom paternity has not been adjudicated.

REFERENCES

Beverly, C. C., & Stanback, H. J. (1986). The Black underclass: Theory and reality. *The Black Scholar, 17,* 24-32.
Blayton, C. C., & Stack, C. (1977 Spring). Income support policies and the family. *Daedalus, 6,* 2, 147-161.
Bluestone, B., & Harrison, B. (1982). *The deindustrialization of America.* New York: Basic Books.
Brewer, R. M. (1993). Theorizing race, gender, and class. In S. M. James & A. P. A. Busia (Eds.), *Theorizing Black feminisms* (pp. 13-30). New York, New York: Routledge.
Carby, H. (1987). *Reconstructing Black womanhood.* New York: Oxford University Press.
Cassety, J., & McRoy, R. (1983, Summer). Gender, race, and the shrinking welfare dollar. *Public Welfare,* pp. 37-38.
Children's Defense Fund. (1983). *Children's defense budget.* New York: Aetna Foundation.
Collins, P. H. (1990). *Black feminist thought.* New York: Unwin Hyman.
Devine, J. A., & Canak, W. (1986). Redistribution in a bifurcated welfare state. *Social Problems, 33,* 391-405.
Frazier, E. F. (1939). *The Negro family in the United States.* Chicago: University of Chicago Press.
Gordon, D., Edwards, R., & Reich, M. (1982). *Segmented work, divided workers.* Cambridge: Cambridge University Press.
Jencks, C. (1992). *Rethinking social policy.* Cambridge, MA: Harvard University Press.
Jewell, K. S. (1992). Use of welfare programs and the disintegration of the Black nuclear family. In R. Staples (Ed.), *The Black family: Essays and studies* (4th ed., pp. 319-326). Belmont, CA: Wadsworth.
King, D. K. (1988). Multiple jeopardy, multiple consciousness: The context of a Black feminist ideology. *Signs, 14*(1), 42-72.
Klaus, M. (1986, July). The work ethic state. *New Republic, 195,* 22-33.

Law, S. A. (1983). Women, work, welfare, and the preservation of patriarchy. *University of Pennsylvania Law Review, 131,* 1249-1339.

Leashore, B. (1993). Social policies, Black males, and Black families. In R. Staples (Ed.), *The Black family: Essays and studies* (5th ed., pp. 334-340). Belmont, CA: Wadsworth.

Manning, R. (1992). *Immigration, industrial restructuring, and African Americans.* Paper presented at the "Multicultural Washington: Changing Complexion of Social Inequality" conference, American University, Washington, DC.

Mead, L. (1986). *Beyond entitlement: The social obligations of citizenship.* New York: Free Press.

Moynihan, D. P. (1965). *The Negro family: The case for national action.* Washington, DC: U.S. Government Printing Office.

Newman, D. K., Amidei, N. J., Carter, B. L., Day, D., Kruvant, W. J., & Russell, J. S., (Eds). (1978). *Protest, politics, and prosperity.* New York: Pantheon.

O'Connor, J. (1973). *The fiscal crisis of the state.* New York: St. Martin's.

Omi, M., & Winant, H. (1987). *Racial formation.* New York: Routledge.

Offe, C. (1974). Structural problems of the capitalist state. *German Political Studies, 1,* 31-56.

Poulantzas, N. (1973). *Political power and social classes* (T. O'Hagan, Trans.). London: New Left Books.

Quarles, B. (1964). *The Negro in the making of America.* New York: Collier.

Rapp, R. (1982). Family and class in contemporary America: Notes toward an understanding of ideology. In B. Thorne & M. Yalom (Eds.), *Rethinking the family: Some feminist questions* (pp. 168-187). New York: Longman.

Sayer, A. (1984). *Method in social science.* London: Hutchinson.

Scott, J., & Black, A. (1992). Deep structures of African American family life: Female and male kin networks. In R. Staples (Ed.), *The Black family: Essays and studies* (4th ed., pp. 204-213). Belmont, CA: Wadsworth.

Simms, M. C., & Malveaux, J. M. (Eds). (1986). *Slipping through the cracks: The status of Black women.* New Brunswick, NJ: Transaction.

Skocpol, T. (1979). *States and revolution.* Cambridge: Cambridge University Press.

Staples, R. (Ed.). (1992). *The Black family: Essays and studies* (4th ed.). Belmont, CA: Wadsworth.

Staples, R. (Ed.). (1993). *The Black family: Essays and studies* (5th ed.). Belmont, CA: Wadsworth.

Thomas, R. (1991). The historical roots of contemporary urban self help in the United States. In M. Lang (Ed.), *Contemporary urban America: Problems, issues, and alternatives* (pp. 253-291). New York: University Press of America.

Tomaskovic-Devey, D. (1993). *Gender and racial inequality at work: The sources and consequences of job segregation.* Ithaca, NY: ILR Press.

Urban League. (1993). *The state of Black America 1993.* New York: National Urban League.

Whitman, D. (1983). Liberal rhetoric and the welfare underclass. *Society, 21,* 63-69.

Williams, R. (1985). *Competition, class location, and discrimination: Black workers and the "new growth dynamic."* Unpublished manuscript, Department of Economics, University of Texas at Austin.

Wilson, W. J. (1987). *The truly disadvantaged.* Chicago: University of Chicago Press.

SUGGESTED READINGS

Anderson, M. (1993). *Thinking about women*. New York: Maxwell.

Brewer, R. M. (1983). Black workers and corporate flight. *Third World Socialists, 1*, 9-13.

Fusfeld, D. R., & Bates, T. (1984). *The political economy of the urban ghetto*. Carbondale: Southern Illinois University Press.

Gordon, D. (1988). Left, right, and center: An introduction to political economy. In R. Cherry (Ed.), *The imperiled economy: Through the safety net* (pp. 9-24). New York: Union for Radical Political Economics.

Gough, I. (1981). *The political economy of the welfare state*. New York: Macmillan.

Lemann, N. (1986). The origins of the Black underclass. *Atlantic, 257*, 31-61.

Murray, C. (1984). *Losing ground: American social policy, 1950-1980*. New York: Basic Books.

Noyelle, T., & Stanback, T. M. (1983). *The economic transformation of American cities*. Totowa, NJ: Rowman & Allanheld.

10

Empowerment Through the "Ordinary" Knowledge/Scholarship/Policy Nexus

Bette J. Dickerson
Philipia L. Hillman
Johanna E. Foster

The preceding chapters of this volume make a collective contribution to the intellectual inquiries and knowledge of African American single mothers and their families. They contribute to the reconstruction of the ideology of Black single motherhood. By expanding the use of the Afrocentric paradigm and methods, the writers have challenged conventional views and promoted the *re*visioning of the experiences of African American single mothers and their families. They have expanded understandings of the nature, extent, and implications of the pluralism of American families. In this chapter, we take these processes a step further through a discussion of a form of inquiry that can link this much needed scholarship with action to achieve the empowerment of African American single mothers and their families. The strategies advocated to foster this empowerment center around four themes:

- Use of Afrocentric theory and methods
- Elimination of false perceptions that influence and inform structural and social boundaries of African American single mothers and their families
- Legitimation of African American single mothers' experiences as points of resistance and potential sources of power

- Possibilities and limitations faced by scholar-activists, in partnership with African American single mothers, when working within the policy-making realm.

THE CONTRIBUTIONS
OF AFROCENTRISM

The contributors to this volume bring voices to the discourse that are not typically heard in the policy-making milieu because the debates usually "highlight notions of difference, marginality and otherness in such a way that it further marginalizes actual people of difference and otherness" (hooks, 1990, p. 125). When this occurs, the patterns of domination "where the 'other' is always made object, appropriated, interpreted, talked over by those in power" are further inculcated (hooks, 1990, p. 175). We have tapped these voices through Afrocentric analyses of selected issues affecting African American single mothers and their families.

Afrocentrism, a paradigm dedicated to centering the standpoint of people of African descent, has informed our understanding of African American single mothers and their families. Specifically, Afrocentrism offers an *interactive* approach to research and empowerment. One of its strengths lies in the recognition of the inextricable relationship between "knowledge for understanding" and "knowledge for action." In the first chapter in this volume, Dickerson explains the purpose and relevance of the required historical and sociocultural immersion that is essential to the Afrocentric approach. Furthermore, she reminds us that not only is applied Afrocentric research undertaken for the specific tasks of discerning the centered standpoint at the heart of the "ordinary knowledge" base of people of African descent and of calling attention to particular social conditions affecting them but also with the intention of developing a *course of action* to positively transform social injustices. Thus Afrocentric scholarly pursuits are liberating because, through a better understanding of their centered standpoint, the participants are involved in a more democratic process of inquiry aimed at increasing their "literacy." The findings from such inquiries result in emancipatory knowledge that can lead to social and psychological "freedom," personal empowerment, and structural change.

Afrocentric scholars are skeptical of the chasm between objective researcher and passive subjects of research and between "expert" scientific knowledge and "ordinary" knowledge (Asante, 1987; King & Mitchell,

1990). Many are scholar-activists equipped with skills for affecting the policy process and with the ability to navigate their way in and out of policy-making spheres quite adeptly using a combination of expert and ordinary knowledge. Using these skills and abilities on behalf of African American single mothers and their families involves privileging their experiences as they define them, legitimating the reality of conditions shaping their lives, and doing so for the sake of promoting their liberation (Spalter-Roth & Hartmann, in press).

Conducting Afrocentric activist scholarship involves learning how to be an ambassador of sorts, a liaison, a translator. This process is somewhat akin to W. E. B. Du Bois's (1986) notion of "double consciousness," or the required capacity of people of African descent to understand the worldviews of both the dominant and other subordinate groups. For Afrocentric scholars attempting to affect change in the policy arena, this dual visioning includes a significant variation: As scholar-activists they are charged with the task of persuading dominant group members to become "doubly conscious" as well as, in this case, to accept and learn from the "ordinary" knowledge of African American single mothers. This is a monumental task given that the dominant group has not been required to understand and accept the worldviews of subordinate groups, particularly those of African descent.

SOCIAL CONSTRUCTIONS
OF BLACK WOMANHOOD

Historical and cultural literacy can break the bonds of psychological oppression caused by the controlling images created by the dominant society—images that limit the freedom to conceptualize the world in ways continuous with one's history and culture (Harris, 1992; see also Dickerson, Chapter 1 in this volume). The self-definition of African American single mothers, therefore, is a critical step toward assuming full ownership of empowering ideas and strategies. One of the major obstacles for scholar-activists is deconstructing the persistent myths of Black womanhood that shape policy makers as well as other scholars and even other African Americans' perceptions of Black single women and their families.

Both historical and contemporary constructions of the African American family, and particularly African American single mothers, have been undertaken using either a cultural deviant or cultural equivalent model (see Dickerson, Chapter 1 in this volume). These approaches define the ideal "family" as a nuclear unit composed of married parents and their immediate offspring, a model based on a patriarchal family type to which all other families should conform (Abramovitz, 1988). This definition ignores the diversity, consanguinity, matrifocality, and blood and fictive extended patterns that are essential elements of many African American families. Conversely, this ideal family structure has not been the most prevalent family type for either African *or* European American families. This notion of the ideal family is based on a type of family that emerged very briefly in the 1950s and was the reality for only a very small number of European American families (Coontz, 1992). The irony is that while African American single mothers and their children have been characterized as constituting an "abnormal" family type, it is actually this idealized nuclear, patriarchal family that is the aberration.

Using these false perceptions in assessing African American single mothers and their families has led to inaccurate questions and insubstantial explanations that serve to support the "deficit model." Not only are African American families headed by women labeled "pathological," but such women have had to mediate their lives around insidiously entrenched notions of Black womanhood. These images are socially constructed, have their roots in the slavery era, and include "the mammy," "the matriarch," "the welfare mother" and "the Jezebel" (Collins, 1990). According to Barbee and Little (1993), the mammy is characterized as the "faithful, obedient servant" and was created and has been maintained to legitimate the relegation to domestic service. The matriarch is characterized as "overly aggressive, emasculating, strong, independent, unfeminine" and is used to strap African American women with the blame for the hardships of the African American families as well as the lack of services and assistance offered to them (i.e., Blacks are strong and thus do not need our help). The welfare mother image is "essentially an updated version of the breeder image that was created in slavery" (p. 185) and describes Black women as lazy, fat, and having numerous children for the sake of increased public assistance. This characterization rationalizes the arbitrary distinction between the "deserving and undeserving poor" and alleviates the state's sense of responsibility of assisting poor Black women and their families (ironically, in absolute numbers, the state is assisting more White women than women of color). Last, the Jezebel stereotype, or the image of Black women as sexually promiscuous and "loose," was created to justify the repeated sexual violence against Black women by slave owners and continues to be manipulated by men of all race/ethnic backgrounds for similar reasons (for a discussion of the contemporary uses of these stereotypes, see Ziegler, Chapter 5 in this volume).

Relying on false perceptions in assessing African American families has led to misguided research questions and unsubstantiated explanations that serve to support the cultural deviant or deficit model of African American motherhood on the part of scholars, and the use of such paradigms has contributed to African American mothers and their children being labeled pathological, aberrations, and social problems by both scholars and policy makers. Through a cultural deviant or cultural equivalent lens the following occur:

1. *Projection,* or the assigning of negative or positive qualities to other persons or groups based not on their standpoint but, rather, on one's own. This conceals diversity and imposes an epistemological perspective contrary to the unique attributes of the group central to research.

2. *Rationalization,* or the assumption by the dominant group that its own standpoint is the only reasonable one for all other groups. This limits real communication between groups.

3. *Denigration,* or the dominant group's refusal to recognize the existence of the other group's standpoint. This relegates the subordinate group's standpoint to a state of invisibility, unimportance, irrelevance. (Karenga, 1989)

In other words, relying on these false perceptions ignores and distorts the realities and diversity of African American mothers and renders their daily resistance and production of ordinary knowledge nonexistent.

SCHOLAR-ACTIVISTS AND AFRICAN AMERICAN MOTHERS: PARTNERS IN RESISTANCE

One avenue through which scholar-activists can work to dispel false perceptions of African American single mothers and the policy implications of these myths is to legitimate the crucial role of women's "ordinary" knowledge. Linking scholarship to African American women's empowerment means verifying their daily experiences as points of resistance and potential sources of collective action for those who are in positions to help expedite social change.

Empowerment consists of "having the specific resources that are required to make, pursue and achieve informed life choices" and encompasses a process that includes (a) gaining some control over one's life by taking part with others in the development of activities and structures that allow increased involvement in matters which directly affect all involved and (b) access to power—the *power to do with* others rather than *power to wield over* others. According to Morgen and Bookman (1988), empowerment "begins when [people] change their ideas about the causes of their powerlessness, when they recognize the systematic forces that oppress them and when they act to change the conditions of their lives" (p. 4). Within this framework, empowerment is "a *process* aimed at consolidating, maintaining, or changing the nature and distribution of power in a particular cultural context" (p. 4). It is a collective expression that requires and assumes organization and united thrusts (Karenga, 1989).

To acknowledge this notion of empowerment is to admit that African American women have used and continue to use strategies of resistance to empower themselves and their families. Resistance is defined as "the accumulated effects of daily, arduous, creative, sometimes ingenious labors, performed over time, sometimes over generations" (Aptheker, 1989, p. 173). It is this ordinary knowledge, or daily experiences, that are not recognized as "true" knowledge in traditional social science or mainstream politics. Moreover, this system of knowledge exists parallel to the dominant system and produces knowledge reflective of the daily survival of African American women (Tandon, 1988, p. 6).

Efforts to resist oppression are not new among African American women and their families; what *is* new in the applied sciences is the recognition of the resultant alternative ways of knowing and subverting systems of domination. The role of scholars interested in promoting and encouraging these acts of resistance is to become involved in the empowering process itself. A commitment to this kind of research requires the validation of these women as "researchers themselves in pursuit of answers to the questions of their daily struggle and survival" (Tandon, 1988, p. 7). As co-researchers, scholar-activists can assist African American women not only in realizing the sources of their daily struggles but in facilitating solutions grounded within their communities (Friere, 1990). Simultaneously, African American single mothers can teach scholar-activists alternative ways of knowing and understanding; they can clarify information that has been distorted and often hidden from stakeholders in the policy arena. Stakeholders are any individuals, groups, or institutions that "have input into the decisionmaking process or are affected by policy decisions" (Majchrak, 1984, p. 28). They may gain or lose as a result of the policy implications of a scholar-activist's work.

It is here that an Afrocentric perspective is particularly useful to challenge systems of domination and empower "subjects" by fostering the development of a critical consciousness. Empowerment is essentially synonymous with consciousness raising, or a process where scholar-activists and mothers *work together* to increase their understanding of the interlocking systems of oppression that affect the lives of African American single mothers. Rather than delineating an arbitrary line between "expert" researchers and "dependent" mothers, a coalition must be built between African American single mothers and those interested in co-researching with them. This partnership can also become "a site of resistance" (hooks, 1990). It is then that scholar-activists can take the lessons learned from these partnerships and move to affect the policy process with and on behalf of African American single mothers and their families.

DECIPHERING RESISTANCE
IN THE POLICY-MAKING PROCESS

Kingdon (1993) characterizes the policy arena as being influenced by three specific sources:

> There are three streams: problems, proposals, and politics. People in and around government recognize and come to concentrate on certain problems rather than others, they propose and refine policy proposals (alternatives), and political events like shifts in national mood, changes in administration, or interest group campaigns move along on their own. These streams develop largely independently of one another. Proposals are generated whether or not they are solving a problem, problems are recognized whether or not there is a solution, and political events move along according to their own dynamics. . . . At certain critical times these three streams come together, and the greatest agenda change occurs. (p. 41)

In a sense then, influencing agenda change requires being able to slip through an "open policy window." This model of agenda setting and policy making challenges the positivist model of rational decision making by public servants, who, void of any other influences, carefully weigh objective research and then, based on the data, legislate the best policy solution.

Instead, scholar-activists must work within a policy arena that is rarely adequately understood within academia, the scholarly domain. The alternative model of policy making proposed here recognizes the need to incorporate the acts of resistance by everyday people as elements of the policy-making process. For example, Kingdon (1993) and Morgen and Bookman (1988) address the critical role played by social movements and grassroots efforts (including boycotts, strikes, and riots) in pulling these "three streams" together. Ironically, although these claimsmaking activities are often misconstrued as disconnected from the "official" political domain, movements that spring from the "everyday" lives of empowered people have been integral to the success of particular social policies (or the failure of them in the absence of effective social movements) (Reich, 1988; Rossi & Freeman, 1993). A salient example of this process was the impact of the activities of the National Welfare Rights Organization in reforming particular eligibility requirements and enforcement policies with regard to the Aid to Families with Dependent Children program (Amott, 1990). In fact, power and knowledge are not separable, one implies the other, and the policy-making process itself serves to reinforce race/ethnic, gender, and class hierarchies unless informed by "ordinary" knowledge (Foucault, 1980).

Recognizing that this method of inquiry is simultaneously a craft, an art, and a political act (Rossi & Freeman, 1993), the work of scholar-activists can influence the policy process by articulating cogent problem definitions, assessing the scope and severity of problems, and conceptualizing issues for policy makers that are reflective of the standpoint of African American mothers and their families. Findings can also be instrumental in mobilizing the formation of particular coalitions around policy choices both inside and outside the official policy arena. Most important, scholar-activists with "double consciousness" are in the unique position of being able to reconstruct knowledge for understanding into knowledge for action in order for their work to be legitimated, recognized, and used in the policy arena. Specifically, this process involves generating a body of *policy-relevant* knowledge that can be drawn on by stakeholders within the policy arena and require one to become equipped in selecting from one's research those elements that can be feasibly translated into policy initiatives.

Scholar-activists participating in the development of policy-relevant knowledge engage in the following steps in conducting research. Many of these steps are also required of scholars conducting basic research, yet there are distinct processes particularly germane to applied scholarship. First, in the preparation phase of policy-relevant inquiries, scholar-activists must have a keen sense of the power relations shaping the problem in question. In a sense, it is necessary to conduct a preliminary network analysis, or a piecing together of all possible stakeholders vested in a policy issue. In applied research, critical stakeholders often include funding organizations, program sponsors, managers or administrators, and obviously clients of services, the potential beneficiaries of proposed policy initiatives. Using an Afrocentric framework, it must be determined how exactly different groups of African American single mothers and their families have a stake in the issues being addressed. Moreover, clarity is needed about how these different groups are related to other stakeholders, especially policy decision makers and resource allocators.

Along with an initial analysis of where the power lies and who has what stakes in changing or maintaining these relations scholar-activists need to have a detailed notion of the various ways that the many stakeholders have defined the problem(s) in question. Familiarity with the underlying values and assumptions that inform definitions is critical. Specifically, to what extent have Afrocentric analyses characterized stakeholders' understanding of the problem or, conversely, in what ways have African American single mothers and their families been defined as the social problem itself? Sensitivity to the extent to which social movements have been instrumental in typifying the issue is required. Furthermore, it is necessary to keep abreast of related policy issues and to be cognizant of the social construction of these issues. These first steps are critical in assessing whether the policy-relevant study is, indeed, policy relevant given the sociopolitical climate and the personal and professional resources at hand.

Once a preliminary investigation has been completed and the conclusion reached that action-oriented research can be undertaken, the second step involves conceptualization of the problem, including a causal model of the problem (why is this happening?), an intervention model (what specific action(s) will solve this problem?), and an action model (how exactly does the intervention alleviate the problem?) (Rossi & Freeman, 1993). When forming the specific research questions, particular attention must be given to the way the scholar-activist's own definitions and underlying assumptions are informed or not informed by Afrocentric theory. Also in this phase are decisions regarding the target population, that is, which group(s) of African American single mothers will be included as co-researchers.

After these and other related decisions have been made, scholar-activists must decide which means of data collection best suits not only the research question, the target population, and their own resources and skills but also the political context. For example, is a cost-benefit analysis the most useful strategy? Is a case study design the most appropriate type of technical analysis given the needs of stakeholders? A focus group? Secondary data analysis? It is in this phase of the research process that scholar-activists must be critically conscious of the ways that they reproduce research *on* African American single mothers and their families rather than *for* or *with* them. In what ways does the relationship between "the researcher" and "the researched" remain fundamentally unchallenged?

Once data have been collected and processed, action-oriented researchers must begin to analyze the implications of their work for policy. During these stages, it is essential to maintain the research copartnership, and take great care not to lose the source of "everyday" knowledge that must be carried into the policy arena. Both the intended and unintended consequences of the research findings must be considered. In this stage, clear communication occurs regarding what course of action may follow if the policy recommendation is ignored (Majchrak, 1984).

The findings must be strategically publicized to various audiences, including those traditionally excluded as research consumers. Because most policy makers rarely use research information directly, it is essential that both direct and indirect dissemination strategies be carried out. In addition to direct contact with decision makers, funders, and program managers, other means of information dissemination must be used, including using, rather than being "used by," the mass media in creative and culturally relevant ways. Besides increasing the chances of being heard and being taken seriously, ambitious communicative efforts encourage policy makers to be more sympathetic to the constraints of research and reduce cynicism. Moreover, close communication with policy makers throughout the research process allows them to catalogue information that can be used when additional "policy windows" open in the future. Just as important, these efforts allow scholar-activists to stay knowledgeable about changes in the policy arena and the constraints under which decision makers work (Majchrak, 1984).

Yet, regardless of the caution and foresight used in generating action-oriented knowledge, scholar-activists have to be realistic about their capabilities within the policy arena. First, they must often work within the boundaries of current debate in order for their policy initiatives to be considered. Scholar-activists may not always be victorious when suggesting, regardless of its technical feasibility and/or fairness, policy alternatives that do not reflect the ideas and goals of the most powerful stakeholders and, perhaps more important, decision makers.

Second, as stressed earlier, without large-scale community support, transformative policy initiatives are moot. In other words, policy alternatives are more likely to be implemented and sustained when accompanied by the power of effective social movements. Without the support of recognizable, sustained community action, transformative agenda change is rarely a feat accomplished by policy makers alone.

Third, scholar-activists are limited to the selection of malleable variables (aspects of the issue that are open to influence and intervention). It is useless to offer policy solutions that are based on variables that cannot be realistically altered. To use an extreme example, a policy initiative that involved changing everyone in the nation to the same race is obviously not a viable policy option because the variable, race, is not changed that easily or that willingly. Related to this consideration, scholar-activists are constrained not only by political feasibility but also by technical feasibility. Often, there may be limited access to the necessary tools of research, resources, personnel, time, and technical skills. There may also be limitations caused by the resources, personnel, time, and technical skills of those officially formulating policy and those implementing it as well as limitations caused by the extent to which the policy recommendations are determined usable by others.

Fourth, as Innes (1990) argues, rarely is research by itself used directly by decision makers. Even when the needs of stakeholders are carefully calculated, policy research is often on the periphery of policy decisions. Particularly disheartening is the realization that, as another set of competing voices in the complex policy process, scholar-activists can be easily ignored. Also troublesome is the possibility that research findings will be appropriated in ways unforeseen, unintended, or unapproved, no matter what sorts of concerted steps may have been taken to ensure that the findings and the resultant recommendations are communicated in a responsible manner. There is an ever present risk of work being misinterpreted, resulting in conscious or unconscious misuse. A particularly salient example of this was the interpretation of the work of E. Franklin Frazier, a scholar who was trying to speak to three distinct audiences, namely, racist scholars, African Americans themselves, and social reformers. Frazier's work was later misappropriated by Daniel Patrick Moynihan in his now infamous 1965 report, *The Negro Family: The Case for National Action* (Platt, 1991).

Last, claims-making activities are complex and constantly fluctuating to mediate the demands of stakeholders within changing circumstances.

This constant shift between standpoints may limit the voice of scholar-activists in that they become perceived as not credible, as lacking a depth of scientific expertise, as operators or "idea brokers." Similarly, with a commitment to Afrocentrism, positivists may claim that there appears to be a limiting contradiction: How can one legitimize the centered standpoint of African American women who are single mothers and simultaneously speak with any authority about optimal national policy outcomes? Because the standpoints of other groups are acknowledged, how can it confidently be said that another "centered" solution to the problem is invalid?

Despite these limitations, the contention is still that the challenging work of scholar-activists has a long history, much possibility, and is much needed. The skills derived from "double consciousness" can be used to navigate the voices of African American single mothers through the policy arena to create a new body of knowledge that is reflective of their lives and useful to all the stakeholders. Examples of this are found in this volume: Leslie highlights how the Eurocentric constructions of "sinful" do not apply to the moral realities of African American teenaged mothers and their families; Ziegler discusses how the mass media have distorted motherhood, especially African American motherhood; and Brewer's work illustrates the complexities of race, culture, gender, and class, examining how their intersections are played out in the lives of African American single mothers and their families. As translators, scholar-activists can take this knowledge and maneuver it through recognized social institutions and practices to generate new realities. Using their "double consciousness" skills, scholar-activists can translate "ordinary" knowledge into the ideas, concepts, and formats understood by government programs or counseling services or child-care providers or educational programs—whichever is called for —to create a unified voice that can be empowering for the mothers, their families, and their communities.

Using the examples above, scholar-activists would discover and realize that the sexual mores of Black women must be understood within the context of the African American pragmatic spiritual ethos. Effective translation would allow the diversity and richness of Black single mothers and their families to be evidenced. The mass media portrayal of African American motherhood would no longer be the primary definitional source. Moreover, once single mothers' realities have been translated and synthesized and aided in becoming infused within social institutions, stakeholders and decision makers could *finally* see how micro and macro social dynamics affect the lives of African American single mothers. These dynamics often leave them in positions of vulnerability that are described as "networks of pathology."

CONCLUDING REMARKS

The holistic inquiries in the preceding chapters underscore compelling reasons to seek alternative options for the empowerment of African American single mothers. Scholar-activists, with "double consciousness" skills and working as co-researchers with African American single mothers, can weave the "ordinary" knowledge derived from the mothers' realities into the dynamics of the social environment to create a new tapestry of knowledge. Addressing social issues in the proposed manner can lead to "freedom" for African American single mothers and their families. The new levels of "literacy" and subsequent actions can generate positive societal change, and practical, relevant policy approaches can then be set in motion to initiate, monitor, and sustain the action initiatives for empowerment.

REFERENCES

Abramovitz, M. (1988). *Regulating the lives of women: Social welfare policy from the colonial times to the present.* Boston: South End Press.

Amott, T. (1990). Black women and AFDC: Making entitlement out of necessity. In L. Gordon (Ed.), *Women, the state, and welfare* (pp. 280-230). Madison: University of Wisconsin Press.

Aptheker, B. (1989). Get over this hurdle, there's another one coming. In B. Aptheker, *Tapestries of life: Women's work, women's consciousness, and the meaning of daily experience* (pp. 167-230). Amherst, MA: Amherst University Press.

Asante, M. K. (1987). *The Afrocentric idea.* Philadelphia: Temple University Press.

Barbee, E. L., & Little, M. (1993). Health, social class, and African-American women. In S. M. James & A. P. A. Busia (Eds.), *Theorizing Black feminisms* (pp. 182-199). New York: Routledge.

Collins, P. H. (1990). *Black feminist thought.* New York: Routledge.

Coontz, S. (1992). *The way we never were: American families and the nostalgia trap.* New York: Basic Books.

Du Bois, W. E. B. (1986). *The suppression of the African slave trade; the souls of Black folks; and dusk of dawn* [Essays]. New York: Literary Classics of the United States.

Foucault, M. (1980). *Power/knowledge: Selected interviews and other writing, 1972-1977.* New York: Pantheon.

Friere, P. (1990). *Pedagogy of the oppressed.* New York: Continuum.

Harris, N. (1992). A philosophical basis for an Afrocentric orientation. *Western Journal of Black Studies, 16,* 154-159.

hooks, b. (1990). *Yearning.* Boston: South End Press.

Innes, J. E. (1990). *Knowledge and public policy: The search for meaningful indicators.* New Brunswick, NJ: Transaction.

Karenga, M. (1989). *Introduction to Black studies* (6th ed.). Los Angeles: University of Sankore Press.

King, J. E., & Mitchell, C. A. (1990). *Black mothers to sons: Juxtaposing African American literature with social practice.* New York: Peter Lang.

Kingdon, J. (1993). How do issues get on public policy agendas? In W. J. Wilson (Ed.), *Sociology and the public agenda* (pp. 40-50). Newbury Park, CA: Sage.

Majchrak, A. (1984). *Methods for policy research.* Beverly Hills, CA: Sage.

Morgen, S., & Bookman, A. (1988). Rethinking women and politics: An introductory essay. In A. Bookman & S. Morgen (Eds.), *Women and the politics of empowerment* (pp. 3-29). Philadelphia: Temple University Press.

Platt, A. (1991). *E. Franklin Frazier reconsidered.* New Brunswick, NJ: Rutgers University Press.

Reich, R. (1988). *The power of public ideas.* Cambridge, MA: Harvard University Press.

Rossi, P. H., & Freeman, H. E. (1993). *Evaluation: A systematic approach* (5th ed.). Newbury Park, CA: Sage.

Spalter-Roth, R., & Hartmann, H. (In press). Small happinesses: The feminist struggle to integrate social research with social activism. In H. Gottfried (Ed.), *Feminism and social change: Bridging theory and practice.* Champaign, IL: University of Illnois Press.

Tandon. R. (1988). Social transformation and participatory research. *Convergence, 21*(2-3), 5-18.

SUGGESTED READINGS

Asante, M. K. (1990). *Kemet, Afrocentricity, and knowledge.* Trenton, NJ: Africa World Press.

Asante, M. K., & Asante, K. W. (1990). *African culture: The rhythms of unity.* Trenton, NJ: Africa World Press.

Brewer, R. M. (1993). Theorizing race, class, and gender: The new scholarship of Black feminist intellectuals and Black women's labor. In S. M. James & A. P. A. Busia (Eds.), *Theorizing Black feminisms* (pp. 13-30). New York: Routledge.

Kershaw, T. (1992). Afrocentrism and the Afrocentric method. *Western Journal of Black Studies, 16,* 160-168.

Index

About the Authors

Rose M. Brewer is Chair and Associate Professor of Afro-American and African Studies at the University of Minnesota. She received her M.A. and Ph.D. degrees in sociology from Indiana University and did postdoctoral studies at the University of Chicago. She has written extensively in the areas of race, class, gender, public policy and African American families. She is the editor of *Bridges of Power: Women's Multicultural Alliances* (with Lisa Albrecht) and is working on a manuscript titled *Race, Gender and Political Economy: The African American Case Since the New Deal*. She was selected as one of ten outstanding teachers at the University of Minnesota, receiving the Horace T. Morse Alumni teaching award for outstanding contributions to undergraduate education in 1993.

Norma J. Burgess is Associate Professor of Child and Family Studies at Syracuse University, where she teaches classes in family history and gender. She recently completed a three-year National Science Foundation fellowship appointment at the Center for Research on Women at Memphis State University, where the issue of sociohistoricism (combining sociology and history) emerged as a key component in further understanding the issues associated with race, class, and gender. Her work primarily involves a sociohistorical analysis of family structures and gender role development among African American women. She is currently researching social psychological well-being among managerial and professional middle class women. She has a master's degree in public affairs and a Ph.D. in sociology.

197

Bette J. Dickerson is Assistant Professor of Sociology at The American University. She has served as Director of the Delta Research and Educational Foundation, Program Assistant for the W.K. Kellogg Foundation, and Program Director for the National Urban League, and has taught for the Jefferson County (KY) and the Louisville Boards of Education. She has been a training and an evaluation consultant for numerous nonprofit organizations, government agencies, and academic institutions on a wide range of issues including cultural diversity, race and ethnic relations, gender and family, and global education. She coedited *Color, Class, and Country: Experiences of Gender* and has authored several book chapters and policy, program, and evaluation reports. She holds an M.Ed. from the University of Louisville and a Ph.D. from the Washington State University.

Sharon Elise teaches courses on race relations, gender, and Black communities in the Sociology Department at California State University, San Marcos. She is also co-managing editor, with Dr. Adewole Umoja, of a new journal, *WAZO WEUSI (Think Black): A Journal of Black Thought.* She earned a Ph.D. in sociology from the University of Oregon in 1990. Her dissertation, "Routes to Teenaged Motherhood: African, Native, and European Americans," explores the racialization of teenaged motherhood, and reexamines the race, class and gender construction of this phenomenon through intensive interviews with teenaged mothers of three different communities in the Northwest.

Johanna E. Foster is completing her doctoral work in sociology at Rutgers University. She earned both a master's degree in applied sociology/social policy, specializing in the sociology of gender and race, and a B.A. in Interdisciplinary Studies/Women's Studies from The American University.

Susan M. George is a doctoral candidate in clinical psychology at Northwestern University. She received her B.S. in biology (human physiology) from the University of Illinois. She has coauthored *An In-Depth Study of High Risk Mothers.*

Willa Mae Hemmons is Associate Professor of Social Service at Cleveland State University and a lawyer specializing in criminal justice. She received her law degree from the University of Illinois and her Ph.D. in sociology from Case Western Reserve University. Her work has been published in a wide range of scholarly publications dealing with higher education, women's rights, and law. An academician and a community advocate, she has given countless hours of service to civic causes and her church.

Philipia L. Hillman is a doctoral student in sociology at The American University, with special interest in race, gender, and social policy. She received her B.A. in public relations from Howard University in 1989 and her M.A. in sociology from The American University in 1993. She is also a public affairs specialist for the Pension Benefit Guarantee Corporation in Washington, DC.

Annie Ruth Leslie is Assistant Professor of Sociology at Howard University, where she teaches courses on the sociology of African Americans and the African presence in the United States. She is the author of several articles on women and Afrocentric moral thought, including "African American Women's Views Regarding the 'Mistake' of Unwed Motherhood." She received her Ph.D. in sociology from Northwestern University in Evanston, Illinois.

Suzanne M. Randolph is Assistant Professor of Family Studies at the University of Maryland, College Park. She holds M.S. and Ph.D. degrees in psychology from the University of Michigan, Ann Arbor. She served as Research Coordinator for the Howard University Normative Study which followed African American infants in interactions with their mothers from birth to age three. She has an extensive background in community-based and basic research related to African American children and their families. She has also studied cross-cultural aspects of family life as a Kellogg National Fellow. She is a Past National President of the Association of Black Psychologists, Past Chair of the Black Caucus of the Society for Research in Child Development, and a member of the American Psychological Association and the National Council on Family Relations.

Dhyana Ziegler is Associate Professor at the University of Tennessee, Knoxville. She is coauthor of the book *Thunder and Silence: The Mass Media in Africa* and editor of *Molefi K. Asante and Afrocentricity: In Praise and in Criticism*. She has also authored several book chapters and has published in numerous academic journals such as the *Journal of Broadcasting and Electronic Media, Journal of Black Studies, Journal-*

ism Quarterly, FEEDBACK Journal, The Journal of Studies in Technical Careers, Thought and Action: The NEA Higher Education Journal, and the *Radio-Television News Directors Association* (RTNDA). She is also a television producer of news shows and documentaries and is a weekly "Commentator" appearing on WATE-TV News in Knoxville, TN. She serves on several professional boards and community organizations and has won numerous local, state, and national awards.